Social History in Perspective

General Editor: Jeremy Black

Social History in Perspective is a series of in-depth studies of the many topics in social, cultural and religious history for students. They also give the student clear surveys of the subject and present the most recent research in an accessible way.

PUBLISHED

John Belchem   *Popular Radicalism in Nineteenth-Century Britain*
Tim Hitchcock   *English Sexualities, 1700–1800*
Sybil M. Jack   *Towns in Tudor and Stuart Britain*
Hugh McLeod   *Religion and Society in England, 1850–1914*
Christopher Marsh   *Popular Religion in Sixteenth-Century England*
N. L. Tranter   *British Population in the Twentieth Century*
Ian D. Whyte   *Scotland's Society and Economy in Transition, c.1500–c.1760*

FORTHCOMING

Eric Acheson   *Late Medieval Economy and Society*
Ian Archer   *Rebellion and Riot in England, 1360–1660*
Jonathan Barry   *Religion and Society in England, 1603–1760*
A. L. Beier   *Early Modern London*
Sue Bruley   *Women's Century of Change*
Andrew Charlesworth   *Popular Protest in Britain and Ireland, 1650–1870*
Richard Connors   *The Growth of Welfare in Hanoverian England, 1723–1793*
Geoffrey Crossick   *A History of London from 1800 to 1939*
Alistair Davies   *Culture and Society, 1900–1995*
Simon Dentith   *Society and Cultural Form in the Nineteenth Century*
Martin Durham   *The Permissive Society*
Peter Fleming   *Medieval Family and Household in England*
David Fowler   *Youth Culture in the Twentieth Century*
Malcolm Gaskill   *Witchcraft in England, 1560–1760*
Peter Gosden   *Education in the Twentieth Century*
Harry Goulbourne   *Race Relations in Britain Since 1945*
S. J. D. Green   *Religion and the Decline of Christianity in Modern Britain, 1880–1980*
Paul Griffiths   *English Social Structure and the Social Order, 1500–1750*
Anne Hardy   *Health and Medicine since 1860*
Steve Hindle   *The Poorer Sort of People in Seventeenth-Century England*
David Hirst   *Welfare and Society, 1832–1939*
Helen Jewell   *Education in Early Modern Britain*

Titles continued overleaf

List continued from previous page

Anne Kettle   *Social Structure in the Middle Ages*
Alan Kidd   *The State and the Poor, 1834–1914*
Peter Kirby and S. A. King   *British Living Standards, 1700–1870*
Arthur J. McIvor   *Working in Britain, 1880–1950*
Anthony Milton   *Church and Religion in England, 1603–1642*
Michael Mullett   *Early Modern British Catholics, 1559–1829*
Christine Peters   *Women in Early Modern Britain, 1690–1800*
Barry Reay   *Rural Workers, 1830–1930*
Richard Rex   *Heresy and Dissent in England, 1360–1560*
John Rule   *Labour and the State, 1700–1875*
Pamela Sharpe   *Population and Society in Britain, 1750–1900*
Malcolm Smuts   *Culture and Power in England*
John Spurr   *English Puritanism, 1603–1689*
W. B. Stephens   *Education in Industrial Society: Britain, 1780–1902*
Heather Swanson   *Medieval British Towns*
David Taylor   *Crime, Policing and Punishment*
Benjamin Thompson   *Feudalism or Lordship and Politics in Medieval England*
R. E. Tyson   *Population in Pre-Industrial Britain, 1500–1750*
Garthine Walker   *Crime, Law and Society in Early Modern England*
Andy Wood   *The Crowd and Popular Politics in Early Modern England*

Please note that a sister series, *British History in Perspective*, is available which covers all the key topics in British political history.

POPULAR RELIGION IN SIXTEENTH-CENTURY ENGLAND

HOLDING THEIR PEACE

CHRISTOPHER MARSH

Lecturer in History
Queen's University of Belfast

First published 1998 by
MACMILLAN PRESS LTD
Houndmills, Basingstoke, Hampshire RG21 6XS
and London
Companies and representatives
throughout the world

ISBN 0-333-61990-0 hardcover
ISBN 0-333-61991-9 paperback

A catalogue record for this book is available
from the British Library.

This book is printed on paper suitable for recycling and
made from fully managed and sustained forest sources.

10   9   8   7   6   5   4   3   2   1
07 06 05 04 03 02 01 00 99 98

Printed in Hong Kong

Published in the United States of America 1998 by
ST. MARTIN'S PRESS, INC.
Scholarly and Reference Division
175 Fifth Avenue, New York, N.Y. 10010

ISBN 0-312-21093-0 cloth
ISBN 0-312-21094-9 paperback

For Margaret Spufford and Patrick Collinson

How came it to pass that you were so ready to distroy and spoil the thing that you thought well of?

Question put to a man who, in the mid-sixteenth century, had participated in the despoiling of Roche Abbey in Yorkshire (British Library Add. MS 5813, reproduced in A. G. Dickens (ed.), Tudor Treatises, *Yorkshire Archaeological Society (1959) p. 125)*

CONTENTS

ACKNOWLEDGEMENTS

This book draws many of its examples from the primary research of other historians, and I would like to express my gratitude to all the scholars whose work has come under the pilferer's eye. More specifically, I wish to thank those who have read the typescript or discussed portions of it with me: Scott Dixon, Ian Green, David Hempton, Patrick Collinson and Margaret Spufford. My wife, Katie, read it at least twice – a uniquely heroic effort. The Queen's University of Belfast and the Leverhulme Trust provided me with time and money, and the book would not have been written without their combined generosity. Finally, I would like to thank all of the students who have taken my 'popular religion' course during the last five years. They have helped to shape my thoughts more extensively than they will realise. I remember well the first tutorial I hosted in Belfast: a nervous young lecturer, convinced that his task would be to prevent sectarian bitterness from boiling over, encountered an equally nervous group of students, each of them deeply anxious to avoid offending the sensibilities of the other participants. I learnt more from them on that day than they ever learnt from me. Sectarian assumptions are, of course, present, but they are not alone.

1

INTRODUCTION

Two Snapshots and an Enigma

Between 1462 and 1479, the inhabitants of villages in the deanery of Wisbech (Isle of Ely) made their presentments to the bishop's consistory court, responding to official requests for information on local misdemeanours of a moral or religious nature. This was a routine procedure, and the evidence is unusual only in that it has survived. Detailed records of ecclesiastical visitations in the fifteenth century are rarely found. The evidence is extremely valuable, and enables us to form an impression of the state of religious affairs at the parish level, from the viewpoint of the parishioners themselves (or at least of their chosen representatives, the churchwardens).[1]

Several locals were accused of sexually improper behaviour. A Whittlesey man, for example, had been consorting with somebody else's wife 'at unusual times'. Others had breached the peace within their communities, and were labelled 'common quarrellers'. In a number of places, there was concern over the state of the church, its surroundings and contents. In Elm, the walls enclosing the vicarage were broken, 'so that swine can enter the churchyard at will'. The vicar there was also reported for keeping back from the church 'one lavatorium [a washing vessel] of pewter'. At Wisbech, the vicar and rector had failed in their responsibility for maintaining the chancel, where the windows were not glazed and some of the church ornaments were damaged. The vicar had also failed to find sufficient surplices for the proper conduct of church services. In Parson Drove, some local servants were accused of breaking 'Maynard Cross', one of the parish's religious landmarks. In Newton, two men had refused to

1

provide a 'lamp' (candle) to burn in front of the church's crucifix, 'as they ought to do'.

The behaviour of certain individuals during service time had also raised a few eyebrows. One servant from Whittlesey 'plays and disturbs Divine Service in the church on Sundays and festivals'. But at least he had turned up, which was more than could be said for the Whittlesey men who had herded cattle, ground malt and sold meat when they should have been in church. The economic motive was presumably strong in such cases, and probably in those of the parishioners who had detained portions of their 'Easter offering' to the church. Similarly, Robert Ward of Newton was refusing to pay the forty shillings he owed to the guild of St Katherine. Only one offence sounds more like that of a principled religious objector: Bartholomew Edmund of Leverington 'refuses to take off his hat in the church there at the time of the elevation of the Host'.

Several of the local clergy were considered negligent in their conduct of services. The churchwardens from Elm reported that 'They have not a priest to administer the Sacrament', and that their vicar had not been resident with them for years. In Whittlesey, one chaplain had defamed another by accusing him of failing to urge the observance of the fast on St Thomas's day. There were also signs that the lay officials of church and guild, responsible for maintaining religious order, were not always treated with the respect they deserved. The aldermen of one Wisbech guild, for example, informed the churchwardens that Thomas Joley had refused to obey them.

Nearly one and a half centuries later, in 1606–8, the same courts and procedures were still in place, and a new generation of fenlanders made their presentments in the deanery of Wisbech. In between, of course, the English Reformation had occurred (or begun) and the world had changed in numerous ways. There are also, however, solid signs of similarity. A second snapshot will permit comparisons to be drawn.[2]

Sex and morality were still important concerns, and generated an arguably more intense anxiety. In Elm, for example, Henry Townsend was living openly with someone else's wife, and John Watson 'useth lewde & filthie behaviour in shewinge his nakednes etc'. Isabella Webster, a little less luridly, was described as a 'common Rayler'. The churchyard in Elm was still causing concern, principally because Richard Roe had thrown his dead cattle into it, 'so that dogges carrye it into every Corner aboute the Church & the Sanctuarye is defiled with Carrion'. In Wisbech, the chancel was 'very much ruinated & so hath continued a longe tyme'. True enough. Clerical garments and ecclesiastical equipment could also still provoke disquiet. Johan Houshold of Emneth was in trouble 'for sayinge publiquely at the Communion table before the cheife of the parishe that the olde surplisse was not better worth then to make a sheete or a smocke of'. The churchwardens of Elm found themselves accused of keeping the Prayer Book and communion chalice at home. Worse still, there was an ugly rumour that some had used the said chalice 'to quaffe in there jolytye'. The wardens utterly denied the second part of this charge. In Wisbech, it was reported that the parish's bible was 'not sufficient', lacking 'all the apostles'.

The behaviour of laypeople on the Sabbath was still not all it might have been. Edward Brigstock of Tydd St Giles was presented for 'unreverently...laughing and Groninge' during the sermon, with Edward Towe, 'a fiddler'. Others skipped church completely, preferring to 'water hempe', hunt ducks or play cards. There was no visible local precedent, however, for the frequent disputes over who sat where in church, nor for the presentments of numerous laypeople for neglecting to receive communion or attend Sunday services. More outrageously still, a Wisbech butcher 'encouraged & sett a dogge upon certaine that were goinge to the Church to heare divine service on the holly day'.

There were still those layfolk who refused to pay 'the money wch was layed for the repaire of the Church', and those whose objections look more conscientious. Early Jacobean Wisbech, for example, had a few individuals who were 'supposed [i.e. believed] to favor the error of the Brownists', and two who 'have separated themselves from our Congregacon' in favour of 'a reformed Churche in Amsterdam'. Other parishes reported the presence of small numbers of Catholic recusants.

Members of the clergy could still fail to match lay expectations. The vicar of Whittlesey was presented because he did not announce holy days and fasts, and the incumbent at Wisbech was said to be 'always absent from us'. In addition, he preached only once a year and 'alloweth us noe preachinge Minister'. Churchwardens, like their ministers, certainly came in for their share of criticism from local people. In Leverington, for example, John Bishop was presented for speaking against the wardens as they put up 'sentences of scripture to bewtifye the Church'. As we shall see, insulting the churchwardens was developing into something of an art form amongst an inventive minority of the English laity.

In the second of these snapshots, there are many signs of a religious environment that had undergone conspicuous change. The documentation is much richer, and it seems that local church government had become more thorough, sophisticated and intrusive in the intervening decades. The hints of physical change are numerous too. In local churches, the 'lamps', crucifixes and images of saints had gone, replaced by scriptural sentences. The laity were now required to receive the communion regularly, and could expect a reprimand if they did not. The religious guilds had been dissolved long ago, and the number of priests and chaplains substantially reduced. The new 'ministers' were expected to preach regularly and with expertise, and to promote a religion centred on the vernacular Bible and Prayer Book. The reformed Church of England recognised many fewer days of feast and fast. Finally, the cases of dissent suggest a greater religious diversity amongst the laity by the early seventeenth century.

Yet there are also many signs of continuity. The impulses, attitudes and priorities of these fenlanders had certainly not been transformed beyond recognition. The citizens of Wisbech and surrounding parishes remained preoccupied with social morality, above all the preservation of peace amongst neighbours. They still paid great attention to the conservation and embellishment of their sacred surroundings, and to the promotion of suitably respectful behaviour when in and around the church. In both periods, they knew how the clergy should behave, both morally and liturgically, and they were not afraid to reprimand those who fell short of the required standards. Many feast days may have been abolished, but the remaining ones continued to punctuate the year and to hold significance. Laypeople worshipped in the same buildings as before, and operated through the same system of jurisdictions and institutions. From both sources, there is a strong sense that the laity were *involved* in the running of the church, even if a minority of them always fell foul of the majority. Some of these continuities may seem rather obvious, but they existed at quite a deep level and are important. As we shall see, the nature of the balance between change and continuity is fundamental to an understanding of the English Reformation.

So much for the snapshots. Now what of the enigma? His name was William Akers, and he too was a man of the Wisbech fens. Akers's story, which ends with his death in 1590, is bizarre, contradictory and confusing. It can serve as an early indication of the fascinating but frustrating interpretative problems with which religious historians of this period must wrestle.

We can get to know William Akers relatively well, for the simple reason that he was a man of unusual passion. Most of his contemporaries pursued their interests far more quietly. In 1581, the Ely Consistory Court was informed that, on Easter Sunday, Akers had spoken evil words of his parson, saying 'that Mr Bowler did preache such a sermone . . . as was not mete for a man to here, And sayd alsoe that if he preached soe in some place he woulde be pulled oute of the pulpit like a rascall'. Mr Bowler, it emerged from other presentments in the court book, was a minister of distinctly puritan leanings. Akers's Easter Day outburst was in fact the climax to a period of alleged disruptive behaviour, during which he had been rebuked by the sidesmen (churchwardens' assistants) for his 'stirringe' ways, and had responded by calling them 'more busye than wise'. He had refused to pay a fine for his offensive conduct. Akers's relationship with local officialdom did not improve in 1582, and he was accused of attempting to ring the church bells 'superstitiouslye', of insulting the churchwardens, and, just before Christmas, of being 'droncken in most beastely and fylthye manner to the ofence of manye people'. In addition, it was reported that he protected his adulterous daughter from authority, that he sowed strife amongst his neighbours, and that he slept in church during Mr Bowler's sermons and services, presumably exhausted from his other activities.

When William Akers came to make his will in 1590, however, he opened with an unexpected page of exceptionally pious pronouncements. Nearly all wills of the period began with some form of religious section, in which the testator committed his or her soul to God, but Akers's preamble was unquestionably out of the ordinary. He declared his belief in the Trinity, praised God in extravagant terms, asked the parson (the same Mr Bowler) to assist with the choice of a burial place inside the church, asserted that he belonged to 'the Elect', and spoke of his firm faith in Jesus Christ as his only saviour. He then prayed for forgiveness of his sins, and for the strength to persevere in faith and to avoid all worldly temptations. Only then did he proceed to bequeath his more tangible possessions, described as 'those blessynges wherewth God of his goodnes & mercye hath Inryched me'.[3]

So what sort of a man was this? Perhaps a consistently devoted, though imperfect, member of the Church of England, who objected to the puritanical liberties his minister took with the Prayer Book. Perhaps a thoroughly ungodly man who passed through a dramatic conversion to fervent Protestant piety in his last years, befriending his former enemies along the way. Perhaps even a closet Catholic (hence the 'superstitious' attachment to church bells) whose remarkable testamentary preamble was actually written on his behalf, but not in his words, by an evangelically Protestant neighbour. These are all possibilities that can also be applied to the population at large. Had the first decades of the Reformation produced a society dominated by puritans, or by 'Anglicans', or by 'church papists', or by irreligious drunkards? We will never know for certain, but it is hoped that this book will provide some guidance, and help to stimulate further discussion.

What is 'Popular Religion', and Does it Matter?

No designation is neutral, and both components of the term 'popular religion' cause problems. 'Popular' has a number of associations, ranging from the seemingly uncomplicated to the obviously controversial. It can be used to refer simply to that which was widespread, or generally liked. But more specifically, it means 'of the people', and thus implies the existence of a smaller elite group whose members did not belong to 'the people' and did not share their values. This in turn suggests the possibility of a social system based around relationships of domination and subordination, and therefore of a popular culture that was imposed on the people from above, rather than growing organically from their midst. 'Popular' can come to mean designed '*for* the people' but not necessarily '*of*' them. The term can therefore imply a two-tier, antagonistic culture, and it is by no means clear for early-modern historians that this is an assumption deserving to be written into the very terminology we use. There is also a danger of implying that 'the people' somehow spoke with one voice. This was certainly not the case, for the world cannot have looked precisely the same to men and women, to old and young, or to rural and urban dwellers.

'Religion' is no better, principally because it is difficult to decide which forms of belief or practice merit inclusion and which do not. In late twentieth-century society, most people understand religion to apply to organised church worship; but what of astrology, fortune-telling, and firmly held beliefs about the dangers of walking under ladders? These all deal with supernatural forces, and with attempts to understand, serve or utilise them. Dictionary definitions of religion as 'the belief in a superhuman controlling power' cannot legitimately be applied in a way that includes God but excludes the black cat. The most famous modern book about early-modern popular beliefs in England made the distinction in its title between 'religion' and 'magic'. One group of commentators subsequently complained that the author, Keith Thomas, had failed to comprehend the power of organised Christian religion, by treating it as

comparable to practices such as palmistry; another group, more anthro-
pological in its instincts, turned this on its head and criticised him for
underestimating the coherence and force of the supposedly 'magical'
beliefs, which had been excluded, without justification, from the 'religion'
category. The issue is still not settled.

Despite these difficulties, it seems that historians will continue to find
themselves stuck with the term 'popular religion'. For those of us interested in the ways in which the early-modern majority gave meaning to, or
found meaning in, their lives, there seems to be nothing more suitable.
Eamon Duffy has recently proposed 'traditional religion' as an alternative,
but the term has distinct limitations.[4] It helps us towards a richer
understanding of the last decades of majority Catholicism in the
fifteenth and sixteenth centuries, but it is much less useful in enabling
us to understand the development of majority Protestantism in the
sixteenth and seventeenth centuries. 'Traditional religion' was a major
component of 'popular religion' in this period, but the two terms are
hardly synonymous. For the religion of the English people to have developed in this period as it did, there must have been a narrow but
powerful current of non-traditional piety flowing through the system.
Duffy's term excludes this current, and so offers only a partial explanation
of a complex process.

The term 'popular religion' is therefore used in this study not with any
great sense of enthusiasm, but for want of something more satisfactory.
The emphasis is primarily upon the people beneath the level of the gentry,
though I certainly do not wish to imply that 'elite' religion was fundamentally different. My focus will be upon the majority of England's inhabitants,
with the result that martyrs, 'puritans' and spiritual misfits may not enjoy
quite the level of attention to which they have become accustomed.
'Popular religion' will be taken to refer to all the varied beliefs
and practices that brought the early-modern majority into contact with
the divine or supernatural. As will become obvious, it is my opinion
that Christianity and the church dominated this interface from the viewpoint of all but a minority of contemporaries. It seems clear, nevertheless,
that many other strands of belief and practice were also woven into
the cloth of popular religion. Using this cloth in a myriad of patterns,
ordinary people fashioned for themselves spiritual coats which they hoped
would keep them warm in the winter, cool in the summer, and happy in
the end.

Another question relates to the importance of all this. Why should we
bother studying a mass of long-dead people whose views, according to

many commentators, counted for little even in their own day? One contemporary writer, admittedly with tongue in cheek, acknowledged that the 'plaine countrie fellow' was not without religion, but portrayed it as 'a part of his coppy-hold which he takes of his land-lord'. The historian A. L. Rowse, with his tongue more conventionally placed, betrayed similar prejudices when he spoke of the 'stupid and backward-looking peasantry' in sixteenth-century Cornwall.[5] What, then, is the point of studying such people? Three justifications come to mind. In the first place, the careful work of social historians is a mark of respect for all the nearly blank faces of the past, the people whose portraits were never painted, and who spoke to posterity only in disjointed snatches recorded here and there. We should study them because they deserve to be studied. Secondly, we study them because, contrary to the opinions reported above, the ordinary people of the early-modern period *did* matter at the time, even if their 'betters' were not in the habit of admitting it. The argument that all meaningful power lay in the hands of the gentry and aristocracy, so that 'the people' simply followed their landlords, is no longer sustainable. Early-modern systems of government also depended on the opinions of more humble local office-holders (churchwardens and the like), and those opinions were shaped from below as much as from above. Many of the seemingly most autocratic royal dictats can only be understood in their admittedly indirect relation to a much deeper social context, one that conditioned governmental possibilities and therefore motives. The 'little people' could and did exert an influence, though it was of course disproportionate to their numbers. To a surprising extent, they governed themselves, ran their own affairs, and their responses to official orders could be highly selective. Early-modern government was a matter not just of dictation and obedience, but of negotiation and settlement. Of course the dice were loaded, but the game was still worth playing.

Finally, historians study the ordinary people of the past for the simple reason that their world is intrinsically fascinating. To some, this may not justify, but it certainly explains. Colourful fragments of a lost world lie scattered around us like the pieces of a vast jigsaw, and the task of reconstruction can obsess (and madden) a mind, just like any puzzle. It is a strange and compelling thing to make partial contact with some of the 'lost people of Europe', people like the mercurial William Akers. In a real sense, they were our ancestors, and the seeds of us were in them.

How Can We Study Popular Religion?

If we are seeking to reconstruct the religion of the majority, and if the majority rarely went 'on the record', then what hope is there of success? It is no easy matter to 'get *within* poor persons', as one seventeenth-century clergyman remarked with frustration.[6] Historians have often dodged the problem by concentrating on those forms of popular religion that were more exotic, enthusiastic, or extreme, and therefore more visible, than the norm. Alternatively, they have felt defeated by the problem, commenting pessimistically that 'Orthodoxy, like happiness, has no history.'[7] Our quarry is certainly elusive, allowing us only fleeting glimpses and never pausing long enough for us to take aim (with camera, not gun), but the religion of the majority is slowly becoming more comprehensible as our equipment and our fieldcraft improve. It is likely that popular religion conceived as the faith of the many will, in the next decade, come to provide a much-needed balance to popular religion conceived as the faith of the unusually committed on all sides.

Patterns of religious belief and practice in sixteenth-century England can be examined through a wide variety of primary sources. Amongst the most commonly consulted are wills, in which testators left their souls to God using a variety of pious expressions, and in which they often made more tangible bequests to the church or to charitable causes. Church court records, such as those mentioned at the opening of this chapter, are another favoured source. They provide detailed information on the religious climate in the localities, and on the parochial response to orders from above. Frequently, the presentments were framed in response to 'visitation articles', another useful source, which consisted of detailed questions from the bishop concerning the state of spiritual affairs in the parishes. The records of other courts, and of central government itself, can also be mined for evidence concerning official dealings with groups of miscreants (rebels, heretics and the like), whose motives were often wholly or partly religious.

More mundane but no less valuable are the records kept by the lay officers of individual parishes, most notably the 'churchwardens' accounts', which offer extensive information on the management of church funds from year to year. On occasion, the wardens also made notes relating to the allocation of church seating and the names of those receiving the communion on given dates. Literary sources can also be taken in for questioning. These range from the cheaper forms of print, especially ballads and chapbooks, through the various forms of clerical literature (for example, catechisms and manuals of piety), to mammoth works of religious propaganda such as John Foxe's famous *Book of Martyrs*. All of these reflect directly or indirectly upon the religiosity of the English majority. Finally, historians are making increasing use of the buildings, monuments and windows that survive from the sixteenth century. In general, the paper sources become more plentiful as the period goes on, while the stone and glass sources move in the opposite direction.

It is certainly true that none of these sources affords us a clear view of our quarry. Standing alongside the ailing testator, for example, there was often a clergyman or professional scribe. We can rarely be sure that the recorded spiritual bequests were truly the considered and voluntary acts of the individual in whose name the document was written. Churchwardens' accounts *are* extremely valuable, but their survival is patchy and we can usually only speculate about the motives behind the figures. When the government of Edward VI ordered parishes to make a series of distinctively Protestant purchases for the church, did the often sluggish local response reflect a rejection of the new doctrines, or a shortage of money, or a pragmatic inkling that the sick, Protestant boy-king would soon be succeeded by a Catholic?

The importance of cheap print as a source cannot be denied, but any investigation is dogged by uncertainties over the size and social composition of the consuming public. How 'popular' was 'popular literature'? Clerical publications and visitation articles are similarly problematic, because they often tell us much more about the standards and objectives of the authors than about the state of religion in society as a whole. And the assorted court records, though amongst the most colourful sources we have, are inevitably biased towards evidence of conflict. They may therefore give a misleading impression of polarity, dispute and excited engagement. There is a risk that historians may end up presenting a sort of 'Match of the Day' Reformation, packed with goals and sendings-off but without the unexceptional interplay of a full, live game.

Scholars in gloomy mood can, therefore, dig themselves into a deep, dark hole from which there seems to be no prospect of escape. It would, however, be a serious mistake for them to abandon all hope. It will have been noticed that the sources, when viewed in their full range, are rich and varied. If approached in an appropriate spirit of critical optimism, they can tell us a great deal. At the bottom of our hole, there are enough bits and pieces for the construction of a makeshift but serviceable ladder.

We must also be aware, in seeking a suitable spirit of enquiry, that our own perspective on the past embodies distortions of its own. As we

examine the evidence of sixteenth-century popular religion, several possibilities need to be borne in mind. In the first place, four centuries of
religious history have driven into us the importance of a fierce and
fundamental divide between Protestantism and Catholicism. This divide
is given physical expression in the streets of modern Belfast, even if English
cities have found other issues over which to risk rupture. The Reformation
chasm yawns large in our minds as we look back, and it is therefore wise to
remember that, in the parishes of mid-sixteenth-century England, it was
something new and peculiar, a distinction that had to be learned rather
than simply inherited. That it often was successfully learned is implied by
numerous examples, such as that of the Protestant Kentishman who, in
the 1570s, said 'if I knew him that would go to mass I would thrust my
dagger in him'. Earlier, in 1536, a Protestant had been shot dead, Belfast-
style, as he went about his business in Cheapside.[8] Some people learned
quickly, but we should not assume that violent polarities over religion
developed instantaneously in the minds and communities of the majority.

Secondly, modern culture places a high emphasis on the acquisition of
knowledge, and upon the development of clear, personal beliefs that can
be held in one's mind and articulated to order. Once again, it may be a
mistake to transport this emphasis back into the sixteenth century, where it
often seems that ordinary people were not at all obsessed with intellectual
knowledge and verbal articulation. As John Craig and Mark Byford
have both argued, historians must be ready to seek meaning in the
seemingly 'inarticulate' actions of contemporary parishioners as they
attended services or contributed to the upkeep of their churches. Religion
for them was not principally about careful, intellectual attention to questions of belief.[9]

Similarly, we seem to set considerable store by intellectual consistency.
'Internal contradiction' is the un-doing of many an undergraduate essay,
and we expect one another to develop a systematic and rational line of
argument on all matters of interest. Sixteenth-century people, in contrast,
often seem to have been adept at living with contradictions. This does not
appear to have been an 'either/or' society, though attempts were under
way to turn it into one. As we shall see, people were able to hold onto
aspects of Catholic belief and practice, while simultaneously learning to
think of themselves as Protestants; they could hate the idea of heresy, yet
treat the local heretics with a measure of sympathy and respect; and
radical dissenters could reject the validity of the established church's
services, yet serve the established church well throughout their lives. It
does not appear that consistency was all.

Finally, we live in a highly literate and highly electronic age. We are bombarded from all sides with visual information, and it is arguable that our imaginative capacities have been undermined as a result. Most of the time, we *receive* images rather than fashioning them in our own minds. Sixteenth-century imaginations must have been more active and more extensively used, and this is something we would do well to remember as we contemplate the impact of a religion of words, Protestantism, on a religion of pictures and rituals, Catholicism. Historians should not be too ready to accept the argument, frequently proposed, that when Protestants removed paintings from the church walls, they rendered official religion inaccessible to the majority. Would they have been so stupid? Perhaps ordinary people responded instinctively to the spoken words of their ministers by making pictures in their heads. Even we, culturally impoverished citizens of the late twentieth century, do not need television screens to form pictures from some of the verbal descriptions provided by early reformers. In the 1530s, for example, one author invited his audience to imagine Jesus Christ, so severely beaten that, from 'the sole of his foote: to the hiest part of his hed was not one place but the skinge and the flesshe was broken, rent and bloody for our sakes'.[10]

Historiographical Outlines (and Battle-Lines)

The varied source material, and the still-controversial atmosphere surrounding the issues at stake, help to explain why historians have proposed very different interpretations of the nature and development of popular religion during the sixteenth century. Inevitably, the concept of the 'Reformation' dominates the debate, as historians ask themselves whether it was an event or a process, whether it was welcomed or resisted, whether the initiative behind it lay with the populace or with their leading governors, and whether it deserves a capital or a lower-case 'r'. Historians are the captives of their sources, and the *r*eformation as it emerges from, say, wills may be very different in tone and texture from the more confrontational *R*eformation found, for example, in many literary sources. Similarly, sixteenth-century religion will naturally not look the same to historians of Protestant, Catholic or agnostic convictions. This is not to say that historians are incapable of rising above their preconceptions to some extent, but that they cannot do so completely (and some hardly seem to try).

Secondary material currently in print covers a vast range, and
'Reformation studies' have emerged in recent years as something of an
academic industry. Approaches vary considerably, from Robert Whiting's
intensive study of a single region during a fifty-year period, to Keith
Thomas's grandly conceived survey of shifts in English popular religion
over two centuries and more.[11] Different scholars concentrate on different
aspects of the field, devoting their attention variously to changes in
popular theology, patterns of church attendance, the activities of radical
minorities, relations between laypeople and the clergy, and so forth.
Underlying this rich variety, it may be useful to identify two distinct but
powerful poles of perception which, while not achieving widespread
acceptance, do clearly exert a forceful pull on the field as a whole. The
majority of historians would resist total identification with either extreme,
but would tend nevertheless to lean a little in their analysis towards one or
the other. As Margaret Aston has suggested, 'Perhaps it is impossible to
study the Reformation for long without becoming aligned – if one does not
start off by being so.'[12]

It will come as no surprise that there is a distinctly sectarian element to
our principal polarity, though it certainly is not possible to draw up the
historiographical battle-lines on the basis of religious identity alone. At one
pole stands A. G. Dickens, who has always portrayed the Reformation as
basically a good thing. The majority may not actively have sought to take
their part in the religious stirrings initiated in Germany by Martin Luther,
but significant numbers of ordinary people are considered by Dickens to
have seen the new light at an early date. They therefore assisted the
reformist clergy and their powerful lay champions in the task of leading
England bravely away from the clutter and confusion of the old religion,
and into a religious world more spartan but more satisfying (and much
better for you). For Dickens, the Reformation had purpose, direction, and
also a certain inevitability. By the end of Edward VI's reign in 1553, the
Protestant clock could not be turned back, and the reformers were 'an ever
growing minority'. It is notable that Dickens does not say that the majority
were convinced Protestants by this date, rather that convinced Protestants
were advantageously placed (Mary's reign excepted) both geographically
and politically. The English majority, in Dickens' estimation, were still
conservative and unenthusiastic about reform in 1553, a date marked by
the death of the nation's most Protestant sixteenth-century monarch.[13]

Professor Dickens's work has been justly celebrated, though its definitively Protestant assumptions now jar somewhat (definitively Catholic
assumptions are more in vogue). At one point, he praises Elizabethan

puritanism for having 'taught men to see Christ through the eyes of St. Paul instead of through a cloud of minor saints, gilded legends and plain myths'.[14] This is hardly a balanced assessment, though we can at least commend the author for not seeking to conceal his bias. Dickens's choice of metaphor is also revealing. We are told, for example, that under Mary 'the forest of Protestantism was spreading relentlessly across the landscape of the nation'.[15] The expansion of a forest is, of course, a natural process, and nowadays seen as a healthy one too. This is the metaphor of a historian who views the religious history of the sixteenth century as primarily about 'the rise of Protestantism', rather than about developing a rounded understanding of the process of change, with all its contrary tides and cross-currents. Other historians, as we shall see, would turn the metaphor around, portraying the Protestant Reformation as a terrible act of *de*forestation.

For the sake of symmetry, it would be pleasing to place Eamon Duffy at the other pole, for his committed Catholicism arms him with assumptions equal and opposite to those of Professor Dickens. Unfortunately, Dr Duffy's positive view of Protestant endeavour after *c*.1570 disqualifies him from consideration. Christopher Haigh is the next obvious candidate. Regrettably, however, he is not a Catholic, though his work has earned him a place in Catholic hearts comparable to that of Jack Charlton on many an Irish mantelpiece.[16] This leaves J. J. Scarisbrick, who meets both the required criteria. His most relevant work bears a title similar to that chosen by Dickens, but beyond this the two authors recognise little of themselves in the other. Where Dickens saw his subject as the spread of Protestantism, Scarisbrick announced in his preface that he was leaving this (seemingly relevant) subject out of the account. This alerts us to the fact that the acute differences between historians often relate to questions of emphasis. There is a reluctance, at both poles, to tell the whole story.

Scarisbrick's Reformation was regrettable, undesirable and undesired. People, he argues, were thoroughly content with the ministrations of the traditional church, despite its imperfections, and there was no groundswell of opinion making fundamental change ever more likely. The Reformation was an act of state, and almost nothing more. Far from bringing the laity to the fore in religious affairs, it radically curtailed their opportunities for involvement, creating a church in which parishioners sat statically in their pews while remote and all-powerful clergy harangued them. The progress of Protestantism, not surprisingly, was slow and uncertain. Scarisbrick's preconceptions, like those of Dickens, arouse suspicion. We are invited to consider, for example, 'a random sample' of late-medieval wills, which are employed to make the point that people bequeathed large sums to a universally beloved church. Yet it is obvious to those with knowledge of the sources that this is not pot-luck at all (unless the pot is a jackpot), but a mouth-watering selection of the choicest morsels.[17]

Christopher Haigh adds further force to this portrayal, presenting us with not one but a set of Reformations, amounting in sum to a process that had no coherence or sense of direction. In his words, 'England had blundering Reformations, which most did not understand, which few wanted, and which no one knew had come to stay.' Throughout the mid-century, ordinary people despised the numerically insignificant Protestants living amongst them, and readily turned them over to the authorities for examination and, if necessary, burning. High political circumstances meant that Protestantism emerged from the tussle as the official, though insecure, religion of the nation, but the majority sought and found ways in which to treat the new communion service as if it were the old Mass. The whole sorry process produced a majority of 'parish Anglicans', but pitifully few believing Protestants. In Haigh's view, Protestantism (for which we can often read 'puritanism') had very little appeal for the majority, and Protestants were always isolated and unpopular figures within their localities. Once again, the author's use of evidence suggests the influence of unspoken bias. For the late-medieval church, a rate of ten tithe disputes per year in the Norwich diocese is dismissed as insignificant, certainly not an indication that the laity resented the church; but in Elizabethan Essex, religious disputes in twelve parishes during an entire decade are presented as evidence that Protestant ministers were deeply unpopular. Late-medieval conformity demonstrates commitment to the church; Elizabethan conformity reveals mere obedience. Historians working at our second pole certainly present us with a different Reformation, but it is not necessarily a more persuasive one.[18]

Most historians inhabit the more temperate zone between these two poles, but all are constantly aware that the bold utterances of scholars like Dickens and Scarisbrick serve to define their field of study. Some historians, like Eamon Duffy, can be said to draw on elements from both ends of the spectrum. He is most noted for his belief that Protestantism was fundamentally unwelcome, destructive, and disastrous in its first decades. The Protestant martyrs of Mary's reign, towering heroes in Dickens's account, are dealt with in a couple of paragraphs, and Duffy almost writes Protestantism out of the picture by subtitling his work 'Traditional religion'. Pre-Reformation Lollardy is similarly dismissed, despite the fact that there was clearly a Lollard 'tradition' too, even if it involved only a small minority. Yet Duffy also holds that, once the memories of a wonderful past had faded, Protestant educators *did* have what it took to make real progress at the grassroots level. The perspective of Margaret Spufford on post-Reformation faith is in many ways similar.[19]

Further variations on the two main themes are numerous. Robert Whiting's study of the Reformation in the west country gathers a wealth of vivid material and argues that, while a rich traditional religion crumbled readily under official pressure, people in general failed to take the new doctrines to their hearts. The solid obedience of the English people lies at the centre of his account, and he, like Scarisbrick, views the impact of Protestant reform as essentially negative. Mid-sixteenth-century people moved from religious enthusiasm into 'conformism, passivity, or even indifference'. Susan Brigden has written a superb narrative of the Reformation in London, recreating for us the many complex twists and turns along the way, and demonstrating the involvement of many of the capital's laity in the process of forging their own religious destinies. The attention granted to the committedly Protestant minority is more reminiscent of Dickens than of Scarisbrick, though Brigden avoids his extravagances of interpretation. Patrick Collinson's immensely subtle and influential work defies all attempts at crass classification. His lifelong interest in the Elizabethan puritans clearly says something about his sense of what was and is important, and we can occasionally hear him gently rebuking scholars of Haigh's 'catastrophist school' for their failure to appreciate that sixteenth-century Protestantism had its popular element and was not necessarily an unmitigated disaster in the parishes. Nevertheless, Collinson recognises that the English majority did not want the Reformation, and absorbed it only slowly.[20]

These are some of the most famous names within the field, though it would of course be possible to mention others. At present, it is also possible to detect the emergence of a new and disparate group of historians who are approaching the old questions in new ways, or asking slightly different questions. Current work on late-medieval piety is soundly dominated by the Duffy line of interpretation, but work on Elizabethan and Jacobean religion has recently been moving in new and interesting directions. A fundamental, underlying question concerns compliance: why did English people, happy with the old church, generally shuffle obediently towards allegiance to the new church? It seems unlikely that work written at either of the historiographical poles will ever provide satisfactory answers (and the answers will inevitably be multiple) to this question. We are therefore fortunate that, every year, less militant scholarship is adding bright new pieces to the puzzle.

Tessa Watt, for example, has contributed a thorough and fascinating account of cheap religious print between 1550 and 1640, and has opened up the possibility of religious change as a gradual, flexible, negotiated process. Work by Jeremy Boulton and Nicholas Alldridge has demonstrated the administrative ability of the post-Reformation church to incorporate its local members, and to provide for their needs and expectations. Martin Ingram's work on church courts has, amongst many other things, revealed the sober and sensible tactics adopted by these institutions in working towards a gradual transformation of English religious norms. Articles by John Craig and Eric Carlson have carried us towards a more sophisticated understanding of the important role of parochial church officers, selected from amongst the laity. The work of Judith Maltby is improving our awareness of the attitudes, often highly committed, of unexceptional parishioners towards the established church in the late sixteenth and early seventeenth centuries. Mark Byford places a similar emphasis, encouraging us to consider the power of continuities, and to avoid treating Protestantism and popular culture as necessarily opposed. These contributions will help us with the crucial problem of understanding how, why, and when the majority of people came to define themselves as Protestant.[21]

And on the other side of the religious divide, Alexandra Walsham's research on 'church papists', those Catholics who periodically attended services of the post-Reformation church, has greatly enhanced our knowledge of a vital category of English believers. They too can provide invaluable clues concerning the compliance conundrum. Finally, the work of Ian Green on catechisms and religious education more widely will add immeasurably to our appreciation of the ways in which the vast majority of people encountered the Protestant Reformation.[22] It seems likely that an older emphasis upon the activities of the most evangelical of educators will be found wanting. This book is indebted to all of the scholars mentioned in the paragraphs above, and to many others besides.

The Narrative Outline

It is not the purpose of this study to provide a detailed chronicle of religious developments in the period. A swift and necessarily superficial overview may, however, be of value to those who are relatively new to the subject. The hundred-year period under view can be divided up in a number of ways, and all such divisions are to an extent subjective and arbitrary. Having said that, a six-part story is discernible, and it is a story possessed of a peculiar and paradoxical pattern, a kind of symmetry in asymmetry.

In the early decades of the sixteenth century, phase one, the religious atmosphere appears to have been relatively stable. The church maintained a state of equilibrium, though Christopher Haigh seems to stretch a point in calling it 'unchallenged'.[23] The late-medieval church clearly did attract significant criticism, even if it would be a serious error to deduce from this that a Protestant Reformation was almost inevitable. Critics of the church came from a variety of backgrounds. There were intellectual humanists like John Colet, who denounced what they saw as the degeneracy of the contemporary clergy and called urgently for 'the reformation of ecclesiastical affairs'. There were many lawyers and laymen whose objections centred on the privileges and financial exactions of the clergy. Most famously, the merchant tailor Richard Hunne was sued in a church court over his refusal to pay a mortuary fee (a payment due to the parish priest on the death of a parishioner). The legal dispute escalated, with Hunne challenging the church's jurisdiction over him, and ended in 1514 when he was found dead in his prison cell. The views of England's 'heretical' Lollards (sometimes referred to by historians as 'proto-Protestants') were also fiercely critical of many of the church's rituals and beliefs, though they clearly constituted only a small minority of England's population as a whole. Lollardy was under attack in the early sixteenth century – a sure sign that the church's leaders were in anxious mood – and there were major heresy-hunts in several localities. Finally, from around 1520, various academics, clergymen and laypeople developed an interest in Lutheran ideas from the continent, increasingly available in printed form, and a new strand was added to existing criticism of the church. Yet it is true that these were all minority currents of opinion, and that the vast majority of English people were happy enough with the established religion.

A second phase began in the mid-1520s, and lasted until the death of Henry VIII in 1547. The prevailing climate during the previous phase may well have proved manageable by the church, but in 1527 it all became vastly more complicated with the fading of the king's love for his wife, Catherine of Aragon. Henry's wish to wed Anne Boyleyn set up a delicate situation in which a king whose religious instincts were predominantly conservative found himself having to ally with reformist clergy and leading laypeople in order to win his prize. This affair of the heart inaugurated a period characterised by momentous acts and momentous contradictions.

On one side of the picture, the 'English Reformation' of national legend took place. The parliament that opened in 1529 passed a series of statutes which transformed the nation's relationship with Rome, and with it the whole tone of official religion. The most constitutionally dramatic year was 1534: the Pope's rights over English people and institutions were radically curtailed (Act of Dispensations); the English clergy became subject solely to the crown (Act for the Submission of the Clergy); denial of papal authority ceased to be a heresy (Heresy Act); the succession was altered in favour of the offspring of Henry and Anne (Act of Succession); Henry was declared supreme head of the Church (Act of Supremacy); and the crown appropriated the right to tax English church livings (Act of First Fruits and Tenths). Developments of similar significance were in progress beyond parliament during this decade. Moves towards the comprehensive distribution of an authorised English version of the Bible took place, and by 1540 all parishes were being ordered to acquire a copy. Those who spoke against the supremacy, or who denied the validity of Henry's marriage to Anne, were pursued and sometimes executed.

From 1535, the monasteries and other religious houses were also under attack, ordered by the government of Thomas Cromwell to surrender their assets and abandon all that they stood for. In the north of England, a major rising in their defence, the famous Pilgrimage of Grace, was put down. Many of the church's traditional institutions, rituals and beliefs were severely undermined by official action. The Six Articles of 1536 omitted to mention four of the seven sacraments, and hardly delivered a ringing endorsement of transubstantiation or purgatory. Royal injunctions issued in 1538 ordered the destruction of images which had attracted offerings or pilgrimages, and banned the burning of candles before images. In 1541, many of the ancient rituals associated with holy days were outlawed, and in 1546–7 acts were passed preparatory to the dissolution of the chantries (endowments for memorial Masses). Meanwhile, Archbishop Cranmer had been working on plans for the introduction of church services in the vernacular, and 1544 saw the introduction of an English version of the litany.

This, however, was merely one side of the Henrician coin, and only very rarely did the leading reformers feel secure in their efforts. The Six Articles of 1539, for example, were far more conservative than the Ten of 1536. They upheld key traditionalist doctrines and practices, such as transubstantiation, communion in one kind only, the saying of Masses for souls, and clerical celibacy. Their passage was seriously damaging to the hopes of Cranmer and his allies. Another highly conservative act was passed in 1543, banning the lower orders from reading the Bible at a time when reformers believed they should be doing just that. And Protestants were never entirely free from the risk of prosecution and execution during one of the traditionalist backlashes. This second phase can suitably be concluded with the burning of Anne Askew, a Protestant gentlewoman, for heresy in 1546. She was not the first to have gone to the flames.

The next two phases coincide with the reigns of two of Henry's children, and are interesting because they involve, back-to-back, the century's most Protestant and Catholic royal campaigns. These took place within an eleven-year period, and can only have been immensely confusing for the bulk of those who witnessed them. Edward VI (reigned 1547–53) was a mere boy, and a sickly one at that. His government was therefore dominated by two magnates in succession, Somerset and Northumberland, who – for mixed motives – attempted to lead the country in a more radically Protestant direction. Traditionalist bishops were removed from their posts. In 1547, chantries and guilds, two of the principal foci of traditional parish piety, were dissolved by statute, and ordered to surrender their assets to the crown. A full English liturgy was introduced in the Prayer Book of 1549, then revised in a more radical direction in 1552. This savagely shortened version presented the communion as a purely commemorative rite (now to be received in both kinds by the laity), omitted the word 'Mass', and drastically simplified the garments to be worn by officiating clergymen. In addition, it removed many traditionalist ceremonies and reconstructed the rites surrounding baptism, confirmation and burial. In Christopher Haigh's words, 'it broke decisively with the past'.[24]

The governments of Edward VI also ordered the transformation of church interiors. All remaining images and statues were to go (1548); altars and rood screens were to follow (1550). Parish officers were told to replace their colourful pictures and figures with clear quotations from the Scriptures, to be painted onto the church walls. Clergymen were now permitted to marry for the first time, and England, in official theory at least, had become a thoroughly Protestant nation. The doctrinal position of the established church was laid down in 1553 with the passage of the Forty-Two Articles. The Eucharistic theology of the second Prayer Book was reiterated, and it was made clear that justification before God was now by faith alone. Good works made no contribution to salvation, and salvation occurred instantaneously at death. Purgatory was dismissed as a vain fabrication. The official position on the doctrine of predestination was spelt out less clearly, and historians devote considerable time to arguing about the meaning of Article Seventeen.

The reign of Queen Mary (1553–8), our fourth phase, involved a rapid religious reversal. The rituals, materials and ideas that had been outlawed under Edward were reinstated by his half-sister. Protestant bishops were deprived of their offices. Parliamentary statutes and official injunctions resurrected the Mass, altars, images, crucifixes, holy days, the old ceremonial, clerical celibacy and the papal supremacy. An attempt was made to relaunch at least some of the religious houses. Most infamously, Protestants were harassed under the heresy laws; many of the wealthier ones fled to the continent, but something like three hundred were burnt in England, including Thomas Cranmer. More positively, the reign – all too short in the eyes of Catholic historians – witnessed a campaign to re-educate and reassure the English laity following the radical Reformation of Edward VI.

Our fifth phase commences with the accession of Elizabeth I in 1558, which brought an end to this campaign. But the Protestant clarity which England's most committed reformers hoped to see was not about to appear. The queen's personal signals were ambiguous from the early years of her reign: she objected forcibly to the traditional elevation of the Eucharistic host in the service marking her coronation, but insisted on retaining the crucifix, another symbol of conservatism, in her chapel. Her somewhat contradictory Protestantism helped to protect England from the ravages of religious warfare then being endured by the French, but it ensured paradoxically that for years the situation was fragile, and the established church faced attack from both sides.

The new liturgy, published in the 1559 Book of Common Prayer, was – like Elizabeth herself – unquestionably Protestant but certainly not dogmatically or straightforwardly so. Its communion service combined the forms of both of Edward's Prayer Books, thus establishing Protestantism in a flexible manner that may have allowed many Catholic believers to participate. The new book also omitted several of the more clearly Protestant, and thus anti-Catholic, references and requirements that had been included in 1552. Use of the Prayer Book was to be enforced under the terms of the Act of Uniformity (1559). Another pillar of the Elizabethan settlement was the Act of Supremacy (1559), which established the queen as supreme governor of the Church, ordered the laity to receive the communion in both kinds, and revoked all the now offensive Marian religious legislation. A set of royal injunctions (1559) further reinforced the whole programme, and Protestant bishops replaced their Catholic predecessors.

The first thirty years of the reign saw continuous agitation on the part of the more zealous Protestants, campaigning over what they saw as the only partially reformed nature of the new Church, and over government efforts to insist on their conformity to the established ceremonial requirements. The mid-1560s were marked by arguments over the wearing of the surplice, unacceptable to the more dogmatic ministers. A number lost their livings over their refusal to use this controversial garment. From the later 1560s, radical Protestants in parliament regularly put forward bills for further reform of the Church, which generally failed and provoked the anger of the queen. Topics addressed by these bills included clerical non-residence and pluralism, amendment of the Prayer Book, abuses in the church courts, and the possibility of greater liturgical latitude for Protestant ministers. The 1580s saw some particularly fierce parliamentary encounters, with the proposal (and failure) of bills that attacked episcopacy and would have introduced a Presbyterian system of church government to England.

This radical, Presbyterian strain had emerged within zealous Protestantism during the 1570s and was associated with the Geneva-inspired clerical activists Thomas Cartwright and John Field. In the same decade, clergymen 'of the hotter sort' in East Anglia began coming together for preaching conferences, known as 'prophesyings', to the alarm of the queen. The Archbishop of Canterbury, Edmund Grindal, was suspended from office in 1577 for his refusal to suppress these initiatives. During the next decade, the radicals organised Presbyterian-style 'classes' in their localities, and a minority of them moved towards actual separation from the established church. Small numbers of separatists were executed in 1583 and 1593, a trend which reflects the influence of John Whitgift, the new and fiercely anti-puritan Archbishop of Canterbury. Whitgift emerged victorious from the inter-Protestant struggles of the 1580s, and the latter part of the decade also saw the deaths of godly Protestant heroes such as John Field and the Earl of Leicester. In 1590–1, another great hero, Thomas Cartwright, was tried in the courts of High Commission and Star Chamber for his allegedly subversive Presbyterian activities.

Throughout these decades, the church was also under threat from surviving and reviving Catholicism. In 1569, the anti-Protestant revolt of the 'Northern Earls' caused great alarm, though with hindsight it looks considerably less dangerous. From 1574, missionary priests were arriving in England from seminaries on the continent, intent on boosting the native Catholic cause. They were soon joined by Jesuits. In 1570, the Pope excommunicated Elizabeth, thereby placing his English followers in a painful dilemma. The vast majority remained loyal to the queen, though a tiny handful added substantially to the atmosphere of tension by becoming involved in plots to kill her and seize the reins of government. The period, not surprisingly, witnessed a progressive turning of the legislative screw, as ever fiercer statutes were passed against Catholics, and particularly their priests. There is a sense in which the energy and anger of the radical Protestants, thwarted in their attempts to achieve further reform, was channelled into increasingly harsh anti-Catholic laws. From the mid-1570s, seminary priests were pursued, and frequently executed for their activities. In 1588, the year of the Armada, 31 priests lost their lives.

Elizabeth's last decade (1593–1603), our sixth and final phase, looks reasonably settled in comparison with the rest of her reign. The situation was still fragile, and the atmosphere could still feel oppressive and unpleasant, but it seems that something resembling religious stability was beginning to develop. Radical Protestants were, by this time, in a much weakened position. Catholicism too appears to have posed a lesser threat. As Diarmaid MacCulloch puts it, 'From the 1590s, persecuted [Catholic] gentry and government persecuting machine seem usually to have settled down to a rather surprising degree of symbiosis.'[25] Perhaps this shift of mood had something to do with simple, generational turn-over; by the mid-1590s, the great majority of England's population had no personal memory of a different kind of church and religious culture. The need for change, and the prospect of change, may have seemed more remote.

Symbolically, the first great defence of what would one day be called 'Anglicanism' was published in 1593, written by Richard Hooker. The Catholics were still a threat, though the unity of their cause was in question as the Jesuits squabbled with secular priests and laypeople over questions of loyalty, jurisdiction and strategy. The government naturally attempted to exploit these divisions, and at the end of the century a small number of secular priests was negotiating with officialdom over the possibility of arranging some form of reconciliation. Nothing much came of the encounter, but it does suggest a mood very different from that which had prevailed in the 1580s. Zealous Protestantism, too, was somewhat quieter and more domestically-orientated than it had previously been. The century ends, therefore, with a phase of fragile equilibrium, not entirely dissimilar in tone to that with which it had opened.

Of course, the religious world in 1600 was more tense and more complicated than it had been in 1500. The emergence of two mutually opposed sets of ideas about how humans might hope to reach God had seen to that. One 'pathway to heaven' led the Catholic believer through participation in the seven sacraments, the performance of penitential good works, and faith in Jesus Christ. Guidance along the way came from other powerful intercessors – the saints, the Blessed Virgin Mary, and also members of the priesthood. The layperson's map to this route was colourful and pictorial, and each step in the right direction was to be marked by a ritual observance or gesture. The alternative pathway took the Protestant believer through a very different terrain. Here, the seven sacraments were reduced to two (baptism and the Eucharist), and their centrality was more cautiously defined. Good works could no longer provide a surge of acceleration; instead, they could only indicate that the traveller was heading the right way. On this second route, guidance came 'only' from Christ, and without Him one was utterly lost. Christ also supplied the map, in the form of Scripture: words written on pages, or pronounced from the pulpit, or recited from memory. Visual images were regarded with a new distrust. And as the traveller proceeded, he or she was to think and reflect, cutting ceremonial gestures to a bare minimum. But having said all this, we should be careful not to exaggerate the starkness of the choice as it was perceived by ordinary people at the grassroots. They were not all prepared to trust exclusively in one map or the other. This attitude bred tensions of its own, but also a kind of stability. By 1600, it seems that some at least of the tensions generated by the development of two rival theological systems were beginning to ease – for the time being at least.

The remainder of this study is not structured along primarily narrative lines, for the simple reason that many others *are*. It can also be argued that a thematic approach may draw us into an exploration of possibilities which sometimes seem to go neglected. This was a period of religious continuity as well as change, and an awareness of the many ways in which the two were juxtaposed and interrelated will help us to understand how and why the English Reformation unfolded as it did. Historians who show an interest in religious continuities are sometimes criticised by certain of their colleagues for seeking to perpetuate the Anglo-Catholic myth of the Reformation, which argues that Elizabeth's Church as conceived by its founders was not really Protestant at all but instead a beautifully reformed version of the late-medieval institution. This line of criticism can be frustrating for social historians who see themselves as neither Anglican, nor Catholic, nor Protestant, but who are interested primarily in understanding a complex and fascinating historical process. The sensation is rather like that of being drawn unwillingly into a bar-room brawl without fully understanding what the fight is about. It occurs to me, an innocent in such disputes, that one way to approach a balanced understanding of sixteenth-century religion may be to consider it in terms of three broad themes, each involving the relationship of laypeople to the church, as they were played out during this most intriguing of centuries. This will inevitably lead to some losses, but it may conceivably produce some gains.

The foremost of several central themes to emerge as a result of this approach is, I hope, encapsulated in the sub-title of this book, which uses an expression taken from the marriage service in the Book of Common Prayer: 'Therefore if any man can shewe any just cause, why thei may not lawfully be joyned together let hym now speake, or else hereafter for ever holde his peace.' At a superficial level, to 'hold one's peace' indicates merely a decision to remain silent. This, as suggested above, was precisely what the majority of England's population seems to have done during the turbulence of the Reformation. Like people attending a wedding about which they had misgivings, the majority decided not to speak out. The famous Prayer Book injunction is notable in that it appears to allow, even to encourage, silence concerning objections which are held to be valid, in the interests of some wider good.

The now archaic use of the word 'peace' identifies that wider good for us. The message, it seems, is that justifiable complaints can and should, in certain circumstances, be withheld in order to promote harmony within the Christian community. It will be argued here that at the very core of popular religion in the sixteenth century lay an aspiration to communal peace. As Mildred Campbell commented, many years ago, good neighbourliness stood 'perhaps first in the criteria by which the social and ethical standing of an individual in a community was measured'. Keith Wrightson and David Levine encountered a testator who, in 1603, made one of his last bequests conditional upon the recipient 'behaving himself honestlie and neighbourlie as a christian should and ought to doo'.[26] The term 'community' is not intended here to imply any cosy, parochial tranquillity during an age of high political turmoil. Rather, it designates a hope and a dream, conceived very much in spiritual terms, that Christians might be able to live together in a state of concord or 'charity'.

This dream found expression in a wide variety of settings, ranging from participation in the liturgies of the church to the customs of 'good fellowship' played out in the alehouse. It was under intense strain during the century of the Reformation, as the preceding paragraphs make clear, and it sometimes seemed to have been shattered. 'Community' was, therefore, continually having to be reconstructed and buttressed. Yet through all this, ordinary people held onto the dream, refusing to relinquish it, as certain Elizabethan clergymen sought to persuade them, for example, that the church and the alehouse were incompatible. At times, of course, individuals 'forgot their duty towards god', as one contrite fornicator from Essex put it, and social–religious conflict was very far from uncommon. There were always, furthermore, those who fell outside the bounds of 'community', and who attracted the hostility of their contemporaries. Amity and enmity were locked into a never-ending dialogue, and one of the characters in James Shirley's mid-seventeenth-century play *The Brothers* spoke despairingly of 'The fierce vexation of community'.[27] But an awareness of the duty to promote peace through reconciliation remained at the heart of commonplace piety, and is therefore central to any attempt at understanding how communities survived the Reformation. The 'social miracle' was even harder to enact in 1600 than it had been in 1500, but it was still something which a majority of England's people hoped to make possible.

The thesis that emerges can perhaps be characterised as a distinctively English version of Germany's 'communal reformation', analysed by Peter Blickle. The differences, naturally enough, are conspicuous. Blickle's portrayal of early sixteenth-century German burghers and peasants as locked into a struggle for communal autonomy against their landlords clearly will not suffice as a depiction of the contemporary English population. Ordinary English men and women were not, therefore, drawn to (selected) Protestant doctrines primarily because of their utility in a quest for political and social emancipation. For Blickle, the early German reformation, in town and country, came 'from below' with a vengeance.

Nevertheless, Blickle's belief in the vital importance of 'community' and associated concepts has obvious importance for historians of England. The people of early sixteenth-century England, like their German counterparts, 'perceived . . . the ideas of the reformation through [their] integration into a communal association'. The reception of Protestantism was profoundly conditioned by consensual and powerful ideas about the importance of 'community'. England's circumstances meant that its 'communal reformation', in comparison with Blickle's German version, was more cautious, more compromising and actually more clearly Christian in its motivation. The Reformation, when viewed through the spectacles of English communalism, had a softer aura than its German sibling. As in Germany, however, concepts of community and neighbourliness provide arguably the best chance of 'understanding the history of how the reformation was received within society'.[28]

2

LAYFOLK WITHIN THE CHURCH

The Centrality of the Church

Perceptions of the nature and extent of lay involvement within the church have varied considerably. Historians used to speak of the Reformation as 'the triumph of the laity' over an all too dominant priesthood. Scholars such as Scarisbrick reject this view, presenting instead a Reformation which suppressed and reduced lay initiative, leaving a clerical elite whose members no longer represented the interests of their parishioners. More recently still, Nicholas Alldridge has argued that, if lay activity within the church suffered any diminution, it soon reasserted itself and flourished again.[1] The purpose of this chapter is to sift and assess the evidence.

Sixteenth-century churches, in both a physical and a psychological sense, generally stood near the centre of their parishes. Recent historians have described the early-modern parish church as 'the locale for the constitution and reproduction of the Christian community', and as the source of an 'immensely powerful field of force'. It is vital to acknowledge this centrality in any attempt to understand the shifting religious patterns of the sixteenth century. As Margaret Aston has put it, 'The Reformation for most believers meant the reformation of their parish church.'[2]

Before and after the Reformation, the local church was a vital forum for the propagation and absorption of moral lessons. Through sermons, rituals and liturgical lessons, people learnt and re-learnt the rules of 'upright dealing', and asked forgiveness for their shortcomings. They were taught how to live, and they expressed their respect for the church by conducting a significant amount of their day-to-day business in and around the

27

church. Testators frequently asked that their bequests be handed out in the south porch of the church. Elementary schooling was often available in one of the rooms connected to the church. In Weaverham (Cheshire), the Jacobean parishioners complained that the keeping of a school within the church itself was causing the spread of fleas and lice amongst the adult congregation. A chamber over the north porch at Mildenhall (Suffolk) served as the town's armoury, while the parishioners of Bury St Edmunds kept barrels of gunpowder in their vestry. The church bells were rung in order to convey a variety of messages – imminent danger, local deaths, or causes for celebration – to the parishioners. The church was also the setting for the election of local officers, from the churchwarden to the mole-catcher. And it was there and thereabouts that, a little less respectably, local children gathered to play. In 1596, the leading parishioners of one London parish decided to lock up the church after weekday services in order to restrict the mischievous antics of 'boyes and others'.[3]

More fundamentally still, it was through the church that people learnt how they might be saved. Of course, the official details and the required duties underwent very substantial change during the period, but – at both ends of the century – there were very few English people who believed that an individual could achieve salvation without attending the services held in their parish church. Spiritual identities were forged in the local church, or at the very least in relation to it. Something similar can be said of social identities, for the church provided a central forum for the establishment of local reputations and interrelationships. People observed and judged the behaviour of their neighbours while attending divine service, and repeated ill conduct could make a severe impact upon one's 'credit' in the neighbourhood. Young men and young women also watched one another at Sunday services, and many a married couple could probably have traced their attachment to the moment when their eyes met across a crowded nave. The way in which one dressed was another important consideration, and non-attenders sometimes pleaded a lack of suitable clothing when they appeared before the ecclesiastical courts.

Special church services, before and after the Reformation, also marked the most crucial stages in an individual's development. It goes without saying that these official rites of passage changed significantly during the sixteenth century. The discontinuities were striking and, to some, traumatic. Marriage ceased to be a sacrament, and Protestant theologians feared that the institution would be under strain as a result. The ritual of exorcism which had been central to late-medieval baptisms was dropped in the Protestant Prayer Books of 1552 and 1559, and the church's burial rites were radically simplified at the same dates. A set of rituals that had begun the day before the funeral and continued for months or even years became a single, final service of burial that rejected outright the possibility that the efforts of the living could in any way benefit the souls of the dead. In the words of Eamon Duffy, 'the boundaries of human community have been redrawn' with the official denial of that fundamental channel of communication between people in the parishes and souls languishing in purgatory.[4] Protestantism shook the world.

The liturgical ground certainly shifted beneath peoples' feet, but it is by no means clear that the earth was in serious danger of opening up – except under the sexton's trusty spade as he prepared the next grave. Some people, it is true, were alarmed at the changes. A traditionalist Yorkshire parson warned in 1535 that, if reformist measures were instituted, 'we should have no more Christian burial than dogs'.[5] The vast majority of people, however, seem to have survived the changes without any acute anxiety. In 1600, as in 1500, they were baptised, married and buried according to the rites of the established church. A crucial factor in explaining this transfer of allegiance must have been the liturgical continuities that rubbed shoulders, or jostled, with the potentially unsettling changes in the Protestant Prayer Books of the mid-century. In baptism, for example, renunciation of the devil still lay at the heart of things; the vicar still made the sign of the cross in water on the child's forehead; and participation in the rite was still treated as a matter of urgency, and probably something that remained essential for salvation. People were still married with a symbolic ring, and the dignity of marriage was strongly emphasised. Similar continuities marked the burial service, despite the fundamental changes in its underlying theology, and Elizabethan puritans disliked the on-going and optimistic assumption that the soul of the deceased was saved, as if all belonged to the 'elect'. It seems, however, that most Elizabethans adjusted gradually but smoothly to the new burial rites, which were described by the Bishop of Durham as 'a great comfort to all Christians'. By 1600, popular attachment to the reformed rites of passage could be extremely strong, and Judith Maltby has recently gathered numerous examples of laypeople ready to confront clergymen who, through scruple or negligence, omitted any part of the official services. It should also be remembered that late Elizabethans passed through these rites in the same buildings and graveyards as their Henrician ancestors had done. The power of this obvious continuity is not to be dismissed lightly.[6]

A similar mixture of change and continuity, minority controversy and majority compliance, emerges in David Cressy's recent analysis of the 'churching' ceremony, which marked a woman's return to public participation in the life of the community following childbirth. This was an old rite whose survival was probably due in no small part to its popularity, though its theological purpose shifted from 'purification' to 'thanksgiving' in the process. It was despised by the most zealous Elizabethan Protestants, who saw it as an offensive 'popish' survival. From our less heated perspective, the retention of the 'churching' ceremony looks like one of the many flexible continuities that encouraged attachment to the reformed church. Wright and Boulton have found statistically high levels of compliance in the later sixteenth century, and some parishioners were prepared to confront clergymen who refused to use the ceremony. One such cleric reported that, in 1584, 'a butcher did beat me in the street because I yielded not to a superstitious coming to church, which his wife used after her deliverance in childbirth'. It was, therefore, a continuity that contributed to conflict, and tensions over 'churching' rose significantly during the 1630s, but in the pre-Laudian period it was also, paradoxically, a stabilising influence because of its links with the past.

In a more general sense, churching, throughout the period, was unusual and important in that it placed women at the centre of a liturgical rite. In a patriarchal age, this mattered. It provided them with an occasion which they could make their own, and Cressy is critical of the argument that 'churching' was essentially an oppressive male institution, a ritual of purification imposed on reluctant women. It might be unwise to deny this possibility entirely, but it is certainly clear that 'churching' became a popular focus for female festivity and piety. It was a time for feasting and conviviality, with women at the forefront. We have recently been told 'There is little doubt that female spirituality was...more intense than men's'.[7] If such a bold statement is valid, then it is clear that the churching ceremony must have fulfilled a vital role.

The parish church therefore watched over and marked the most important occasions in an individual's life. It was also the most important venue for the propagation and consolidation of hierarchical values. In theory, the whole community attended church regularly and simultaneously. No other institution could make such a claim, and it is therefore not surprising that in church, more than anywhere else, people received and expressed their sense of place. In a variety of ways, before and after the Reformation, the precise contours of the social hierarchy were negotiated and displayed in church. The community came together, but it also revealed its many ranks and subdivisions.

In the early sixteenth century, the place people occupied in parish processions and the order in which they received the holy bread on Sundays were both carefully arranged to affirm the local hierarchy. In the later sixteenth century, church seating was coming to fulfil a similar function, as we shall see. One Elizabethan yeoman told his vicar of his wish to receive the communion the following Sunday, but then backed off deferentially when he heard that the more eminent 'Mr Talmage' was planning to receive on the same occasion. Once inside church, ordinary people were expected to rise from their seats in order to acknowledge the arrival of their betters. The young were expected to show respect for the old, and one youth from Littleport (Isle of Ely) was presented to the church courts in the 1570s because he had been discourteous to Elizabeth Dove and her mother as they arrived at, and departed, the church: 'he let the mother passe bye, not putting of his cappe to her, but when the daugh- ter...came againste him [i.e. passed nearby] he moved his cappe to hir and smiled at hir, bothe goeing and comeinge'.[8] This example, seemingly trivial to us, demonstrates clearly the vital role played by the church in the construction and maintenance of a hierarchical community.

Participation in Church Services: the Opportunities

Any analysis of sixteenth-century church services will inevitably be dom- inated by the repeated and far-reaching changes of liturgical direction that occurred as a result of royal command. Once again, however, it may also be useful to keep our eyes and ears open for signs of continuity: rituals, beliefs and emphases that were retained through the turmoil, and that perhaps made the transition from old to new more manageable in the localities. This section also needs to be manageable, and will therefore concentrate primarily on the development of the main, Sunday services held in England's parish churches. These were, after all, the backbone of parish Christianity and the most regular occasions upon which ordinary people encountered the holy. Historians have often failed to consider the significance for popular religion of the official liturgy, though several recent commentators have begun to set the record straight (or at least to skew it in a different direction). As Eamon Duffy has argued, 'the liturgy was in fact the principal reservoir from which the religious paradigms and beliefs of the people were drawn'. It marked time on a daily, weekly and yearly basis for a society that possessed few clocks. 'For townsmen and countrymen alike, the rhythms of the liturgy...remained the rhythms of life itself.'[9]

Before the Reformation, English men and women were required, under ecclesiastical law, to attend Matins, Mass and Evensong on Sundays, with regularity and respect. The main Sunday Mass was, without doubt, the centrepiece of the liturgical week, and was conducted largely in Latin. Let us imagine a typical parish service of c.1520. It commences with the blessing of salt and water, and a procession during which holy water is sprinkled on the church's altars and on the congregation. The priest, in his vestments, then recites the 'Confiteor' (confession of sins) and certain Scripture lessons. He next pronounces a solemn prayer in English, calling upon the congregation to pray for all their earthly leaders, for each other, and for the souls of the dead. The priest then prepares bread and wine for consecration, as the high point of the service approaches. The 'sacring' is a particularly solemn phase of the Mass, and one of the church bells is tolled so that people know that the moment of elevation is near. The priest recites the 'canon', a long prayer of consecration centring on Christ's words at the last supper, and involving the ritualised 'elevation of the host' for adoration by the people. Through the mysterious process of 'transubstantiation', the bread and wine are changed into the body and blood of Jesus Christ.

The priest then kisses the corporas and the chalice (vessels for the bread and wine respectively) in turn, followed by the 'paxbred' (a sacred tablet or disc). The paxbred is then passed amongst the congregation in order of seniority, and kissed by everyone in turn. The priest next recites the Lord's Prayer, before receiving the communion and dismissing the congregation with a blessing. Finally, he recites the 'In principio', taken from the opening of St John's Gospel. The service then closes with the distribution amongst the people of a 'holy loaf' of bread, baked by each household in rotation and believed to have protective powers.[10]

Historians seem to know little about the frequency of sermons within the standard Sunday services of late-medieval England. Certainly, there were numerous pulpits and a system for the licensing of preachers. Sermons were therefore far from unknown, and the official expectation was that they would take place four times a year, at least. Sermons could also be lively: one priest gave performances sufficiently animated that he is said to have died from injuries sustained while preaching. Yet it appears that many sermons were less inspired, and even Scarisbrick has described the vivid allegorising of much pre-Reformation preaching as 'ultimately sterile'.[11] Colourful tales of saints and miracles predominated, and preaching of any sort was probably a rare occurrence in the majority of rural churches. Pulpits, it should be remembered, were also used by priests when they urged the congregation to pray for the souls of the dead.

The music for the Mass was provided by the parish clerk, local chantry priests, and – where resources were available – an organ and a choir. In the cathedrals and largest churches, the accompanying music could be elaborate and polyphonic, but in the smaller rural churches attended by the bulk of the population, it must have been far simpler. Most commonly, it consisted of plainsong, including the intoning of psalms, with a simple, improvised vocal accompaniment. At no point in the service did members of the congregation sing for themselves.

The laity did, however, take part in a variety of ways. They were expected to make occasional Latin responses, and to pray privately at a number of points (for example, during the Confiteor, the Gloria, the offertory and the Sanctus), and we can imagine the service being punctuated periodically by the muttering of Aves, Pater Nosters and elevation prayers. One homely and touching example of the latter opened with the lines, 'Jhesu Lord, welcome thow be / In forme of bred as I the[e] se[e].'[12] Literate members of the congregation might carry with them to church printed works containing specific prayers, designed to assist them in their devotions. At the sacring, layfolk were expected to kneel with their hands raised, and to gaze upon the host as it was elevated. They were also to stand up when the gospel was read, and to participate reverently in the rituals accompanying the passing of the paxbred and the holy loaf. Duffy has portrayed these ceremonies as substitutes for actual reception of the communion, which was usually restricted to the priesthood. In the symbolism of paxbred and holy loaf, he sees one example of the fundamental centrality within the Mass of corporate harmony, and of human, as well as heavenly, bonding. 'What all these dramatic Sunday ceremonies have in common is an emphasis on the location and maintenance of blessing, healing, and peace within the community.'[13]

The middle decades of the century saw the Mass adjusted, translated, abolished, reinstituted, then abolished again – this time, as it turned out, more permanently – in 1559. These were confusing years in the parishes of England. In the late 1530s, Thomas Cromwell ordered that a much higher importance be attached to sermons and to the education of the laity in the basics of faith. In the Henrician portion of the 1540s, Cranmer was preparing the way for the introduction of an English Prayer Book, and in

1544 an English version of the 'litany' was printed for use in parish churches. Celebration of the Mass, however, remained largely traditional at this time. The reign of Edward VI marked a far more decisive break with the past, and the main Sunday service was transformed, first relatively gently and then quite radically, in the Prayer Books of 1549 and 1552 respectively. By the end of the reign, the experience of church attendance must have seemed very different to the laity. The second Prayer Book dropped the word 'Mass', and much of its structure. Services were now to be conducted wholly in English, and sermons were to become more frequent and more central. Symbolically, the sacring bell was banned, but parishes were permitted to ring a bell just before the sermon. Other casualties included the parish procession, the sprinkling of holy water, much of the traditional Latin music, the old priestly garments (except the surplice), the pax, the holy bread, and the elevation of the host.

It was envisaged that reception of communion would remain a regular feature of the service, but it was now to be administered regularly and in both kinds (bread and wine) to the laity. The minister should not take communion alone, and ordinary wheaten bread was to replace the special wafers of old. Transubstantiation was now repudiated, and Christ was no longer deemed to be physically present in the bread and wine. The words spoken by the minister as communion was administered to members of his flock were now purely commemorative, and the exchange was to take place at a wooden table in the body of the church rather than at a stone altar. As we shall see, this was by no means the only change to be ordered in the organisation of church interiors.

The 1552 order for the celebration of Holy Communion became obsolete in the following year with the accession of Queen Mary. The Latin Mass returned to the parish churches of England, though several historians have noted that the old services were not often restored in all their richness. In 1556, orders were still being issued for the reintroduction of parish processions, implying that many communities had so far failed to bring them back. It has also been remarked that the Marian authorities were willing to learn from what they saw as the more worthwhile reformist initiatives of recent years. In particular, the Marian church placed considerable emphasis on sermons, and followed the Edwardian church in printing books of official 'homilies', for use by priests who were not qualified to preach for themselves. Marian Catholicism was not, therefore, the reactionary, blinkered beast portrayed by an earlier generation of historians.

The Elizabethan settlement of 1559 abolished the Mass once'more, and shunted the country back towards Protestantism. Given the repeated

liturgical reversals of recent decades, it must be assumed that the new
services were greeted at first with a certain degree of fatigue and even
scepticism. To combat such feelings, the traditional requirement that all
adults attend church services every Sunday was now backed by a parliamentary Act of Uniformity (1559), which ordered that non-attenders pay a
fine of twelve pence for each offence. More sensitively, the unavoidable
misgivings of traditionalists – undoubtedly a majority in 1559 – were
answered, partially at least, by the retention of certain ancient features,
such as kneeling at key points in the service, and the wearing of the clerical
surplice. The Prayer Book of 1559, by a combination of accident and
design, was also in some ways more flexible and ambiguous than the 1552
version, upon which it was based. The settlement was definitely Protestant,
as Duffy and MacCulloch have both argued forcibly, but it was also
designed to encourage the conformity, if not necessarily the enthusiasm,
of most conservatives; in time, such people might learn to love the
reformed services and to absorb their Protestant messages.

The new services inevitably took several years (at least) to settle into
place; but by c.1580, the Sunday service must have felt considerably less
'new', and may even have begun to generate an aura of permanence. It is
worth noting that, by this date, a majority of the population had no
personal memory of the pre-1540 period during which Catholicism had
felt established and secure. The Elizabethan settlement, though always
dogged by controversy, was the most stable liturgical system they had
experienced. The demographic structure meant that a high proportion –
perhaps more than half – of the population was under twenty years of age,
and had therefore been baptised into the Elizabethan church. It may be
instructive to reconstruct a typical Sunday service of the mid-Elizabethan
years, for comparison with the parish Mass of c.1520.

In 1577, the chronicler Holinshed wrote a brief but valuable summary
of the standard Sunday morning service.[14] He began, 'After a certain
number of psalms read, which are limited according to the dates of the
month, ... we have two lessons, whereof the first is taken out of the old
testament, the second out of the new.' This was in fact an extremely
compressed description of the 1559 Prayer Book's 'ordre for morning
prayer'. In this, the minister began by reading selected sentences from
Scripture 'with a lowde voyce'. He proceeded to lead the congregation in
a 'general confession' of their sins, for which they were instructed to kneel.
The minister then pronounced the absolution, which beseeched God 'to
graunt us true repentaunce and hys holy spirite'. Here, and throughout
the service, the laity were required to pronounce in unison a varied series

of responses to the minister's words. There followed a group of psalms, to be 'sayde or song' (the Prayer Book did not specify by whom). Next came the two lessons, which again were allowed to be sung 'in a plaine tune after the maner of distinct readinge'. The first lesson was to be followed by a recitation in English of the 'Te Deum' ('We prayse the, O God...'), and the second by the 'Benedictus' ('Blessed be the Lord God of Israel...'), also in the vernacular. The entire congregation then stood to pronounce the Creed, before 'devoutlye knelyng' for certain prayers, one of which was the Lord's Prayer, to be spoken by all. After further brief prayers, the service concluded with the three 'collects', which asked for God's blessing on the Queen, for peace, and for the granting of grace to live righteously (and safely).[15]

This was not, however, the end of the laity's morning devotions. Holinshed went on, 'After morning prayer we have the litany and the suffrages.' This was a long series of short prayers, in which the people, following their minister's lead, pleaded for mercy, protection from sin and the earthly hurt which followed it. It ended with prayers specifically tailored to periods of drought, excessive rain, dearth, war, and plague. These were selected and recited as the times required.

'This being done,' Holinshed continued, 'we proceed unto the communion, if any communicants be to receive the eucharist: if not we read the decalogue, epistle and gospel, with the Nicene creed..., and then proceed unto an homily or sermon, which hath a psalm before and after it.' In most parishes, the communion was probably offered mainly on important feast days, so that the normal Sunday morning had the sermon rather than the Eucharist as its centrepiece. Holinshed was in fact describing the pre-communion stages of the Prayer Book's 'ordre for the administracion of the lordes supper', and it seems to have been customary by this date for this to be employed regularly on Sunday mornings, even when nobody was to receive the sacrament. The reference to the psalms before and after the sermon is an addition to the Prayer Book order, and probably refers to the communal singing of unaccompanied metrical psalms that is known to have been highly popular by this date. By 1580, they were the only music likely to be heard in the majority of parish churches.

An octogenarian, attending such a service in 1580, would have noticed many striking discontinuities with the parish Masses of his or her youth. The services were now in English, 'that each one present may hear and understand the same', as Holinshed proudly explained. The music had changed, becoming simpler and more participatory. The vicar's attire had also been simplified. The communion was no longer celebrated every week, but when it was, the laity were encouraged to receive it in both kinds. Sermons and homilies were now a more regular feature of church attendance. Much of the structure of the Mass had been dismantled. There was no procession and no paxbred.

But our ancient parishioner might also have drawn comfort from a considerable body of familiar liturgical routine. At an obvious and funda-mental level, Sunday services happened inside the same building as before. The vicar in his surplice still spoke, and the people uttered their responses. They also stood, knelt and sat during different phases of the service. Music remained an accepted way of praising and appealing to the almighty. The preservation of Christian community through the performance of 'com-mon prayer' and the inculcation of social virtue remained central object-ives of the liturgy. Members of the congregation still confessed their sins at the outset, and asked forgiveness throughout. They were still asked to concentrate on texts such as the Ten Commandments, the Creed and the Lord's Prayer; while the Te Deum and Benedictus even retained their Latin titles, though the words themselves were now in the vernacular. The royal injunctions of 1559 had also allowed, and even encouraged, the traditional habit of bowing at every mention of Jesus Christ. And Eliza-bethan Christians, like their Henrician forebears, continued to pray for their governors, for peace, for protection, and for salvation. It is arguable that the basic nature of these continuities renders them more, rather than less, important to our understanding of the process of Reformation. It should also be reiterated that the vast majority of those attending mid-Elizabethan church services were not octogenarians, and may therefore have needed these links with the past a little less intensely than their elders.

Certain details had been left somewhat vague in the Prayer Book, and the consequent measure of flexibility must also have eased the passage from old to new. There was, of course, a tactical drawback in this policy, and many parishes – particularly in the north and west – responded to the settlement's vagueness by clinging to rituals and practices that were no longer strictly permissible. In 1570, for example, a traditionalist parish clerk in Kingston-upon-Hull found himself in trouble for providing too much organ music during local services, thereby reducing the time avail-able for the sermon. He clearly regretted the Reformation's intended simplification of church music, though he said in his defence that he never left the minister with less than two hours for his homilies![16] The Prayer Book's relatively broad approach was expressed in the first instruc-tions accompanying the first of the printed services: morning and evening prayer were to be conducted 'in the accustomed place of the churche, chapel, or Chauncell'. This was not unduly prescriptive, and the use of the word 'accustomed' reflected a sensitivity to the emotional pull of the past upon the present.

Other matters too were loosely defined. The Prayer Book was ready to countenance the congregational singing of psalms, but did not expressly ban the more traditional chanting of anthems or setting of portions of the service to music. It was unclear whether the communion table should stand in the nave or the chancel, and whether it should be moved to a different location when not in use. Such ambiguities and continuities are vital in explaining the impressively smooth (but geographically varied) process by which the new services became accepted, despite the fact that there is little evidence of widespread dissatisfaction with the old services. This was clearly Protestantism, but in a flexible guise.

Historians such as Christopher Haigh tend to ignore or deny the possibility that the opportunities for lay participation in the Elizabethan services may have been attractive and exciting to many people, or may at the very least have helped to make the changes acceptable. They argue instead that sermons were long, pews were hard, and old rituals were sorely missed. The Prayer Book's only advantage was that, because of its compromises with the past, it could be distorted by conservatives into something like a version of the Mass. Eamon Duffy has also attempted to overturn old arguments about the exclusion of the laity from the late-medieval Mass, by arguing that the traditional services absorbed, stimulated and comforted virtually all the people virtually all of the time. The services in Latin, the offering of the communion in one kind only, and the presence of a rood screen which stood between the laity's nave and the priest's chancel, are all given a positive gloss. People may not have entered the chancel to watch the priest perform the miracle of transubstantiation on Sundays, but they 'passed visually' into that sacred space.[17]

These arguments form an important riposte to the assumptions of a previous generation of historians, but the new interpretation, like its predecessor, is unhelpfully one-sided. Though the majority of the late-medieval English population certainly were not thirsting for change, they may – after an inevitable period of shock and disorientation – have found some of that change relatively absorbing and therefore tolerable. In our Sunday service of *c.*1580, they spoke more than their grandparents had done; the proceedings were conducted in their own language, which must have counted for something; the minister now addressed them regularly and directly through his sermons or homilies; they provided their own music in a way utterly unknown half a century before; and the clergyman no longer received the communion alone. It cannot be doubted that many changes *were* deeply regretted, but others, like congregational psalm-singing, swiftly attracted popular enthusiasm. John Jewel, admittedly a biased observer, spoke of congregational singing spreading rapidly outwards from London in the 1560s. By the early seventeenth century, numerous sources attest to its deep roots. In Temperley's words, the metrical and musical psalms had become 'a treasured part of popular culture'.[18]

The main Sunday morning service was the focal point of a normal liturgical week, both before and after the Reformation, but it is also important to mention the other weekly services, both obligatory and voluntary. On Sundays, late-medieval laypeople were expected to attend Matins and Evensong as well as the Mass. During the week, parishes held regular 'low' Masses, usually for the souls of specific deceased parishioners or in honour of favoured saints. These Masses were simpler than the Sunday celebrations, and were conducted at one of the smaller altars set in the nave of the church. Weekday services therefore allowed members of the laity to witness the miracle of the Mass at closer quarters. In the Elizabethan church, parishioners were required to attend evening prayer as well as the lengthier morning service. Ministers were also to conduct public prayers on Wednesdays and Fridays, though attendance at these was not compulsory under the 1559 Act of Uniformity.

Reception of the communion by the laity was a matter closely related to the principal Sunday services, but for clarity it needs to be considered separately. Before the changes of mid-century, ecclesiastical law obliged people to take the communion once a year, at Easter, and 'in one kind' only (bread without wine). The Edwardian Reformation introduced communion in both kinds for the laity, and applied pressure towards more regular reception. The 1552 Prayer Book banned the clergy from receiving the communion unless joined by a good number of their parishioners. Its successor, the Book of 1559, retained this instruction, and ordered that 'every Parishioner shall communicate, at the leaste thre tymes in the yere, of whiche Easter to be one'. As Jeremy Boulton has observed, however, the canons of 1571 and subsequent dates urged the enforcement only of the requirement to receive at Easter.[19]

The Elizabethan communion service mixes a predominant Protestantism with traces of tradition in a way that, by now, is becoming familiar. Attention has often focused on the words spoken by the minister as he delivered bread and wine to each communicant. This was, of course, intended as a profoundly important moment in the spiritual life of the recipient, and it is therefore deeply significant that the Elizabethan form of words purposefully sought to encompass the feelings of radicals and traditionalists alike. It combined the expressions from the 1552 Prayer Book, which spoke only of 'remembrance', with those from the 1549 version, which allowed the possibility of Christ's 'real presence' in the bread and wine. It deliberately did not explain the precise sense in which Christ inhabited the Eucharistic elements. There is no doubting the essential Protestantism of the service, seen for example in the use of the vernacular, the lack of a specific moment of consecration, the employment of a wooden communion table rather than a stone altar, the emphasis on lay reception of the sacrament (and in both kinds), and the command that ordinary bread should replace the traditional communion wafer. It should also be noted, however, that when Elizabeth I issued her injunctions in 1559, she softened considerably the Prayer Book's specification concerning the replacement of stone altars by wooden communion tables, and expressly ordered that the bread should, 'for the more reverence', be presented in a form much closer to that of the traditional wafers.[20]

Even without these adjustments, the continuities within the communion service were pervasive: the emphasis on repentance, love and charity; the importance attached to worthy reception ('notorious evil livers' were to be excluded); the spiritual perils of unworthy reception; the order that parishioners were to receive the communion kneeling; the stress laid upon the Easter communion; and the centrality within the service of the Ten Commandments, the Creed, and the readings from Epistle and Gospel. In addition, the parishioners continued to make their financial contributions to the (now higher) costs of bread and wine. Much had changed, but much had not.

Throughout the century, the church also celebrated a number of additional feast days or holy days, and required that the laity attend special services held on these occasions. This basic stipulation did not change, though the ecclesiastical calendar itself underwent substantial transformation across the decades. The late-medieval liturgical year involved a rich and complex series of festivals, about fifty in all, each of which had its own customary services and rituals. The greatest of these were colourful, vibrant and symbolically powerful affairs, in which the laity had numerous opportunities for active participation.

At Candlemas, or the feast of the Purification of the Virgin Mary (2 February), the people carried candles to church before Mass, where they were offered to the priest for blessing. Parishioners then processed around the church with lighted candles – quite a spectacle for those enduring the winter without the benefit of light-bulbs. Ash Wednesday marked the start of the Lenten fast, and each individual was daubed by the priest with a mixture of holy water and blessed ashes, while being reminded of their mortality. Palm Sunday was marked by a special parish procession around the churchyard, in which the laity carried branches, and flowers were strewn over the choir. Good Friday involved the people in 'creeping to the cross', a ceremony in which they and the clergy crawled barefoot to the altar, where they kissed the crucifix. The crucifix was then laid in a special Easter sepulchre, where it stayed until Sunday. On this date, the sepulchre was opened and the crucifix was carried triumphantly around the church.

On the feast of Corpus Christi, parishes held major processions in which the consecrated host was carried through the town or village. The Rogation Days, in the early summer, were full of festivity and religious ceremony. For three days, laypeople participated in processions around the boundaries of their parish, carrying crosses and banners, stopping for gospel readings and to hear their priests bless cherished landmarks and crops. Many of these feast days also involved communal eating and drinking (often ending a period of fast), special Masses, and music as elaborate as the local resources would allow. It is difficult to read Duffy's loving evocation of all this ritual without accepting that it must indeed have brought great excitement and comfort to the lives of ordinary people.[21]

The early English reformers, however, considered this comfort to be illusory. All this calendrical clutter, they argued, had led people to worship the representation more than the represented, the crucifix rather than the crucified. The souls of participants were therefore imperilled, and the bodies would be better employed in honest labour. The rescue mission, conducted in the tussle and turbulence of the mid-century 'years of uncertainty', aimed to create a far simpler liturgical year. Feast days in honour of the saints were under attack as early as 1536, when an Act of Convocation ordered a reduction in their numbers. In 1545, Henry told Cranmer to suppress the ceremony of 'creeping to the cross', amongst others, but he subsequently cancelled the order. Edwardian injunctions, proclamations and Prayer Books attacked England's festive traditions more committedly and consistently; on 6 February 1547, for example, the government banned not only 'creeping to the cross' but the use of candles at Candlemas, ashes on Ash Wednesday, and palms on Palm Sunday. By the end of the reign, a number of the less important saints' days had been abolished. Edward's successor, Mary, restored fewer of them than might have been expected, so that Elizabeth inherited a liturgical calendar somewhat simpler than that of her father's reign.[22]

The official position adopted in the Elizabethan settlement was, as on other matters, a version of that which had prevailed under Edward VI. Elizabeth's injunctions banned parish processions, with the notable exception of the Rogationtide rituals. Even these were to be simplified: neither crosses nor banners were to be carried, and the priest was to wear secular dress. It seems clear that the end of most processions must have meant a considerable reduction in the potential for lay participation on holy days. Amidst all this talk of conspicuous discontinuity, however, it is wise to remember that not all was utterly transformed. The 'holy days' permitted in an official list of 1560 were considerably more numerous than those allowed by Edward, and popular medieval saints like George and Cecilia made a comeback. This added to the thirty-seven holy days specified in the 1559 Prayer Book, and Ronald Hutton speaks of 'a profound ambiguity concerning the number of seasonal feasts in the calendar and the pastimes which were to be encouraged or discouraged on them'. He considers it likely that, in practice, the Elizabethan clergy permitted the retention of some at least of the accompanying ritual, as long as it moved out of the church.[23] The Prayer Book, furthermore, still specified for each of its holy days the appropriate additions to the standard church services, and still insisted that parishioners come to church on these days.

This survey of the laity's many responsibilities for involvement in the liturgical life of the church also needs to take account of several more voluntary opportunities. Late-medieval people, for example, could exert a direct influence on the liturgy by giving or leaving money to finance the celebration of extra Masses, often held on weekdays. The grandest of such gifts, made by dying parishioners, founded 'chantries', institutions which then supported the saying or singing of special Requiem Masses for their souls. Other people made smaller gifts to support extra Masses in honour of the Blessed Virgin Mary or of a favoured saint. In all such cases, it was open to the laity to specify which collects, prayers and extra gospel readings they wished to be included in the services. Chantries were abolished in 1547, but other opportunities for lay influence survived the Reformation. Before and after, a testator could also leave money to finance the preaching of one or more sermons following his or her death. Parishioners were also able, usually through their churchwardens, to report their clergymen to the higher church authorities for any failure to conduct the liturgy according to duty and in an acceptable manner. Another vital opportunity for lay influence over worship – the supply and maintenance of church decorations and fittings – will be reserved to a later section.

Participation in Church Services: the Response

It is time now to consider the ways in which people responded to this abundant but shifting opportunity. There are, of course, many cases of a hostile and aggressive reaction to liturgical change. In 1536, for example, the parishioners of Beverley were alarmed when their priest, following orders, omitted to announce the imminence of St Wilfrid's day when he celebrated Mass on the previous Sunday. They challenged him openly as he stood in the pulpit, and were advised of the new rules. After the service, 'the whole parish was in a rumour and said that they would have their holydays bid and kept as before'. In the same year, thousands of northern people rose up in defence of traditional religion. Yet the overwhelming impression is that the parishes of England complied with the many changes they were ordered to endure, despite their anxieties, frustrations and misgivings. This point has been made most forcefully by Robert Whiting, who describes popular responses to the repeated liturgical reformations as 'predominantly acquiescent'. When, in 1537, two Cornish fishermen with the excellent names of Carpisack and Tregoslack tried to raise a force in defence of the abrogated holy days, they found few people willing to don any of the two hundred jerkins they had optimistically purchased as armour.[24]

Historians have formed divergent opinions of the extent to which the official church's services attracted and engaged the attention of the English population. The central problem is a general lack of statistically reliable evidence on matters such as church attendance. This vacuum often throws us back on more qualitative evidence, and creates an opportunity for historians to present educated assumption as established fact. This criticism can be levelled at pessimists and optimists alike. On the gloomy side, Keith Thomas has famously argued that 'a substantial proportion' of the population was hostile to organised religion and rarely if ever went to church. The poor, he says, were notoriously absent. And Peter Clark once made the unprovable statement that, under Elizabeth, absenteeism was rising as fast as population levels. Duffy's assumptions are far more positive, but not necessarily more reliable. We are told, for instance, that 'Virtually every town in England had had its Jesus Mass on Fridays ..., *well attended* and often a major focus of establishment piety' [my italics], but we are not presented with any evidence for this high level of attendance. Interestingly and surprisingly, Scarisbrick – one of Duffy's greatest admirers – had previously argued that many late-medieval people probably did not go to church regularly, and probably appreciated only the elevation of the host when they did.[25]

Contemporary commentators were similarly varied in their opinions, and similarly guided by their underlying assumptions. Their statements were not remotely objective, of course, and were often motivated by political anxiety, by a wish to fire the hearts of the majority with godly zeal, or alternatively by a desire to portray their own preferred liturgical options as more warmly received than all the rest. It is possible, therefore, to collect comments claiming both high and low attendance levels from virtually any decade. In the early 1560s, for instance, Sir Nicholas Bacon lamented the laxity of popular church attendance, but Sir John Chichester reported happily that in Devon 'the service in the church is well received and done for the most part of the shire'.[26] The validity of such assessments is very difficult to judge.

There is now, however, a considerable body of work that attempts to look more closely and cleverly at the subject of church attendance, and that enables us to build a reasonably reliable picture. The researches of Martin Ingram, Eric Carlson, Patrick Collinson and Nicholas Alldridge (together with John Morrill and Donald Spaeth for the seventeenth century) are all of immense value here.[27] The pre-Reformation portion of the picture is seriously out of focus, for the surviving sources simply are not adequate to the task. Margaret Bowker has deduced high levels of attendance from the rarity of ecclesiastical court prosecutions for absenteeism, but this rarity may well reflect a relaxed attitude to prosecution rather than genuinely impressive conformity. One mid-fifteenth-century cleric complained that the people 'come to matins no more than three times a year' and that, even then, they grumbled that the dawdling priest 'keeps them from their breakfast'. Norman Tanner was struck by the levels of non-attendance in the Lincoln and Hereford dioceses, and spoke of 'many people' who were accused of neglecting their most basic duties. Positive evidence on such matters is always more difficult to find, but it does exist: one late-medieval letter-writer noted incidentally that 'the more part of al the parisch' had been present at Mass on Easter Eve.[28] Overall, it seems most plausible to think in terms of reasonably high levels of conformity, and of a fairly non-intensive system of detection and prosecution. Those who found themselves in the courts were probably only the most persistent and defiant offenders.

Our knowledge of attendance levels in the middle of the sixteenth century is similarly vague. Robert Whiting has used negative contemporary reports to suggest that attendance was declining from the 1530s, in reaction to the period of change and challenge that commenced at this time.[29] An alternative reading is, as ever, possible, for it was also in the century's middle decades that anxiety and insecurity were at their height, as official policy changed direction again and again. Commentators may have been particularly disposed to see the church as half empty rather than half full during such a phase. Nevertheless, it does seem plausible to argue that the 'years of uncertainty' would also have been those during which ordinary laypeople were least inclined to attend their churches with regularity and enthusiasm. They must have felt that they did not know what to expect if and when they passed through the porch.

Whiting's account of popular religion in the south-west stops in 1570, at which point – in the author's judgement – enthusiastic attachment to the established church was at a very low ebb.[30] More recently, scholars have come to view the Reformation in a rather longer time-span, and have seen 1570 as more a starting point than an end. This makes considerable sense, for the Elizabethan church may at this time have begun to feel a little more sturdy than any of its recent predecessors. Nevertheless, conspicuous examples of low attendance in this and subsequent decades are still encountered. On one occasion in the first years of the seventeenth century, Archbishop Tobie Matthew – hardly an ecclesiastical unknown – arrived to preach in a rural church, but found 'neither priest nor people' ready to hear him. Individual absentees are also dotted through the records of the church courts, trotting out a wide range of excuses. In 1582, for example, a Wisbech man said his recently slack attendance at church was due to a fear of arrest for debt. His churchwardens, unconvinced, added sardonically, '& yet he can passe freely from alehouse to alehouse dayely without interruption'. In Essex, another lover of the alehouse explained, perhaps with tongue in cheek, that he could not get into church because of the crowds. Some decades later, a Wiltshire absentee promised generously that he would 'henceforward resort more often to the church when the weather is fair and that he hath not any extraordinary occasions to be absent'.[31]

Such cases notwithstanding, several historians are currently proposing a more positive view of church attendance than that taken by Peter Clark. Martin Ingram, for example, has used ecclesiastical court records to argue that between the 1570s and the 1620s, standards of religious observance may have improved steadily as the ecclesiastical authorities nudged the population towards regular weekly attendance. Of course, some contemporaries resented even a nudge, like the Ramsgate boatman who, in 1581, declared 'It was never merry England since we were impressed [i.e. forced] to come to the Church.' The clear implication, interestingly, is that this pressure to attend was a new thing. It is true that local officers were generally reluctant to apply the strictest of criteria – occasional absentees were often not pursued, and family members could be treated leniently if the head of the household attended – but a consensus was developing that required individuals to engage with their church on a weekly basis. Ingram's mildly positive view has been reinforced by Nicholas Alldridge, who argues, on the basis of a sophisticated study of parochial administration in Elizabethan and Jacobean Chester, that *minimum* levels of regular attendance varied from parish to parish between 51 per cent (a low 2.2) and 83 per cent (a good first). Even the authors of Protestant complaint literature, which accused the populace of dreadful religious laxity, nevertheless accepted that attending church on Sundays was part of the weekly rhythm of ordinary lives.[32]

Overall, it seems likely that levels of church attendance in 1500 and 1600 were roughly comparable, though slightly higher standards may have been more widely accepted by the latter date. In between, it may well be the case that levels of observance had fallen for a time, but the Elizabethan church was demonstrating an ability to turn any decline around, albeit gradually. Throughout the century, parishioners were liable to react unfavourably to any attempt to force upon them a puritanical rigour when it came to weekly attendance, but the majority were willing to come to church with what they considered reasonable regularity. They did not expect to be presented to the courts for a single lapse in attendance, but they accepted that repeated absence would and should earn a reprimand. Stricter standards naturally applied to the clergy, and the people of Great Abington (Cambridgeshire) were perplexed when they turned up for church one day in 1585, only to find that the vicar was absent: 'We were all at the churche and our minister was at the Alehouse', they reported with indignation.[33]

A similar portrayal of relaxed but reasonably impressive expectation and performance can be presented as we move on to look at standards of behaviour once inside the church. Several historians, led again by Keith Thomas, would have us believe that early-modern parishioners behaved abominably at services, turning them into 'a travesty of what was intended'. This, however, is to mis-read incidents of misbehaviour as reflections of contemporary norms (in fact, they were almost the opposite).

Of course, there were numerous and sometimes colourful examples of arrant misconduct, and no account of village life should be without a couple. In 1511, people in Woodchurch (Kent) were annoyed at the behaviour of Roger Harlakinden, who 'janglith and talkithe in the chirche when he is there and lettithe others to say [i.e. prevents others from saying] their divociones'. A century later, in Ely, a local drunkard named Thomas Redder made a heroic effort to appear at divine service, but detracted from his achievement when he 'emptied his Gordge in the churche there in prayers tyme'. As Martin Ingram has observed, however, cases such as these were not at all common.[34]

There were also, throughout the century, incidents suggesting personal indifference to the services on offer. Robert Whiting introduces us to a shoemaker from Axminster who, in 1535–6, said he 'would never go to the church for devotion, or holiness of the place; but because other men did such, to keep them company'. A similar lack of theological engagement characterised the Ely man who, in 1588, stood up during the sermon and asked the churchwardens 'yf they woulde or coulde helpe him to a privie aboute the Church'.[35]

Others, before and after the Reformation, used the church to conduct sometimes fierce tussles about status, and these too have sometimes been used to suggest a lack of respect for sacred space. It is perhaps more plausible, however, to argue that people who fought their social battles in the church in fact did so because the church mattered to them. In the early sixteenth century, these disputes often centred around the precise placing of people in parish processions, or the order in which they received the paxbred. On the Sunday before All Saints Day in 1522, an Essex man warned the presiding lay official 'Clerke, if thou here after gevist not me the pax first I shall breke it on thy hedd.' A week later, the clerk bravely resisted this intimidation and was duly clobbered, 'causing streams of blood to run to the ground'.[36]

Disputes could also centre on the allocation of church-seating, and this form of competition became increasingly common as seats were introduced more widely during the century. In 1588, the year of the Armada, an equally apocalyptic confrontation was disturbing the village of Sutton (Isle of Ely). The main parties were the wives of Edward Gunton Senior and George Gunton respectively, who had 'divers and sundrie tymes in servis tyme contended the one with the other for the same seates to the greate disturbance of the congregation'. These women evidently cared deeply about their personal share of the parish's sacred and communal space, but so too did George Gunton himself. On 'holye Thursdaye', he weighed in against his wife's adversary, 'and did leane upon her with his elbowe in such violent manner as she was not well a yeare after'. A little later, Robert Banks of nearby Cottenham declined to sit in his appointed seat, 'but would sit in the lap of Robert Rivers'. This was a competitive gesture, rather than an affectionate one. These parishioners had clearly lost sight of the standards of acceptable conduct, but their vision was clouded more by a form of commitment to organised religion than by apathy or hostility. One disgruntled Wiltshire widow even quoted the Bible in defence of her refusal to accept a new seat.[37]

The majority of parishioners, and therefore the behavioural norms, will never present themselves directly to us. They were the people who turned up, mumbled their responses, knelt and stood as required, listened and left. Perhaps they occasionally fell asleep during a long sermon, and they doubtless muttered to one another at times. Theirs was the 'stolid conformity' of which Martin Ingram has written. Since they do not speak to us, historiographical interpretations are largely a matter of educated intuition. It seems to me most likely that their behaviour in church was generally good, and that they were not there purely under duress. Their attachment to the church was probably basic, unsophisticated, but actually quite strong. It is surely significant that when the Elizabethan puritan author George Gifford dreamt up a fictional no-hoper named Atheos, he endowed him with a warm and robust attachment to the Prayer Book and the official Homilies.[38] Furthermore, Atheos was a caricature, and even in Gifford's mind he was at the reprehensible end of the popular religious spectrum. We can reasonably deduce that the majority, though manifestly not zealots, were committed members of the church. There is little reason to suppose that the Reformation changed this situation fundamentally.

The sixteenth century may, however, have witnessed a slight tightening of expectations where behaviour in church was concerned. It seems likely that there was, in the late-medieval church, a fairly high threshold of tolerance for unscripted congregational sound and movement. Duffy describes situations in which different services were conducted simultaneously in the same church, and refers to 'the bustle, activity and loud gossip' that occurred during services.[39] We know, furthermore, that ranks of wooden pews were only gradually coming into fashion. By 1600, standards had shifted somewhat, and parishioners were expected to remain in their seats and to focus more attentively on the proceedings. It would be a mistake, however, to see this transition as solely a consequence of the Reformation. Other factors – bureaucratic development, state formation, and even furniture manufacture – were also involved. These matters are, however, some way beyond the scope of this study.

From within the ranks of unexceptional Christians, there emerged those whose commitment grew stronger, more fiery. Some of these people turned towards principled dissent or subversive manipulation of liturgical orthodoxy, and they will be considered later. Others expressed their commitment through the established church, coming to know the liturgy intimately and prepared to challenge their clergymen if they deviated from it. The zealous conformists, in their post-Reformation form, have been examined by Judith Maltby in an important article. She, like Mark Byford before her, calls them 'Prayer Book Protestants' and argues persuasively that they were a significant force within the church. In 1604, one group in Chester complained that their puritan vicar would not permit them to make their customary responses during the liturgy, and they spoke proudly of a tradition which had lasted 'for forty years last past and more' (in other words, since the Elizabethan settlement). Elsewhere, committed conformists followed the services in their own copies of the Prayer Book. Others were angry that their minister discouraged them from kneeling during the Lord's Prayer, and by the early decades of the seventeenth century they saw themselves as the defenders of 'the ancient order of our Church of England'. Maltby argues that these enthusiastic conformists spanned the social spectrum and were fairly widespread. We should certainly learn to think in terms of substantial groups within most parishes who, before and after the Reformation, were deeply attached to the liturgy.[40]

Recent work on the reception of communion in early-modern England has also produced some relatively positive findings. Of course, there were always those who failed to take the matter seriously enough, like Edward Garner of Croydon-with-Clopton (Cambridgeshire) who, in 1613, 'did much abuse himselfe the same daie he tooke the Communion, by pissing thorowe a baye in the Church porch upon a maides backe'. A little later, one Buckinghamshire man rather missed the point of 'communion' by bringing his own bread and wine and refusing to share it. He was certainly not alone in resenting the contributions required towards the costs of the Lord's Supper. But such people were far from typical, and the indignant tone of both presentments expresses what was, throughout the period, a consensual view that taking the sacrament was something to be done with due respect. Certainly, there is evidence from the beginning and end of the sixteenth century to suggest popular enthusiasm for this key moment of lay participation, though it may have waned somewhat in the bewildering middle decades. Duffy has made the case for the late-medieval period,

arguing that the idea of 'taking one's rights' at Easter was firmly embedded
in the minds of parishioners. For the Elizabethan decades, we might think
of the Hertfordshire vicar who expressed concern over his flock's *over-
eagerness* to receive. A few decades later, in the 1630s, two godly authors
complained that people 'will by no meanes be kept from receiving this
sacrament'.[41]

It is also clear that many people knew of the potential spiritual benefits,
and of the dangers, of receiving unworthily. Dotted through the records of
ecclesiastical justice are cases in which individuals explained that they had
not taken the communion because of unsettled disputes with others. In
1584, for example, Richard East of Suncombe (Oxfordshire) 'admitted
that he did not communicate this last Easter because his conscience was
troubled by the evil speech of Katherine Ginacre, but doth not refuse the
Lord's table upon any scruple in religion or otherwise'. The official
position was indeed that those who were not 'in charity' should not
receive. The system was clearly open to abuse, but we should not assume
that a majority of these people simply fabricated their excuses. As Arnold
Hunt has argued, the function of the Lord's Supper as 'an instrument of
reconciliation' was 'firmly rooted in popular culture'. The late seventeenth-century antiquarian John Aubrey apparently agreed: he noted
that 'In Danby Wisk in the North-Riding of Yorkshire, it is the custom
for the Parishioners after receiving the Sacrament, to goe from the Church
directly to the Ale Hous and there drink together as a testimony of charity
and friendship.' We cannot be certain, of course, that this was precisely
how the parishioners themselves would have put it. Nevertheless, the
suggestion of a church–alehouse continuum is interesting, and may come
as a shock to social historians more accustomed to treating the two
institutions as the enemy command-centres in a war between the godly
and the rest.[42]

Justifications for non-reception that drew on the rhetoric of broken
charity were not, of course, a product of the Reformation. And there
were other broad continuities too, particularly in the pattern of annual
reception that emerged as the norm within the Elizabethan church. Most
people probably took the communion once a year, at Easter, as they had
done in the late-medieval period. After the Reformation, additional com-
munions were sometimes offered on other big feast days (Christmas,
Whitsunday and sometimes Palm Sunday), and in a minority of parishes
on a more regular monthly basis. But these supplementaries seem generally to have been received only by a voluntary minority of local people,

often the more wealthy. Before the Reformation, too, unusual individuals like Margery Kempe had also taken communion more regularly.

Towards and into the seventeenth century, local administrative mechanisms for noting and pursuing those who failed to make an annual communion grew more sophisticated. In many places, reception levels may have improved as a result. To the joy of historians, something like statistical analysis at last becomes possible for a handful of parishes. Jeremy Boulton has revealed that levels of annual reception in the highly populous and demographically turbulent parish of St Saviour's, Southwark, were between 80 per cent and 98 per cent in the early seventeenth century. This was an extraordinary achievement in such an environment, and was possible only because of a sophisticated system involving special communion tokens and staggered attendance. Boulton also concludes that it could not have worked without a substantial measure of popular cooperation. In other words, parishioners were not present merely because they had to be. Hunt believes that compulsion had a higher role to play, but he too is positive about the reception levels that were being achieved by the beginning of the seventeenth century. Easter was the dominant occasion for taking the sacrament, and one commentator reported in 1604 that 'few, or none, absteine at this time'. This amounted to a maximum fulfilment of a minimum obligation.[43]

Such a healthy situation cannot have existed everywhere, but Palliser's assertion that communion was 'an infrequent service attended only by the more prosperous' begins to look misleading. At Ely, in the first decade of the seventeenth century, reception levels also seem to have been impressive. The most negative evidence is usually provided by contemporary clerics in pessimistic mood, and it must be interpreted accordingly. And even they agreed that ordinary people viewed the Lord's Supper with reverence, seeking to settle disputes in advance of reception, donning their best clothes for the occasion, and attempting to behave with unusual sobriety for the remainder of the day. To the godly author Jeremiah Dyke, these gestures were shallow and inadequate. To us, however, they amount to 'compelling evidence of a genuine regard for the sacrament', as Hunt has put it. Overall, then, we can detect the familiar mixture of change and continuity, and, once again, a reasonably positive sense of engagement between ordinary people and their church.[44]

Our information on the extent to which people fulfilled their liturgical obligations on feast days is thin by comparison. Church attendance on the minor feast days does not seem to have been systematically scrutinised, either before or after the Reformation. Suggestive evidence can be discovered here and there, now and then, but its reliability is difficult to gauge. One Kent man admitted in 1543 that he crept to the cross on Good Friday 'more for company than for devotion'. Robert Whiting has observed that the abrogation of several lesser feast days in 1536 was accepted by the majority with barely a murmur. But Eamon Duffy would dispute any suggestion that observance of these days was in any way lax or mechanical, and he points out that early Elizabethan bishops had to complain that on Good Friday 'some certeyn persons go barefooted and barelegged to the churche, to creepe to the crosse'. There was surely nothing apathetic about maintaining a ritual that had now been outlawed. It may well be that the greatest of the feasts were enthusiastically observed, while the lesser ones attracted a smaller or less intense level of participation. The same observation can probably be applied to the post-Reformation church, which in any case demanded a less vibrant and colourful involvement. Hutton argues that Rogationtide was generally observed, as the Elizabethan settlement required. Donald Spaeth, writing on the post-1660 church, reckons that people often ignored all but the biggest holy days. In 1615, the vicar of Balsham (Cambridgeshire) had explained to the diocesan consistory court that he had given up conducting services on 'half holy day eves' because of poor attendance. He promised to try again. But the bleakest case of neglectful observance comes from Wiltshire where, in 1628, the churchwardens in one parish admitted that nobody there observed the holy days.[45]

Committed members of the laity could also, as we saw earlier, make voluntary gifts which had a direct bearing on what went on in church. As a result of the Reformation, the dominant forms of such bequests clearly shifted from the foundation of chantries to the supply of sermons. This transition directly reflected the official demise of efficacious good works, purgatory and its associated prayers for the dead, and the newer emphasis on a lively faith forever tied to the lessons of Scripture. A couple of examples will illustrate the change. In 1531, a London dyer named William Bowden made a religiously traditional will, which included provision for a priest to say Mass for his kin every day for seven years. The priest's salary was to be £6 13s 4d per annum. Bequests of this nature were very widespread in late-medieval England, though Duffy's assertion that it was 'standard practice' for testators to request the use of particular prayers or Gospel readings seems more doubtful. In 1572/3, Agnes Spylman of Thaxted (Essex) bequeathed a more modest 6s 8d to the local vicar, asking him 'to make 1 honest and learned sermon at the time of my burial when the people may be taught and learned the way to salvation'.

In both cases, the testators revealed the strength of their attachment to the church by exerting an influence over the services that would be held in their absence.[46]

The transition between these two types of giving was not, however, smooth or straightforward. Most noticeably, late-medieval gifts for clerical intercessions were found in a high proportion of wills (though only a minority of the population made wills); Elizabethan bequests for the support of sermons, in contrast, were not. Robert Whiting summarises the percentage figures for intercessory bequests in wills of the 1520s: 70% or higher in Lancashire and the dioceses of Durham, Exeter and York; around 60% in the archdeaconry of Huntingdon and in Suffolk; 44–49% in Somerset; 22–26% in the archdeaconries of Lincoln and Buckingham; and something like 20% in London.[47] Historians rarely bother to express the numbers of Elizabethan testators requesting sermons as a percentage, so unusual were they. But before we conclude that interest in the liturgy had plummeted, we should note that this is not really a comparison of like with like. Before the theological changes of the mid-sixteenth century, it was believed that memorial Masses were capable of reducing significantly the period of time that would be spent by the testator's soul in purgatory. It is small wonder, therefore, that they were commonly provided for. Protestant theology did not endow sermons with the same direct power, despite their centrality within reformed policy. Furthermore, sermons were supposed to happen as a matter of course in the Elizabethan church, but if late-medieval Christians wanted Masses celebrated specifically for their souls, they had to make the necessary arrangements themselves. It is inappropriate, therefore, to interpret the changing levels of provision as evidence of a simple deterioration in lay attachment to the services of the established church.

The middle decades of the century were, as in so many other areas, characterised by confusion and anxiety concerning these forms of giving. Bequests for intercessory Masses and prayers entered a steep decline in the 1530s, largely because of fears for the future of any money that was invested. The late Henrician and Edwardian regimes regarded the chantries with a mixture of suspicion and greed, and they were dissolved by statute in 1547. Prior to this date, the pragmatic people of England began to abandon their traditional investments, and some even sought to dissolve existing chantries before the government did it for them. It has also been noticed that, when chantries became legal again under Mary, investment in them did not begin to approach its former levels. The current orthodoxy is that this is explained more by a general feeling of dazed culture-shock following the experiments of the Edwardian regime, than by any significant weakening of traditionalist beliefs.

We can only speculate about the personal motives that drew sixteenth-century people to leave money for chantries or sermons. The dominant recent work on late-medieval intercessory giving has tended towards a very positive interpretation, emphasising the continual flow of funds into the church, the augmentation of official services, and the contact fostered by chantries between the dead and the living, the laity and the clergy, and so on. Correspondingly, it has attempted to deny the role played by fear of purgatorial suffering, selfish desires to privilege oneself or one's family, and a not necessarily welcome sense of obligation. It certainly cannot be denied that the intercessory system was a vital source of income for thousands of local churches and clergymen, and that post-Reformation giving towards sermons never came anywhere near matching it. The system evidently worked.

Yet it seems unduly charitable to examine only one side of the motivating coin. Patrick Collinson has recently wondered why the system collapsed as swiftly as it did, if it was indeed so deeply cherished and enthusiastically accepted. It is even possible to use examples cited by the optimists to suggest certain darker possibilities. Clive Burgess, for example, mentions one priest in fifteenth-century Bristol who 'procured, moved and stirred' ailing parishioners to give money and property to the church. He persuaded one woman to hand over her very dwelling house in return for certain church services, to the considerable annoyance of her son.[48] Might not this type of priestly pressure have been common, and might it not have led to many intercessory bequests that were not quite as enthusiastic as they look on paper? It would certainly help to explain why intercessory bequests faded so rapidly, once they were no longer officially legitimate. It is not the aim of this book to dispute the generally warm commitment of late-medieval people to their church, but there is now a case for interviewing them a little more critically.

What, then, can we conclude about the participation of the laity in sixteenth-century church services? A balance sheet of opportunities before and after the Reformation suggests a rough parity, despite the many changes that were encountered. Late-medieval people had their processions, their colourful festivals, their annual communion, their involvement in weekly rituals like that of the paxbred, and in annual ceremonies such as the 'creeping to the cross'. They could shape the liturgical routine through intercessory bequests and investment in special Masses. Their sense of commitment was probably rendered more intense by the music and the spectacle. And yet, the services they heard were largely in Latin, the music was performed by others, and the priest generally received the sacrament alone. A few decades later, much had changed, but Elizabethans had their congregational psalms, their vernacular services and sermons, their extensive responses, and their annual communion in both kinds. Their liturgy, like that of their ancestors, focused their minds on corporate values, charity, reconciliation, the majesty of God and the sacrifice of Christ. In 1600, as in 1500, the English majority looked to the official church's rites of passage for comfort, a measure of protection, a sense of contact with their ancestors, and the public legitimation of fundamental life-changes. At the close of the century, there was less colour and less splendour in English church services than there had been at the opening, but it seems likely that the old warmth had come to settle again on the new, Protestant, liturgy. This was a process made possible by the highly distinctive Elizabethan settlement, which was like nothing else in Europe. The English majority were certainly not fiery in their faith, but they cared. And as each generation faded into the next, they made the adjustment as positively as they could.

Church Materials

There can be no doubt that the fittings, furnishings and equipment of the English parish church changed dramatically between 1500 and 1600. There were, as ever, a number of basic continuities, but a Henrician husbandman entering a late Elizabethan church would have been struck by the transformation more forcibly than by the continuities. Amongst other things, he would have noticed a marked change in the balance between image and text. At both ends of the century, local churches were equipped through a combination of local initiative and externally imposed obligation, but here too the balance had shifted.

In the early sixteenth century, the items necessary for orthodox worship formed a very considerable list. At the most basic level, the church itself needed to be maintained in a serviceable condition, clean and secure. All the indications are that the late-medieval period was one of the great ages of church-building and improvement in England. The chancel, site of the stone 'high altar', was separated from the nave by a rood screen, over which was placed a loft for the permanent display of a crucifix and statues of Mary and John. The screen itself was decorated with colourful paintings of the saints, each displaying a specific emblem designed to identify him or her for observers. The surviving rood screen at Eye (Suffolk) has a different saint painted onto each of its wooden panels: St Helen, St Edmund, St Ursula, and so on.

Laypeople had the specific and substantial responsibility of maintaining the condition of the nave. This, the main body of the church, was often lavishly decorated with wall-paintings of the saints and other subjects. In the church of Stratton Strawless, a fairly typical Norfolk parish, there were images of Sts Margaret, Anne, Nicholas, John the Baptist, Thomas Becket, Christopher, Erasmus, James the Great, Catherine, Petronella, Sythe, Michael the Archangel, and the Trinity. Representations of the Virgin Mary were particularly common, and were additionally adorned with jewels, gowns or girdles. Medieval saints provided a galaxy of heroic role-models for men, women and children alike. Their paintings were often strategically placed, like the wonderful St Christopher, once white-washed but now restored, who watches benevolently over 'travellers' as they arrive at church through the south porch at Willingham (Cambridge-shire). Considerable effort went into the provision of 'lights' or candles to burn in front of images of the saints. The stained-glass windows, too, presented images of the saints, the Trinity, the seven sacraments, and so forth. The visual impact of all this must have been extremely impressive, and parish churches possessed an atmosphere that was rich, powerful and perhaps rather heavy. Occasionally it was too much, and the churchwar-dens of Wooton (Kent) were ordered in 1502 to whitewash the church walls, described as 'so dingy that the parishioners sitting in the nave can scarcely see the sacrament of the altar'.[49]

There would have been benches in the nave, often with visual encour-agements to piety carved at their ends, but in most parishes not yet the orderly ranks of pews with which we are now familiar. At the opening of the century, permanent pews, often quite elaborate, were generally the preserve of the local gentry, though it is clear that more organised seating was already spreading before the Reformation. The nave also contained smaller, wooden altars and chapels, often set up by chantries or guilds, at which weekday masses were conducted by the parish's supplementary chaplains. In some places, there was also a shrine displaying holy relics. In the west country, for example, a pious late-medieval tourist could have looked upon a piece of the Crown of Thorns (Bodmin), pieces of the Holy Cross (Tavistock), the head of Genesius the Martyr (Launceston), the remains of Sidwell the virgin (Exeter), and a snippet of the Virgin Mary's hair (Tavistock). Less exotically, the nave housed the stone font, central to the rite of baptism and sometimes decorated with representations of the seven sacraments. Aural contributions to the ambience came from an organ in the nave, and church bells in the tower. Overall, Scarisbrick has characterised the late-medieval parish church as 'a "mysterious succession" of semi-independent spaces' that 'had to be explored, walked round and into' and 'could not be taken in with a single sweep of the eye'.[50]

In addition, the proper conduct of services required a great many smaller items: containers for the sacrament, needed on those occasions when it was taken to sick people or carried in procession; an assortment of crosses and banners for use during festivals; wooden or stone 'sepulchres' for the Easter rituals; numerous decorated vestments and altar cloths; a Lenten veil, to be hung in the chancel during the weeks before Easter; frames in which candles could be set; items needed for Mass, such as chalices, holy-water sprinklers, censers, pyxes and a paxbred; manuals, missals, psalters, legends, processionals and other service-books; lecterns for the books; and a bier for carrying the corpse at funerals. The purchase and maintenance of objects great and small required the churchwardens to operate a basic financial system which absorbed contributions both voluntary and compulsory, both in cash and in kind, from the body of parishioners. The staples of this system were gifts of lands, goods or money, the rents which sometimes followed, 'church ales', annual dues, and rates or collections organised locally. Beat Kümin has recently produced the most sophisticated analysis of this system so far available.[51]

The twists and turns of the mid-century resulted – ultimately but not inevitably – in a comprehensive transformation of English church interiors. The changes began in the late 1530s, with official attempts to reduce the adoration of images. Reformers steadily hardened their attitudes to images, moving from the view that some of them were too frequently abused to the view that all were, by definition, an abomination. The most abrupt changes were ordered by Edward VI. The abolition of purgatory and the cult of the saints rendered thousands of paintings, roods, shrines, and chantry chapels redundant at a stroke. Destructively, the 1547 injunctions, reinforced by later decrees, ordered the whitewashing of walls, the removal of images, the snuffing out of almost all candles, and the levelling of stone altars. Constructively, they commanded parishes to paint scriptural texts and the royal arms onto their church walls, and to see to it that they equipped themselves with a wooden communion table, a parish chest for the collection of alms, a pulpit, and copies of the Bible, Homilies,

Prayer Book and Paraphrases of Erasmus. Meanwhile, the government opened a threatening campaign to acquire the more valuable of the old church's implements. Special commissioners were appointed to oversee the compilation of inventories of local goods, with an eye to confiscating them or at least grabbing the proceeds of any sales.

This process was never completed, and Queen Mary ordered a thorough reversal. Parishes were now required to blot out Protestant texts, themselves only recently painted over the old pictures of the saints, and to re-equip themselves for Catholic worship. Bishop Bonner's visitation articles of 1554 listed a daunting number of liturgical items that were now to be obtained again. Four years later, Elizabeth came to the throne and the majority of Edward's Protestant commands were re-issued. The previous ten years must have been the most turbulent and bewildering that English parishes have ever endured.

By the later decades of the century, matters had settled to some extent, and several scholars have recently reported that levels of locally-initiated investment in church improvements were beginning to pick up again. An impeccably organised church of the period would have looked something like this: the physical division between chancel and nave might remain, though the paintings on the screen have gone (or been defaced), and the lofts have been removed along with their statues; the imposing 'doom' paintings that used to face late-medieval parishioners from the wall over the chancel arch have been replaced by the royal arms; stone altars are absent, having been superseded by moveable wooden communion tables; the nave's rich paintings have been whitewashed, and scriptural texts (notably the Ten Commandments) now occupy their place; the windows contain clear glass, and let more natural light into the church; organs are now more rare, though parish churches still make regular use of their bells (non-superstitiously, of course); pulpits, by this time, have a far higher prominence than they had in the late-medieval decades; the presence of extensive seating is a corresponding development, for it reflects the importance of facing and hearing the preacher; the flickering candles of the past are no more, and the extra altars in the nave have been removed. Scarisbrick's 'mysterious succession of spaces' has become 'a single, open auditorium in which the faithful could assemble to hear the minister proclaim the word of God, plain and unadorned'.[52]

Church interiors had, therefore, become much simpler in appearance. The smaller items required for services at this date were also considerably fewer in number. In 1571, the Archbishop of York asked all of the parishes in his province to ensure that they had the following: an official Prayer

Book and psalter; a large English Bible, the two Books of Homilies, and the Paraphrases of Erasmus; a table of the Ten Commandments; 'a fair linen cloth' for the altar table; a 'comely' silver communion cup with a lid that could double up as a plate for the communion bread; a 'decent' large surplice, with sleeves; a secure coffer, with locks, for keeping the parish registers; and a strong chest for the alms.[53] The provision of church materials was still supported and administered locally, though it appears that a higher proportion of funds was raised through compulsory rates than had been the case half a century earlier.

This, then, was the officially acceptable norm, and a thoroughly Protestant norm it was too. In the words of Patrick Collinson, English church interiors had been 'devastated, totally remodelled'.[54] Yet this was not the whole picture, and to understand how and why this was so we must look more closely at the nature of the local response to the official decrees of the sixteenth century. How quickly, and with what attitudes, did local people undertake this remodelling?

At the extremes were attitudes which can be readily characterised as committedly Catholic or committedly Protestant. During Mary's reign, for example, the good people of Morebath (Devon) – wives, young men and maidens – made several 'voluntary' collections to help their priest equip his church for restored Catholic worship. Ten years later, northern Catholics rose against Elizabeth's Protestant regime, and altar stones that should have been dismantled reappeared miraculously from unknown hiding places. Protestants, too, could comply and resist as circumstances required. The church officers of Rye responded promptly and enthusiastically to the orders of Edward VI's regime, and in 1548 paid out 33s 4d (a substantial sum) 'for clensying the chaunsell from poperye'. And one 'merry fellow' in Marian London mocked the freshly painted rood in St Paul's Cathedral with a humorous speech designed to imply that the Catholic restoration was likely to be just a temporary thing: 'I hope that ye be but a summer's bird, in that ye be dressed in white and green.' More directly but less appealingly, another Protestant drew his dagger on a priest and tried to snatch the St Sepulchre's sacrament as it passed by in the Corpus Christi procession in 1554.[55]

The majority of parishes, however, responded with something between readiness and reluctance to the commands of all governments, perhaps moving from the former towards the latter as one mid-century reversal followed another. Whiting's account of the Reformation in the west country is essentially a tale of ordinary people doing what they were told, despite their evident enthusiasm for the old religious system.

Inevitably, there were geographical variations across the country, reflecting the greater strength of Catholicism in the north and west of the country. But it seems that the response of the majority of parishes can best be described as dutiful but unhurried, whether the orders of the moment were reformist or traditionalist. Most parishes did what they had to, but rarely immediately and rarely with a zeal that went much beyond the letter of the law.

Historians with a particular commitment to the view that the Reformation had almost no grassroots support – Duffy and Haigh, for example – present Marian compliance as swift and enthusiastic, but Edwardian or Elizabethan compliance as generally procrastinatory and reluctant. Although there was certainly a contrast, it can be drawn a little too clearly. Roods and images were often slow to return under Mary, just as Scriptural texts had been slow to appear on the walls during Edward's reign. Many parishes can hardly be said to have leapt with zest into the task of restoring the equipment for Catholic worship in the mid-1550s, though it cannot be doubted that the instincts of the majority remained solidly traditional at this date. The same was true a decade later, when some parishes, having obediently dismantled their roods, then drew crosses onto the church walls to fill the void. In general, it can be said that parishes destroyed things more quickly than they constructed or replaced things, but that they did neither in a rush. Liturgical items were frequently sold or hidden in advance of government investigations, and concealments were often inspired by traditionalist feeling. But on many occasions, these were exercises in hedging parochial bets, or in financial survival, rather than examples of zealous defiance. Compliance was the order of the day, and Scarisbrick speaks of statues and roods appearing and disappearing in these decades 'without great drama or disorder'.[56]

An example will add colour to this portrayal. In early Elizabethan Cornwood (Devon), the parishioners eventually removed their rood loft, but not before one William Warren had insisted that 'he would see the queen's majesty's broad seal first..., before that he would mell withal'. This was outward stubbornness beyond the norm, probably informed by an awareness that the royal visitors had no remit to remove the cross from its position above the screen. Warren's reluctance to witness the end of the loft was shared by other leading parishioners, but they complied when punishment loomed, and Robert Hill urged his neighbours, 'let us agree together and have it down, that we may be like Christian men again of holy time'.[57]

Arguably, this example reveals a climate in which a basic traditionalism and an equally basic obedience were brought into conflict as never before, with compliance generally trumping conservatism at moments of particular pressure. This should alert us to the existence of vital components of the contemporary spiritual mind-set that were not directly dictated by the Protestant–Catholic dichotomy. The prominence of corporate harmony within pre-and post-Reformation church services has already been noticed, and can also be seen in this example. Obedience was another such component, and it is an important but rarely noticed fact that this was, for sixteenth-century people, an unquestionably *religious* duty. It would, of course, be a mistake to overlook substantial and religiously-motivated risings such as that which took place in the south-west in 1549; but, as Whiting has emphasised, the majority of people in this mainly traditionalist region were highly compliant. They accepted the view that 'God's most holy word pronounceth a plain sentence of eternal damnation upon all such as be seditious rebels against their kings or magistrates', though their obedience could certainly be manipulative and partial.[58] These were areas of significant consensus amongst early-modern Christians, and they are often overlooked. The vast majority of people cared about their religion, but perhaps not quite in the way that some modern historians, with their own denominational identities firmly defined, might suppose (or wish). For all, these were spiritually difficult times. For some, they were times in which religious conflict could not, in conscience, be avoided. For most, however, they were times in which a stressful adjustment simply had to be made with as little damage to the Christian community as possible.

We should not present local compliance as a blind and one-dimensional attitude. The majority of mid-century English people, if they had been left to their own devices, would not have sought a Protestant transformation of their churches. They were happy enough with what they already had, even if they were probably not as joyously devoted as some recent writing would have us believe. Their basic sense of satisfaction conditioned their obedience, leading to a style of compliance that left more of the old in place than leading English reformers would have wished. Arguably, the partial spirit of compromise that ran through official pronouncements of the period also served to encourage this attitude. As a result, late sixteenth-century churches, though obviously Protestant, may also have displayed several signs of a very different past. In a sense, this amounted to a negotiated settlement in which official orders were obeyed, but not quite to the letter.

Many churches, for example, still had thoroughly traditional stained-glass pictures in several of their windows, despite a 1559 order that such things be destroyed ('so that there remain no memory of the same'). As the Elizabethan Protestant clergyman William Harrison explained, a consensus had been reached under which, because of the high costs of replacement, coloured glass was being retained until it decayed of natural causes. Under James I, a visiting theologian remarked on the continuing abundance in England of window-images depicting Christ, Mary and the apostles, and in 1629 at least one woman was still in the habit of bowing to a stained-glass picture of God in her local church. Late medieval benches, fonts and memorials, with their religious carvings and inscriptions, may also have been widespread. Margaret Aston has spoken of a high degree of latitude in practice, and John Morrill has described intense Protestant anxieties in the 1640s concerning the survival in parish churches of traditional items such as candles, tapers, crosses, images, and objects connected with the Virgin, the Trinity or the saints.[59]

The extent of these survivals emerges most clearly from the journal of William Dowsing, appointed by parliament in 1643 to tour Suffolk in search of superstitious and idolatrous church decorations. He destroyed something like 7000 items in 150 churches (an average of nearly 50 per church). Dowsing found crosses on steeples and in chancels; inscriptions asking the living to pray for the dead; and various representations of God, Christ, the Holy Ghost, angels, apostles, the Virgin Mary, 'and seven Fryars hugging a Nunn'. Admittedly, many of these objects were found in windows or in the roof, and therefore well above eye level, but their presence in such numbers is striking none the less. In Dowsing's journal, we observe once again the paradox of the sixteenth-century Reformation, which mixed latitude and rigour in such a way as to draw the majority along while storing up trouble for the future.[60]

It appears, therefore, that many such items, though anathema to zealous reformers, were nevertheless part of the very fabric of Elizabethan and Jacobean worship. As Tessa Watt has commented, historians often pay insufficient attention to the visual left-overs of the medieval church.[61] Like the continuities that were written more officially into the Elizabethan settlement, they must have eased and influenced the transition to Protestantism.

Bearing these suggestions in mind, we can also take a fresh look at predominant attitudes to the maintenance of church materials in the period of the Reformation. Historians, usually supporting one 'side' or the other, tend to present us either with high levels of investment that crumbled, or with corrupt forms of investment that were replaced by simpler but more satisfying forms. Arguably, it may be more appropriate to think in terms of a solid reserve of popular enthusiasm for the physical well-being of the church that suffered an entirely understandable decline during the middle decades of the century, but then began to recover reasonably impressively towards 1600. We have frequently heard, in recent years, of the late-medieval period's high levels of communal investment in new and improved church buildings. The church at Bodmin, for example, was rebuilt in the late-medieval period, with contributions from 460 parishioners. Whiting calculates that, in eight widely-dispersed counties, well over two hundred parishes undertook major building work in the half-century preceding the Reformation (though he neglects to tell us how many parishes did not).[62]

We are now beginning to hear more regularly of the increasing levels of investment that marked the late Elizabethan and Jacobean decades. The main problem with Whiting's argument that the Reformation led to mass apathy is a failure, so far at least, to look beyond 1570. At this date, people and parishes must still have been reeling under the impact of four decades of almost continual and directionless religious change. The evidence of a rediscovery of the old reserves comes from the subsequent decades. White, Yule, Collinson, MacCulloch and Kümin have all drawn attention to new work that was being done on pulpits, seats, wall-texts, screens, communion tables, church towers and bells around the turn of the century.[63] This is strong evidence of local commitment to the upkeep of essentially Protestant parish churches, and it looks like a renewed version of an older sense of attachment. At Sherrington (Wiltshire), to give just one example, it is still possible to see 'a fine set of 11 texts, including Creed and Lord's Prayer, 1624, placed in appropriate places of the church'. Yule also estimates that 1000 Jacobean pulpits are still in existence.[64]

It is undoubtedly true that the late Elizabethan style of investment was less vibrant and colourful than its medieval predecessor, but then it should always be remembered that the official injunctions of the reformed church expressly condemned the older forms and asked that spare money be given to the poor instead. When this is taken into account, the decline in levels of investment looks rather less catastrophic. Of course, there were plenty of Elizabethan and Jacobean churches whose fabrics were reported to be defective or inadequate at visitation, but it is by no means clear that there were substantially more such buildings than there had been a century earlier. And post-Reformation defects could cause local consternation, as in 1604 when parishioners from Bottisham (Cambridgeshire) complained that their chancel had not been 'whited' and that 'the stoles or seates there, and the floare, are undecent and unhansom'.[65] The responsibility rested with a local farmer, who had purchased the rectorial rights, and it seems that his neighbours cared.

Throughout the century, the laity within each parish shared responsibility for the maintenance of the church fabrics, and they made their contributions in a variety of ways. They paid locally calculated rates. They participated in church ales. They sometimes held one of a variety of church offices – that of churchwarden being the most important. Skilled local artisans helped to repair faulty bell mechanisms, locks, doors, pews, and so forth. Those without specific skills could do their bit by assisting in the task of cleaning the church. Before 1547, people also contributed to the upkeep and enhancement of the church through their membership of local guilds, which often shared some of the costs.[66] But the most direct opportunity ordinary people had to support the fabric of their local church was by making personal gifts or bequests, and the work of several recent commentators enables us to build up a reliable impression of the extent of such giving across the century.

Few would dispute the statement that, in the late-medieval period, the physical appearance of the church attracted bequests at an impressive level. Nineteen out of every twenty testators in late-medieval Norwich left something to one or more parish churches, and there was no significant decline in giving until after 1517. In Herefordshire, 75 per cent of testators in the period 1500–39 remembered their parish churches. Bequests in the three counties of the diocese of Lincoln were similarly frequent. The proportion was around 50 per cent in the dioceses of Durham, York and Exeter. A few qualifications need, however, to be added. Andrew Brown has detected a slight reduction in the sums of money given by people in the diocese of Salisbury before the onset of reform, and it seems that levels of giving in some other parts of the south had already peaked by the late fifteenth century. It should also be remembered that only a minority of late-medieval people made wills, and they were generally of unusual wealth, so our figures refer to proportions of the privileged, not of the population as a whole. Nevertheless, these figures are all we have, and they suggest generally impressive levels of investment.[67]

Bequests and gifts were made in a wide variety of forms. Cash sums were given simply to the 'high altar', or to support specific building projects, or to finance the construction of particular additions to the church fabric. One eminent Salisbury man asked that a picture of Jesus sitting on a rainbow be painted on the wall over the high altar in Horton.

An alderman from Hull asked for the installation of a state-of-the-art mechanism above the high altar. This device would cause angelic images to descend at the sacring, and rise again at the end of the Pater Noster. Others made provision for beads that could be hung on existing images, for new images to be placed on pulpits, and for torches that would burn over their memorial stones. One man wanted torches like those that had burned for his late spouse, 'savyng where my wife had vi torches I will have viii'. This somewhat self-centred approach was not unusual, and prosperous testators regularly required that representations of themselves be placed in stained-glass windows, alongside those of the illustrious saints. Others were at pains to express the corporate function of their gifts. In the 1480s, a Bristol widow bequeathed a hearse-cloth to her church, 'for the love and honor that sche had un-to all-myghty god and to all Crystyn Sowlys and for the Ese and socour of all thys parysche un-to whom she owyd her good-wyll and love yn her dayes'.[68]

Only rarely are we given such a clear and personal statement of the motivating factors behind a specific legacy. Recent writing has often emphasised the most positive motives, presenting a 'best practice' view of late-medieval legacies. It is indeed appropriate to allow these optimistic options the centre-stage. Like the Bristol widow, those who gave were driven by interrelated desires to glorify God and to benefit their communities. Several commentators, most notably Clive Burgess and Eamon Duffy, have explained in sophisticated detail how these motives worked in practice. Attention is drawn to 'the positive participatory character of pre-Reformation penitential practice'. People gave in order to shorten their own time, and that of all Christian souls, in purgatory. But they also enhanced the lives of their surviving neighbours in a variety of ways. Many holy objects had a protective capacity, and could shield devotees from harm. They also improved and beautified the liturgical round, thus fostering harmony within the community and the prospects of salvation for all. In turn, the living would be stimulated to offer their prayers for dead benefactors. Crucially, the 'community' was not merely one of the living, but was understood to encompass the dead, the saints, the Blessed Virgin, Jesus, and God himself. The Golden Legend, a treasured text, spoke of 'the debt of interchanging neighbourhood': people honoured the saints, and the saints defended them against everything from the plague to the toothache. Burgess speaks of a series of 'circular flows' which linked living and dead, givers and receivers, poor and rich, laity and clergy, in a thoroughly impressive corporate system.[69]

There are weaknesses, however, in an interpretation which seeks to deny the simultaneous power of rather less cheery possibilities. People must have been motivated by negative factors too, and it is a mistake to feel that we must choose between optimism and pessimism in this regard. Arguably, the real strength of the system was that it made it impossible to distinguish between the two sets of factors, thereby ensuring that even those driven predominantly by selfishness would continue to give, and thus to enhance the spiritual lives of all. People were inspired 'by fear as well as fervour, by pride no less than piety', as Glanmor Williams has written of bequests to the church in Wales. Many were driven first and foremost by a desire to earn prayers for themselves and their kin, adding 'and every Christian soul' as a compulsory afterthought. Others were motivated, partially at least, by a wish to augment their own social glory. And should we dismiss out-of-hand the reformist complaint that people could become so devoted to the saints and their images that they lost sight of the centrality of Christ? Even Scarisbrick concedes the existence of 'near-idolatrous devotion to the saints'.

An extremely unsettling fear of the pains of purgatory, and of hell, was another more negative factor that has been unhelpfully dismissed in recent analyses. Each week in church, people saw not only comforting images of saints and the conspicuously saved, but terrifying representations of the damned enduring the pains of hell. Duffy points out that few wills express any sense of hysteria, but it should be added that such formal documents were hardly likely to be the place in which people poured out their deepest fears. Finally, the presence of a priest at most late-medieval will-makings may well have constituted a significant pressure to make the appropriate gestures. Priests were powerful figures, and quite capable of injecting compulsion into moments of apparent voluntarism. As Moir has pointed out, mid-century declines in the level of bequests to the church and in the number of occasions on which clergymen were present at will-makings moved hand in hand, somewhat suspiciously.[70]

The striking collapse of giving to the church during the middle decades of the century can be explained primarily as the result of confusion, pragmatism, legal change and economic downturn. People stopped making their gifts either because they were no longer permitted to, or because they could not afford to, or because they had no confidence that any donations would be used as they intended. It is significant that, even under Mary, the level of bequests failed in many areas to approach its former levels. For Duffy, the explanation of this failure was that traditional religion was in a state of shocked uncertainty, and that the five years of

Mary's reign were insufficient for the older patterns to reassert themselves. He is in no doubt that, had the reign been longer, traditional religion would have settled down once more. This is probably an accurate assessment, though the lower than customary levels of Catholic giving under a Catholic monarch do seem to cast a little doubt on the currently dominant view that late-medieval devotion was, *in general*, profoundly voluntary and enthusiastic. But the case is dented, not holed.

By the middle years of Elizabeth's reign, there is no doubt that 'voluntary' gifts to the church, from the living and the dying, were running at a far lower rate than had been the case before the 1530s. In Herefordshire, for example, the percentage of wills containing bequests stood at 57 in the early sixteenth century, 23 under Edward VI, 38 under Mary, and 18 in the 1590s.[71] This was probably fairly representative, though statistics covering the whole century are hard to come by. It is clear that a testamentary donation to the local church was no longer 'common form'. Bequests that would have an impact on the appearance of the church now tended to refer to personal funeral monuments rather than to liturgical items, decorations, or building works.

The impression of a substantial decline needs, however, to be qualified in a number of ways. In the first place, there was still a significant minority of testators who did remember the church, sometimes in generous and creative ways. In 1590, for example, the widow of an Essex clothier set aside forty shillings 'to be bestowed to buy the Book of Martyrs and to set the same in a grate in some convenient place in the church to remain for the use of all the people for ever'. Secondly, levels of giving seem to have been stabilising by 1600. The decline had been arrested, and in the early seventeenth century was turning around. Some historians feel able to be reasonably positive. Martin Ingram, for example, tells us that 'Many testators' in the Wiltshire village of Keevil 'made some small bequest towards the upkeep of the parish church' in the decades either side of 1600.[72] Thirdly, parish churches needed far less liturgical equipment under Elizabeth than they had under Henry VIII, and it is not therefore surprising that fewer testators made provision. Fourthly, will-making was gradually extending downwards on the social scale, so that the pool of testators included more people with less wealth than had previously been the case. Such people were naturally less likely to make bequests to their church. Lastly, and most importantly, local administrative systems had changed substantially, and a higher proportion of the costs of church repair and improvement was now being raised through compulsory rates than through voluntary gifts. As we have already seen, new work was increasingly taking place in the late Elizabethan and early Jacobean years, but it was financed in a less *ad hoc* fashion. For these reasons, it can be suggested that the sixteenth-century decline in bequests to the church was nothing like as disastrous as the bare statistics imply.

Nevertheless, changes in the local systems by which ecclesiastical fabrics were maintained must have had a major impact upon the attitudes of ordinary people to the upkeep of their church. It does seem, for example, that Protestantism was less successful than Catholicism in stimulating parishioners to make voluntary gifts to the church. Several other factors were also involved, but the abolition of holy intercessors like the saints, of purgatory with its sense of a close contact between living and dead, and of the belief that good works could make some contribution towards an individual's salvation, may have combined to reduce the motives for generosity. On the other hand, it should be remembered that good works were still of vital importance as the 'fruits' of salvation, and that motivating factors such as the duties to glorify God, to promote corporate harmony and to set an example to all were still powerful. Similarly, less positive motives such as fear and the pursuit of personal glory through posthumous display survived the Reformation.

Other aspects of the transformation may also have altered the nature of popular engagement with the fabric of the church. During the century, the dominant forms of giving became less personal, less direct, and less voluntary. And church interiors, like the services held in them, were expected to become less varied and localised. The repeated parliamentary acts of 'uniformity' were so-called with good reason. It may well be that obligatory rates and the promotion of sameness generated attitudes to the physical church that were somewhat less lively and creative than had once been the case. Martin Ingram, usually more positive than most about the efforts of the post-Reformation church, has suggested that compulsory rates and duties may have generated 'a minimalist approach to devotion'.[73] The argument can, however, be pushed too far. It has already been suggested that not all late-medieval 'voluntary' gifts were forthcoming without pressure of one form or another. We might add that rates can actually be treated as expressions of majority commitment and communal responsibility within a parish, an argument that Haigh proposes for Mary's reign (but not, one imagines, for those of Edward or Elizabeth). It should also be noted, finally, that several of these broad changes should not be attributed too directly to the coming of Protestantism. Beat Kümin has argued that late-medieval local administration was already making more use of compulsory rates, and already diverting its emphasis from church fabrics towards more 'secular' concerns such as poor relief and road maintenance. The observation that the balance was shifting all over Europe, in Protestant and in Catholic countries, is equally telling.

Overall, it is difficult to propose any readily digestible summary of the changes and continuities within popular attitudes to church fabrics. Certainly, any simplistic account of a transition from vibrant commitment to dull, grudging obedience will be inadequate. There were conspicuous changes in practice, but there were also some significant continuities of impulse and equipment. Some of these were permitted in the Elizabethan settlement (the buildings themselves, surplices and screens, for example); others were grasped rather than granted (stained-glass windows and carved bench-ends). Perhaps these were minor things, but they mattered in smoothing what for many was potentially a painful transition. Official theology shifted drastically, but several of the most powerful reasons for looking after one's local church were not changed beyond recognition. For ordinary people at the parochial level, the difference between good works which contributed directly to one's salvation and good works which bore witness to one's salvation may have meant less in practice than it was supposed to mean. In the final analysis, it seems likely that most Elizabethans, like their Henrician ancestors, treated the physical well-being of their church with a warm, but not fanatical, regard. The essential pragmatism and resourcefulness of their piety is well illustrated by the way in which outlawed church fittings were sometimes recycled in order to meet other needs. In the 1560s, several parishes in the Lincoln diocese converted their rood lofts into communion tables or pews, while others burnt them to 'make a plummer's fier which mended the churche leades'.[74]

Church Office

Throughout the early-modern period, the laypeople most directly involved in the maintenance and general running of the local church were the handful (at any one time) who held parochial offices. The most important of these offices, and one that has recently been attracting scholarly attention, was that of churchwarden. Churchwardens, who normally served in pairs, were essentially the administrators and overseers of parochial affairs, and their duties were extensive. They were required to maintain the fabrics of the church in good condition, and (from 1538) to keep registers of all baptisms, marriages, and burials in the parish. They organised a

variety of fund-raising exercises, including the levying of rates and the
staging of 'church ales'. They managed any lands or livestock that had
been bequeathed to the parish, seeking to ensure a decent income from
rents. They were also responsible for decisions over expenditure, and
churchwardens' accounts recorded payments for a great variety of causes:
poor relief; the purchase of items for the church, such as communion
books, bell ropes and surplices; work done on the church, from basic
cleaning to the provision of wall-decorations; the supply of bread and
wine for the communion; and travel expenses for attendance at the
ecclesiastical courts. Such records make it clear that these amateur officers
handled large sums of money and took many important decisions.

At the end of each term of office, the outgoing wardens were required to
present the records of their transactions to an assembly of parishioners. At
all times, they were considered accountable to the wider community, and
were expected to act in the interests of that community. This responsibility
extended to the supervision of church attendance in its widest sense. The
wardens were expected to monitor their neighbours' conduct during
services, to notice any absentees, and also to spot any irregularities in
the liturgical conduct of their clergy. Churchwardens also had a significant
'policing' role to play outside the church, and theirs was the task of
reporting the moral misdemeanours of their neighbours to the ecclesiastical courts. They regularly presented their responses to the bishop's articles
of enquiry, which solicited information on many areas of parochial life.
Churchwardens, therefore, were busy people.

Their basic brief remained the same throughout the century, though the
job shifted in several significant ways. Most obviously, the objects of the
churchwardens' attentions changed with the transformation of church
interiors, the abolition of chantries, and the reshaping of the liturgy.
Over the century, their duties were certainly increasing, as almost every
regime passed legislation requiring a closer and wider attention to detail
on the part of local officers. It has been suggested that, increasingly, they
became servants of the Tudor state, and a vital link in the chain of
command. The churchwardens' responsibilities for church attendance,
poor relief, military provision, registration, general monitoring, and even
pest control were all more intense in 1600 than they had been in 1500.
They also came to spend proportionately less time concentrating on
church fabric, and more time on matters we might consider more 'secular'. The Reformation was not the only, nor even the primary, cause of
this: these trends pre-dated the religious changes, and comparable developments also took place in Catholic countries. Kümin presents the

changes in English parish government as a momentous shift from parish autonomy to royal autocracy, from local discretion to officially imposed compulsion. This may be, however, to exaggerate the case somewhat, particularly by underestimating the degree to which post-Reformation churchwardens were still able, in practice, to operate with considerable flexibility in the fulfilment of their obligations.

Another important office to survive the Reformation was that of parish clerk. The pre-Reformation clerk was 'an assistant in lower orders with an intermediate position between laity and clergy', and unlike the churchwardens he received a wage (collected by rates levied in the parish). 'Generally', Kümin tells us, 'he was expected to carry the holy water on different occasions and to assist at mass, but he could also be responsible for bell ringing, washing of church clothes, visiting the sick, or cleaning the church.' Parish clerks were also intimately involved in the provision of music, whether as singers or organists. By the close of the century, some of these duties had become redundant or reduced and the role may consequently have been less prestigious, but a holder of the office in Cambridgeshire described parish clerks as those who 'have sytten in the Chancell there & have helpen the minister to synge & saye divine servis'.[75] There is in this statement a strong sense of continuity through change. Elizabethan clerks still led the responses and organised the music, even if the responses were now in English and the music was now congregational psalm-singing.

Members of the laity also played their part in the running of parochial affairs through a variety of lesser offices. The 'questmen' or 'sidesmen' were the churchwardens' assistants and shared their responsibilities in ways that were arranged locally. Some parishes had officially-appointed 'dogwhippers', whose unenviable task was to 'preserve order amongst the canine attendants at church'. Many late-medieval parishes were also served by a range of minor officials, often appointed through the local guilds. In 1538, twenty-two individuals in Spelsbury (Oxfordshire) held office as 'keepers of the lights'. In other words, they maintained the candles that burned before the church's images of Sts Anthony, Erasmus, Catherine, and so on. In addition, a typical parish appointed a sexton (assistant to the parish clerk), a bedesman (who prayed for the souls of parish benefactors) and perhaps a general 'waxwarden'.

The temptation, grasped enthusiastically by Scarisbrick, is to assume that the Reformation destroyed much of this opportunity for layfolk to serve their churches. Certainly, the keepers of the lights went into retirement. Nevertheless, one of the most detailed investigations of parish government in the later sixteenth and early seventeenth centuries presents an impressive challenge to this view. Nicholas Alldridge, writing about the city of Chester, speaks of 'a proliferation of new lay officials drawn from the ranks of urban commoners' in this period. These included overseers of the highways, overseers of the poor, additional sidesmen and collectors for the poor. In the hundred years between 1540 and 1640, he estimates that the number of parish offices increased very substantially (though he presumably excludes those connected with the late-medieval guilds from his calculations). Occasionally, Eric Carlson adds, parishes even had officers 'to view the comers to the church'.[76]

Other parishioners may not have held titled offices, but nevertheless served the church in a variety of ways. In theory, all parishioners belonged to an annual assembly that reviewed the outgoing churchwardens' accounts and chose their successors. In practice, this task was often done by a smaller, more select group of locals, sometimes known as the 'Four Men', the 'Five Men', or something similar. Other, less privileged, locals did their bit for the church (and for a fee) by cleaning the floors and furniture, carrying out repairs, constructing wooden chests, washing the vestments, or painting the walls. Such tasks provided work, and contact with the church, for a variety of people, skilled and unskilled. In some parishes, these jobs were established on a more formal basis: one London parish, in 1558–9, paid salaries to a clock keeper, a clock maker, an organ keeper, a scavenger, a launderer and a 'conduct'.[77]

Selection processes for parochial offices were quite varied, but detailed information is often difficult to find. Some posts – those of parish clerk and sexton, for example – were held on a long-term basis by particular individuals, probably appointed in the first place by the parishioners with the consent of the priest or minister. Others, most importantly the offices of churchwarden and sidesman, were occupied for fixed terms. In these cases, the appointments were made at the annual parish meeting, about which we know less than we would like. Eric Carlson has provided the best analysis we have of the various methods of election and terms of office. Elizabethan and Jacobean canons attempted to regulate these matters a little more closely (by insisting on annual elections, for example), but there was no attempt to impose a rigorous uniformity, and local custom was allowed to prevail. Churchwardens were expected to have the backing (or at least the consent) of vicar and parishioners, with the latter having the greater say. In 1594, the lay residents of Fen Drayton (Cambridgeshire) explained that, by tradition, their curates 'every year successively were present at the election of the churchwardens . . . and amongst the parishioners did yield their consent . . . to the election by the said parishioners made, and did sometime name a churchwarden, but if such a man ... was disliked by the parishioners they (the said parishioners) would and did name another man'. The canons of 1604, however, placed clergyman and flock on a more equal footing for the first time, by specifying that if they could not agree, then each should choose one of the two wardens.

Beyond this, parishes displayed a wide variety of methods in the appointment of their churchwardens and questmen. Elections were held at different times of year, and sometimes they certainly were not held annually. Some parishes changed their wardens every year, while others kept the same individuals for longer periods. Carlson also mentions parishes which, in the seventeenth century, allowed the existing church-wardens to choose their successors. Other parishes chose their wardens on two-year terms, but staggered the appointments so that one of the two had always served in the previous year. In rural Cambridgeshire, each parish evolved its own system of election, then operated it in a flexible fashion so that no clear rules can be detected. No system was infallible, and one man from Landbeach told his churchwardens that 'there was a scarcity of wise men when [they] were put in office'.

Most analysts agree that, throughout the sixteenth century, a majority of the titled church offices were held by individuals of middling social and economic status. Churchwardens were not the very wealthiest inhabitants of their parishes, but they were certainly comfortably and solidly placed on the local ladder. It seems, then, that a measure of prosperity was considered a qualification for this office. Sidesmen were generally less prosperous, though this may sometimes have been simply because they were younger. There does seem to have existed an informal hierarchy of offices, and a system of progression from the lesser posts to the more prestigious ones. Wealth was not the only qualification for a place on this hierarchy. Age also played a part, and Carlson suggests that marriage and the successful management of a household were important stepping stones to service. Newcomers to a parish were evidently expected to prove themselves before they could be considered. And the overwhelming majority of officers were male, though there may have been a few more exceptions to this rule before the Reformation than after it. Unusual religious commitment, however, does not seem to have been a significant consideration, and Carlson has characterised the 1200 churchwardens of his study as conventionally pious, rather than extravagantly so. In 1582, the parish of Weaverham (Cheshire) elected churchwardens who were 'bothe Reputed & taken for Religion Lyffe and Conversacon very

Suffycient and honest men'. In most circumstances, certainly, parishes would surely not have elected individuals whom they considered to be morally degenerate (though we all make mistakes).[78]

These qualifications obviously restricted the extent of popular participation in the main offices, though many of the lesser ones were more open. Furthermore, service to the church through casual labour or through attendance at parochial meetings widened the pool considerably. There is some debate over the general level of participation, and particularly over any changes in that level during the period. Scarisbrick has emphasised the participatory nature of late-medieval parish government, and has suggested that Protestantism reduced lay opportunities for meaningful involvement. Kümin's detailed investigation of ten sets of churchwardens' accounts has followed this lead, and provided more substantial detail. In particular, he argues for a shrinking participation during the early-modern period, as 'select vestries' of a few prosperous men replaced the big communal assemblies of the medieval past. In essence, he concludes, parish government became much more oligarchical. If the Reformation augmented lay control of the church, it only did so for gentlemen and local elites. Nicholas Alldridge, on the other hand, has proposed a very different interpretation of developments in the parishes of Chester between 1540 and 1640. For him, the extent of participation grew as the Reformation took hold, and he estimates that, at any one time, a third or more of eligible locals had excercised public office. Andrew Brown, in his study of the diocese of Salisbury, has also spoken of 'the rapid expansion of parish offices in many places'.[79]

It is not easy to resolve this difference of opinion. It seems possible that Kümin's picture is slightly overdrawn (for the pre-civil war period, at least), though we cannot yet be sure. Does he perhaps exaggerate the numerical levels of attendance at pre-Reformation parish assemblies, having been lulled into an unduly optimistic frame of mind by the (admittedly appealing) rhetoric of 'whole parish' participation? Paradoxically, does he underestimate the continuance and power of this rhetoric into the seventeenth century? Robert Whiting, for example, argues that a form of select vestry was already widespread in practice during the early sixteenth century: 'The leading roles were usually played by a small council of parishioners.' And Eric Carlson, writing about the period after 1560, considers that smaller governing councils were designed to save the wider body of parishioners from 'molestation and troubling', and that people considered select vestries to be acting for (and presumably accountable to) the entire parish. In other words, this was oligarchy by consent. In any case, he finds 'no formal evidence' that select vestries operated in Elizabethan or Jacobean Cambridgeshire.[80] Until Kümin produces a sequel work dealing with the post-Reformation century, these observations must stand as potentially substantial qualifications to his thesis. Nevertheless, it seems unlikely that future research will reduce to nothing his notion of an oligarchical drift. Parish government was changing, but not quite as dramatically as Kümin suggests.

Another feature of some recent writing has been the argument that, because of the less than popular Reformation and the attendant changes in parish government, people became increasingly reluctant to hold local offices. Before the Reformation, it is claimed, they had been far more enthusiastic. This point has been made by Haigh, Whiting and Kümin. Admittedly, there were some good reasons for avoidance of office in the Elizabethan period. Onerous duties were mounting. Service was no longer accepted as a 'good work' that would ease one's pathway to heaven. Officers might be expected to employ temporarily their own money for parish expenses if the need arose. And, to cap it all, churchwardens and sidesmen seem to have suffered more verbal abuse than any other group in the country. Early-modern men and women put considerable energy into their insults, and their efforts are frequently recorded in ecclesiastical court books. Church officers of the period were called, amongst other things, 'fools and asses', 'drunckards and whoremasters', and 'knaves, Rascalls, dungheld drudges, base slaves'. Frequently they were called 'more busy than wise' and challenged to 'do what they could'. William Chambers of Reach (Cambridgeshire) fell out with his wardens, 'and thretneth there to have them by the cares in the church'. Robert Banks of Waterbeach declared 'We have two churchwardens. I would one of them were hanged up against the other.' And the churchwardens from nearby Ely reported that one man had told them 'he regardeth us noe more than he did the droppings of his tayle'.[81]

Nevertheless, there is actually very little evidence to substantiate the claim that post-Reformation parishioners were more reluctant than their predecessors to hold office. Of course, there are documented incidents, and they naturally become more visible with the increase in surviving records from the mid-sixteenth century. In 1577–8, for example, George Bower of Prescot (Lancashire) was fined two shillings by the parish 'because he refused to be churchwarden according to custom'. But the two historians who have looked into this question in greatest depth – John Craig and Eric Carlson – both conclude that church office was rarely avoided. As in the late-medieval period, it was more an honour than a burden (though it was that too), and election represented a significant communal vote of confidence. There were even cases in which people allegedly bribed their way into office. Carlson presents one such incident, and the same allegation may conceivably help to explain the behaviour of one Cambridgeshire man who reportedly 'quarrelled and wrangled with John Tubbs Inquirer [questman] in the Chancell at the Communion table sayeinge that he came in by his office at the arce'.[82]

If most individuals were reasonably content to hold office, can it also be assumed that they performed adequately during their terms? Certain incidents imply a negative answer. Carlson introduces us to one Cambridgeshire churchwarden who became so angry with his vicar (over the removal of a pew) that he repeatedly referred to him as 'Mr Fucker' and took to urinating in the church. William Noble, one of the sidesmen from Elizabethan Ely, was involved in a still more unsavoury incident, aided by his friend Thomas Smattersgill. They 'did shave of[f] all the heare [hair] from the privities of one Harry duffeild Barber..., the sd. Duffield beinge then droncke'. Then, warming to their task, they 'did rubb...his privities wth bay salte and water'. In their defence, they explained that Duffield's genitals had been hanging out when they found them, and that only 'some' of the hair had been removed.[83]

Most recent assessments, however, have rightly concluded that such cases are wholly unrepresentative, and that the majority of church officers took their duties seriously enough, despite the undeniable difficulties of their position. They were caught, sometimes unhappily, in a whole set of clefts: between laity and clergy, or parish community and diocesan authorities, or social superiors and inferiors, or the state and the locality. A churchwarden, during his term of office, could anticipate being treated by his neighbours with either a certain reticence or a measure of loud-mouthed, tale-telling verbosity. When Robert Smith, sitting with friends in a Cambridgeshire victualler's house in 1597, reported that Thomas Dearmer 'hath had to doe' with another man's wife, one listener warned him to 'take heede what you saye' because one of the churchwardens was nearby. To this, Smith retorted 'I care not whoe is in the howse, for I speake it to that end.'[84]

One Elizabethan member of parliament complained that churchwardens, 'being simple men and fearing to offend, would rather incur the danger of perjury than displease some of their neighbours'. There was certainly some truth in this, yet it would be an error to interpret such comments as evidence that church officers were consistently failing in their responsibilities. It was more a matter of differing opinions about the definition of those responsibilities. The agitated MP probably believed that parochial officers should report, or 'present', all offenders. Within most towns and villages, however, there existed a consensus that only the more notorious or resistant offenders should be pushed into the courts. As Carlson points out, official pronouncements provided some justification for this attitude by insisting, for example, that those who failed to attend church should be 'admonished' and encouraged to reform before being presented in court. There are indications that this was precisely what happened to many offenders, unless their sins were considered so serious that preliminary admonitions were pointless. Socially elevated miscreants were, of course, in an advantageous position, but it is not difficult to find evidence that church officers did attempt to tackle some, at least, of the sins of their superiors when it seemed necessary. One brave man in Devon intended to report a local gentleman for getting a local woman pregnant, 'thoughe he wore a cheyne of gould three or iiii tyme double about his necke'.[85]

Church officers certainly did not apply the strictest possible definition of ecclesiastical laws and injunctions, but they quite definitely possessed a solid conception of their official duties, and behaved accordingly. One has only to read through an Elizabethan court book to realise that the churchwardens were on the look-out for wrong-doing, and ready to pursue the perpetrators. They would hardly have attracted so many inventive insults if they simply ignored the wrong-doing of their neighbours. Instead, they developed their own understanding of the boundary lines between tolerable and intolerable misdemeanours, and their attitude was influenced by their paradoxical position within and without the community; but this may have been more a strength than a weakness. Furthermore, it was a system which most bishops and high-ranking diocesan officials understood well. Puritans, not surprisingly, disliked the negotiated flexibility of these processes, and they frequently sought to impose their own more rigorous standards. But the dominant popular attitudes were sturdy, none the less. Church officers, in the main, handled the pressures upon them fairly well and performed to the satisfaction of bishops and neighbours alike. As Ingram has put it, they provided 'a valuable filtering mechanism' and showed 'a robust regard for distinctions between the serious and the trivial'.[86]

The system of church offices, great and small, clearly made an important contribution to the collective lives of many sixteenth-century settlements. At the most basic level, it kept the church clean and presentable. Church office also provided a reasonably wide cross-section of the local population with opportunities for close contact with the affairs of the parish church, and this must have augmented a popular sense of attachment. It may also have provided a channel for the expression of potentially damaging social tensions. Relatively humble sidesmen could, and did, report the misbehaviour of wealthy yeomen and even gentry. And parishioners of low social rank were entitled to make demands upon their office-holding betters. Alldridge speaks of 'pressure from below with a vengeance', and mentions a Chester tanner who referred to an officer of much higher social standing as his hireling ('I pay his wages'). Church office could also provide a controlled forum for the negotiation of disputes over local religious policy, as suggested by the orderly vote held in Edwardian Southwark about whether or not to dismantle the rood loft in advance of official orders. In this case, a comfortable majority decided to wait. John Craig has pointed out that the Elizabethan churchwardens' accounts for Mildenhall (Suffolk) record payments reflecting both puritanism (for example, the purchase of a Geneva Bible) and traditionalism (2d 'for franckensens one Christmas day in the churche').[87]

Church office was also important in providing local people with mechanisms by which they could negotiate and enforce their own moral consensus, though inevitably there were tensions within (and beyond) this. It can also be argued that the web of offices helped to construct and reinforce communal values. In Alldridge's Chester, for example, the carefully graduated system of church rates ensured that all inhabitants contributed something, but that many received back from the system much more than they gave. There was a place for everybody. John Craig, writing on Suffolk, has emphasised the importance of church office in representing and binding the 'corporate body of parishioners'. Finally, it should be emphasised that the system provided the parish with considerable flexibility in the management of its own affairs. External directives mounted in the sixteenth century, but they were still implemented with considerable discretion. Kümin is exaggerating when he argues that, by the late sixteenth century, 'the days of relative autonomy had come to an end'.[88]

Many social historians will find the tone of the above assessment too positive, and it should be remembered that the system also had its dark side. Church office has been seen as one of the principal means by which local elites sought to discipline and control the lower orders. This may have been increasingly true in the late sixteenth and early seventeenth centuries, owing to a combination of economic distress and puritan ideals in historiographically controversial proportions. It is, then, possible to argue that the system of church office alienated more people than it satisfied, particularly towards the bottom of society. This is, nevertheless, a debatable point and one that has been crudely overstated in many an undergraduate essay.

The church office system survived the Reformation in its essential structures and characteristics. Inevitably, there were numerous changes, and parish government probably became gradually more oligarchical and more heavily influenced by external directives. Both trends were less radical and rapid than is sometimes supposed, and both owed more to wider factors – economic, social and political – than to the Reformation. Offices connected with the guilds disappeared under Elizabeth, but other minor posts swelled to fill the vacuum. Even Kümin, who emphasises discontinuity, concedes that 'the basic income regimes' of most parishes 'remained surprisingly unscathed'. The fund-raising focus shifted from church ales towards church rates, but the transition took place across several generations and was generally managed without extreme stress. The wealth and status of the average office-holder did not change during the century, and frequently there was even some continuity of individual personnel through the turbulence of the 1540s and 1550s. This situation can be contrasted with that which prevailed in the more traumatic 1650s, when the staff of many parishes changed completely in the aftermath of civil war.[89]

Confession and Catechism

Members of the laity also had opportunities, or responsibilities, for engagement with the church through confession and catechism. The former was abolished as a compulsory duty during the Reformation, but the latter survived, and developed substantially. The two practices, as we shall see, were dissimilar in a number of ways, but can conveniently be placed together because they both constituted the most formal occasion for close and obligatory contact between individual parishioners and their clergy. It may be valuable to assess, briefly, the nature of this contact in sixteenth-century England.

Confession, in the late-medieval church, was a fundamental element in the sacrament of penance, and thus of crucial significance in the transmission of grace from God to humans. For a person to be saved, it was necessary to have been confessed (assuming the opportunity had presented itself). But confession also had other functions, including the propagation of proper moral values. Eamon Duffy has emphasised the educational service provided by this sacrament. It was a chance for the priest to assess an individual parishioner's knowledge of the basic articles of faith. Confession, in Duffy's words, was also 'a time for practical re-assessment, reconciliation with neighbours, and settling of spiritual accounts'.[90]

The practice of confession can be reconstructed (in a somewhat ideal-ised form) using a combination of pastoral manuals and surviving pictures or carvings. Every individual was to make confession at least once a year, and visual portrayals reveal the church as the normal setting. Hooded priest and kneeling parishioner conducted their interview close to the rood screen, while other penitents waited nearby. There were no confessional boxes in England during the sixteenth century, so we may assume that the voices of confessing parishioners were hushed (and the ears of their neighbours pricked). The basic procedure as laid down in instruction manuals required the penitent to confess his or her sins, then to be quizzed on the core articles of faith (such as the Creed and the Lord's Prayer) and questioned about the possibility of other, unconfessed sins. In conducting this investigation, the priest was to use the check-lists supplied by the Ten Commandments, the seven sins, the corporal works of mercy, and the five senses. Having done this, our model priest pronounced absolution and imposed an appropriate penance, usually involving the recitation of specific prayers. Keith Thomas adds that the priest had a duty to listen to everything his charge said, regardless of its relevance. It was 'notoriously common' for penitents to run through the sins of their neighbours, as well as their own, while they had the priest's ear.[91]

As Duffy admits, many confessions were probably rushed and abbre-viated versions of this procedure. It is certain that very few parishioners went beyond annual confessions, which came to be heavily concentrated in Lent. There was a growing literature designed to assist priests in the proper conduct of their confessional duties, but it seems unlikely that the majority of clergymen made attentive use of such works. Inevitably, therefore, there was a considerable gap between ideal confessions and actual confessions. 'Pastoral realism ... demanded that the confession be kept within manage-able dimensions: in a time-honoured formula the penitent was to be brief, be brutal, be gone.' On the other hand, it must be remembered that confession was only one of the ways in which late-medieval people received religious instruction. Besides church services, there were wall-paintings, carvings, memorials, dramatic performances, and so on. All of these provided reinforcement for the lessons of confession.

We know next to nothing about the popularity of confession, or about the extent to which annual participation was rigorously enforced. There certainly were incidents in which priests refused the communion to individuals who had not made their Lenten confession. And there were many printed and manuscript 'primers' which offered to help penitents prepare themselves for confession, implying a market for such advice. It is doubtful, however, that these had any major popular impact. There is also evidence that people took the matter of their final confession before death extremely seriously, and were terrified at the prospect of dying 'unshriven'. But isolated outbursts point the other way, and one west country Protestant declared, in the 1530s, that 'he had as lief to [i.e. he might as well] be confessed to a post or a stone as to any priest'.[92] Late-medieval clerics regularly complained about the extent of popular ignorance, implying a perception that the educational impact of confession was limited. Nor does there seem to be much evidence of people standing up in defence of compulsory confession when it was abolished under Edward VI. Peter Marshall speaks of 'its sudden and ignominious decline'. We might conclude that the majority performed their duty, but not with any profound enthusiasm. Those whose devotion went significantly deeper were probably a small minority. Intriguingly, Marshall has used the evidence of testamentary bequests to confessors in order to suggest that women were twice as likely as men to belong to this minority. It is not clear at present whether this demonstrates that female piety, in general, was deeper, or alternatively that something about the confessional satisfied specific needs that were experienced disproportionately by women.[93]

Despite the apparent rarity of profound attachment to confession, its impact on the populace should clearly not be underestimated. Later in the century, numerous Protestant spokesmen regretted its passing, evidently feeling that the pastoral baby had been thrown out with the sacramental bath water. Recent historians have tended to agree, and Patrick Collinson has seen the abolition of compulsory, auricular confession as a disastrous error on the part of the reformed church. For Burgess, confession was one of the elements that bound the laity and clergy together in a 'circular flow', though it has to be said that the sacrament suggests a rather unbalanced power relationship.[94] In summary, there seems little reason to doubt Duffy's assessment of confession as 'an immensely valuable pastoral and educational tool'.

The post-Reformation church did not abandon the idea of confession completely, and the Elizabethan clergy were officially required to 'exhort' those with troubled consciences to come forward and confess. Crucially, this now became a voluntary responsibility, and the sources do not permit us to assess the extent of the practice. We know that visitation articles regularly enquired whether the appropriate exhortation was being made, and whether the confidentiality of subsequent confessions was maintained, but it is impossible to tell whether this implies widespread interest in the matter, or widespread neglect. Other mechanisms also developed to fill part at least of the gap. The business of the church courts expanded as these institutions took on more of the work of moral policing. Keith Thomas has identified the spiritual diaries of the seventeenth century as a continuation of the instincts encouraged by pre-Reformation confession. Some godly clergymen of the period also kept 'commonplace books', in which they recorded the details of confidential discussions held with troubled laypersons. By the seventeenth century, guidance for those in spiritual difficulty was also printed in the form of 'cases of conscience', which provided sets of hypothetical situations for all occasions. For the majority of people, however, such aids were probably encountered very rarely. As Thomas has said, 'this activity was too informal and uncoordinated to be capable of filling the gap left by the confessional'.[95] The godly clergyman Richard Greenham kept a commonplace book, but regretted the demise of compulsory confessions.

Not all was lost, however, and a glance at the development of formal catechising in the centuries after the Reformation should be drawn into the account before we conclude too gloomily. For those requiring something rather more than a glance, Ian Green has recently produced a monumental survey of this important subject.[96] An initial word of explanation is also necessary. Duffy uses 'catechism' and other associated terms in a general sense, to describe the various ways in which the late-medieval church sought to communicate its messages to the laity. In this sense, the 'catechetical preoccupations' of the church were expressed through confession, art, sculpture, preaching, and so forth. Green, however, uses 'catechism' in a more specific sense, referring to the formal, educational exercise (and resultant texts) encouraged by the post-Reformation church. The different usages reflect a definite historical change of emphasis, as the dissemination and testing of specific (if basic) religious knowledge amongst the laity became a higher priority for the church. It is possible to treat post-Reformation catechism as the preservation and enhancement of the educational aspects of confession, and thus as something which helped to replace it.

Regular catechism was compulsory under the terms of the Edwardian and Elizabethan religious settlements, and was supposed to take place 'openly in the church', before evening prayer on Sundays and holy days. It was aimed primarily at the youth of a parish, and was described in the 1559 Prayer Book as an essential preparation for the rite of confirmation. It also served a variety of other functions. Ideally, it would help members of the laity to understand the contents of sermons, church services and the Bible more fully. It would lay the basis of a solid religious knowledge, and anyone unable to demonstrate their possession of this knowledge could, in theory, be barred from participation in the church's services of baptism, marriage and Holy Communion. Catechism also aimed to teach people of their moral duties, and thus to promote virtuous living amongst them.

The official Prayer Book catechism was easily the dominant version throughout the early-modern period, though it spawned many supplementary commentaries and 'unofficial' catechisms. By the end of the sixteenth century, the publishing of printed catechisms ranging in length from slim pamphlets to weighty volumes had become a large-scale commercial enterprise. During the decades either side of 1600, the 'question and answer' format, in which vicar and catechumen take part in a scripted interview, was becoming the norm. The Prayer Book catechism serves as the best example of the genre at its most basic level, and people all over the land were expected to memorise its contents. Children are first asked to list the promises that were made on their behalf by their godparents during the service of baptism (to forsake the devil, to believe the Creed, and to keep God's law). They are then required to recite and explain the Creed, followed by the Ten Commandments. They are reminded that it is only by God's grace that they can fulfil their spiritual responsibilities. The interview concludes with a recitation and explanation of the Lord's Prayer.

The contents of this catechism are, then, very basic and marked by a complete absence of theologically controversial material, and Green has demonstrated that this conspicuous avoidance of contested ground was also characteristic of the vast majority of supplementary or alternative printed catechisms throughout the early-modern period. At the most basic level of catechism, people were being asked to learn a small core of key texts which emphasised 'good living' and the very essentials of Christian belief. This finding has significant implications for all those interested in the ways in which Protestantism, and religion in general, were put across to the majority during these centuries.

As with confession, the reality of catechetical practice is difficult to reconstruct, but Green has gathered together much of what can be known. He believes that compulsory catechism took time to establish itself, and rarely occurred as often as was officially required, but that by the early 1600s it was taking place 'moderately frequently' in most churches (and also in elementary schools). Parishes with no catechising seem to have been rare by the close of the sixteenth century, though some places had settled into a pattern of catechism only during the period of Lent. At the other extreme, godly ministers like Richard Greenham catechised more regularly than was required, adding Thursday to the official schedule of 'Sundays and holy days'. In general, catechism probably started when children were approximately seven years old, and ended when they were in their late teens. By the late sixteenth century, ministers could draw upon a great range of additional catechisms, but the basic units of Creed, commandments and Lord's Prayer (with the addition of a section on the two sacraments of baptism and communion) remained the same. As the genre developed, Green argues, authors became more sensitive to the capacities of ordinary people, more skilful in their educational technique, but certainly not more likely to present parishioners with controversial material.

There were many longer and more complex printed versions, but the majority of people encountered catechism in a basic and reasonably digestible form. Whether it was a clearly and consistently 'Protestant' form is a more debatable question. Basic catechisms did not place great emphasis on justification by faith alone, and said virtually nothing about predestination. They adopted an optimistic attitude concerning the numbers of those who would be saved, and sometimes even implied that 'good works' might be efficacious. They treated the communion as more than merely a remembrance, and taught that Jesus was present in a real but spiritual sense (thus stopping well short of transubstantiation). In sum, they presented people with a version of Protestantism, but certainly not one that was unequivocal or dogmatic.

Of course, not everybody welcomed the idea of compulsory catechism with open ears, and clerical authors often complained about the lack of popular enthusiasm or receptiveness. The church courts also dealt with instances of lay resistance. In 1605, for example, a Hereford man was reported to have complained 'It is a frivolous thing that children are to be sent to be catechised, and not hard [heard] of before.' And one woman in Wiltshire was even less receptive, resenting particularly the intention of her puritan vicar to catechise both young and old (a sign of particular zeal).

She provides us with an entertainingly jaundiced description of a catechism class: 'when once he ... takes his green book in hand we shall have
such a deal of bibble babble that I am weary to hear it, and I can then sit
down in my seat and take a good nap'. Others found the classes traumatic
rather than dull, like the poor boy who ran out screaming when his vicar
warned that he had the devil on his shoulder.[97]

There are, however, more positive signals concerning the reception of
catechism. By the 1580s, pirate copies of one of the simplest versions were
being produced in huge numbers, a sure sign that there was a market for
them. Godly ministers sometimes described the wild success of their efforts
amongst everyone from gentlemen to milkmaids. In the seventeenth century, there were also cases in which parishioners felt strongly enough to
insist that their ministers made use of the official Prayer Book catechism,
rather than of some unauthorised version. We might also add that even
the most frustrated clerical commentators often acknowledged that the
basic texts had been widely learnt. Their complaints were generated by
the perceived mis-use of these texts, or by a popular failure to take the next
steps into more rigorous forms of piety. Overall, we should probably
accept Green's 'moderately optimistic' assessment. Post-Reformation catechism picked up slowly, but eventually (especially from 1600 onwards)
made an important contribution to the dissemination of basic religious
knowledge. The avoidance of complexity and controversy may well have
left elements of the old 'works' theology in place, but catechism amongst
the majority probably helped to foster a sense of commitment to the
church.

In juxtaposing late-medieval confession with post-Reformation catechism, we are not comparing like with like. Nevertheless, there is a
clear relationship between the two activities, especially in the way they
brought layfolk into close contact with their clergy, and certain conclusions
can be drawn. Clearly, officialdom had shifted its emphasis towards the
systematic dissemination of religious knowledge amongst the laity. It was
the didactic element of Henrician confession that emerged as the centrepiece of compulsory clerical–lay contact a century later. Elizabethans were
expected to seek out the vicar for themselves when they required spiritual
counsel, and they were thus required to take greater responsibility for their
personal morals. Post-Reformation catechists dropped traditionalist check-
lists such as the seven deadly sins and the seven works of mercy. And
Elizabethan catechism fitted into a wider context of visual aids (Scripture
texts on church walls, pulpits, gravestone inscriptions, and so on) that was
very different from the earlier setting (paintings, carvings and statues).

It would, however, be an error to ignore the continuities. Confession was no longer sacramental and compulsory, but it was still encouraged. Elizabethan clergy were to concentrate on Creed, Commandments and Lord's Prayer, just as their predecessors had done. Moral duties still played a more important role than sophisticated theology, and it was still assumed that the prospect of salvation was available to all. Clerical commentators remained frustrated with the popular response to their efforts (is this the lot of all educators?). The predominant attitudes of the laity to confession and catechism alike were probably luke-warm, rather than red-hot or ice-cold. Several continuities emerged through practice rather than policy. Green explains that in the seventeenth century, catechists lowered their sights somewhat, modifying the zealous ambition of the first generation of reformers. The tradition of Lenten catechising is also intriguing, and strongly reminiscent of the seasonal pattern of late-medieval confession. Older customs began to reassert themselves within a substantially changed context, as part of the curious and protracted process of negotiation that was the English Reformation.

The People and their Clergy

Inevitably, the clergy found themselves at the sharp and uncomfortable end of religious developments in sixteenth-century England, and their position as a group underwent numerous and profound changes under the Tudors. By 1600, there were fewer of them, and it no longer seemed to visitors that London contained 'an infinite number of priests', as it had done in 1531. Haigh estimates that, overall, clerical numbers fell from 40,000 to 10,000 during the century. England still required roughly the same number of parish incumbents, but had lost a wealth of monks, friars, nuns, and supplementary chantry or guild priests, all casualties of the Reformation. In late-medieval Norwich, 10 per cent of all the sons mentioned in the city's wills were clerics of one sort or another. By 1600, the figure was much smaller (and nobody has bothered to calculate it). There were, admittedly, some new opportunities for unbeneficed ministers in the form of lay-initiated 'lectureships' and chaplaincies, but these cannot have matched the extra options of the past.[98]

The role of the parish clergy had, of course, changed very substantially with the reformation of the liturgy. The focus had shifted from the celebration of the Mass to the delivery of sermons, and the messages that they were required to communicate had altered in numerous ways. No longer did the parish clergy mediate between their parishioners and their God in the same direct and powerful manner. Theologically, they lost their absolute and fundamental importance in the future of souls, and clergymen were no longer to be regarded by the populace as 'higher than the angels'. Their appearance had changed with the simplification of clerical vestments, and the typical vicar now had a wife, where before he had been celibate. The financial and legal privileges of the clergy had been reduced by parliament, and the country's leading gentry had also gobbled up many 'advowsons', which gave them considerable power over the appointment of vicars to specific benefices.

By 1600, a much higher proportion of the clergy were university graduates (roughly 40 per cent overall), and vicars with advanced educations had become virtually the norm in the more prosperous counties of the south-east. Many post-Reformation clergymen were of a 'new breed' in other ways too, and approached their task with a measure of uncompromising zeal that would have been highly unusual in a late medieval priest. Such men were the famous clerical 'puritans' of English historiography. Elizabethan clergymen were also somewhat less likely than their Henrician forebears to be local sons of the soil, and a proportion of them spoke with accents unfamiliar to their congregations. The status of the parish clergy had therefore changed socially as well as spiritually, and it has been argued that the consequences for relations between priests and parishioners were formidable.

Understandably, the changes have tended to eclipse the continuities in historiographical analysis. As usual, however, there is a different picture on the other side of the coin. Most interestingly, the majority of parishes passed through the ding-dong turmoil of the mid-sixteenth century without changing their vicars. Comparatively few resigned or were deprived as a consequence of repeated switches from official Catholicism to official Protestantism (though there was one substantial Marian purge, in 1554). In the first twelve years of Elizabeth's reign, for example, only 10 per cent of parish priests in Whiting's west country were removed from their posts. This was a substantial minority, but it hardly compares with the situation in Scotland, where many more parishes suffered sharp discontinuity during the very different Reformation settlement of the 1560s. In England, continuity of personnel is predominant wherever we look. At Heydon in Essex, the ex-monk William Sheppard, whose ministry has been inventively reconstructed by Mark Byford, tended to the local flock between

1541 and 1586. One Northamptonshire vicar remained in his parish from 1524 until 1570. Occasionally, we can even catch the comments of such people. Under Edward VI, for example, an Exeter clergyman swore never to say Mass again, but did so when Mary came to the throne. At this point, an eminent layman reminded him of his former promise, and was told 'It is no remedy, man, it is no remedy.' Thirty years later, a Berkshire minister, who had once been a friar, was heard to say that 'if ever we had mass again he would say it, for he must live'.[99]

No single, clear lesson can be drawn from this clerical continuity, for its causes were multiple. The religious establishment could not afford to dismiss thousands of serving clergymen at a time. Individual priests could not afford to abandon the livelihoods for which they had trained, and had no wish to desert the people to whom they had ministered. The turbulence of the mid-century also caused a dramatic fall in the number of ordinations, which may have had the effect of improving career prospects for existing clergymen. Yet their decisions to stay must also tell us something about the nature of the English Reformation, which, for all its changes, never quite sought to obliterate the past in its entirety. For many clergy, enough was retained to tip the balance (just) in favour of a personal resolution to stay put and help the laity through a difficult period.

This had the dual effect of compromising the message of Protestantism and of making that message more palatable. Some of the conservative clergy continued, in performing the liturgy, to make thoroughly traditionalist gestures, such as kissing the communion table or elevating the host. Overall, however, Mark Byford may be right to conclude that the presence of familiar clergymen within the reformed church was 'more likely to have eased the transition from the old world to the new than to have encouraged the persistence of active Catholicism'.[100] Eventually, as these men died out in the last third of the century, the situation changed, and clergymen who had been trained as Protestants came to fill the vacancies. But by then, a new generation of laypeople was also growing out of the old, and the impact of the change was once again reduced. The English Reformation, in practice, was a gradual, partial, piecemeal, and often reluctant affair, but it evidently worked.

There were other continuities too. The Elizabethan parish clergy belonged to a church that retained its basic episcopal orders (bishops, priests and deacons). The ideal vicar was still a man with soothing pastoral skills, and a responsibility to apply them in the interests of peace and harmony. As John Bossy has argued, the early-modern clergyman was first

and foremost regarded by his flock as 'a settler of conflicts'. His duties of
rebuke and reassurance, as required, were fundamentally the same. He
was still to avoid unseemly entanglement with 'worldly things'. It also
seems possible that the emphasis on post-Reformation clergymen as outsiders has been overdone. Ian Green has shown that a majority of grad-
uate clergy later worked in the regions of their origin.[101] The physical
appearance of the parish clergy had changed, but it had not done so
drastically, and official injunctions still required them to wear their distinctive clerical garments even when not in church. The clergy remained
accountable to their congregations, and members of the laity were
required to report any sins, omissions or inadequacies noticed in the
conduct of their vicars. Lay-appropriated advowsons were an innovation,
but leading members of the local laity had always influenced the make-up
of the parish's clerical body through chantries and the like.

It is difficult, furthermore, to detect any major change in general
standards of clerical behaviour and ministration across the century.
There were, of course, numerous shortcomings on both sides of the
Reformation, and an irresponsible historian would have little difficulty in
compiling a catalogue of hopeless cases: clergymen who smuggled women
into their houses disguised as men, or who celebrated the communion
while excommunicate, or who loved 'drynkyng, ryotinge and playinge at
unlawful games'. In 1590, one Norfolk man alleged that he had seen his
vicar, the unReverend (and well-named) Mr. Crotche, 'so nere his wyffe
betwixt hir leggs that they wer fylthelie joyned together'.[102] The vast
majority of clergymen, however, were probably 'of good conversation',
and adequate to the responsibilities placed upon them. While it is true that
a new breed of 'puritan' clergymen had emerged in Elizabethan England,
it may well be a mistake to regard them as in any way typical. They have
certainly dominated recent research, and their energy endowed them with
an importance that was out of proportion to their numbers. Historians of
the evangelical tendency in post-Reformation English religion are often
reluctant to concede that their interest is in a minority of clerical practi-
tioners, but this is surely a statistical certainty. Most Elizabethan vicars,
arguably, were not as zealous as we have been led to believe, but nor were
they necessarily lacking in commitment.

Examples are dotted through the record, even though the less fiery
clergy inevitably attracted little attention from the creators of our sources.
Many were 'honest ministers, well able to catechise and privately to
exhort, though they have not the gift of utterance and audacity to preach
in the pulpit'. We should not assume that the only alternatives to puritan

ministry were lax or stubbornly conservative ministry. In Wiltshire, there
were few clerical puritans, but plenty of vicars committed to peace-making
and the improvement of standards of religious observance amongst the
laity. We might also mention the Northamptonshire vicar who, arriving at
a new parish in 1605, found that one of his primary roles was to mediate
between mutually hostile Protestant and Catholic factions.

These mild-mannered ministers could be highly effective in encouraging
conformity and a kind of osmotic conversion. Under Elizabeth, one
Catholic propagandist lamented the way in which his potential recruits
among the laity often decided to attend the services of the established
church, having observed that the local minister and his wife were gentle
and honest people. The reformed Church of England was built upon such
decisions, albeit gradually. William Sheppard's ministry in Heydon presents a remarkable example of this gradualist Reformation. His instincts,
like those of the mid-century majority, were basically traditionalist, and
they evidently remained so at his death in 1589. Yet he conformed without
resistance to the new Prayer Book, 'responding fruitfully to the phenomenon of religious change', and became a kind of semi-Protestant. To
Byford's account we can add that Sheppard evidently owned a copy of
the *Sick Man's Salve* by the celebrated Protestant Thomas Becon, for his will
includes a preamble transcribed from that work. The vicar's version,
however, pointedly omits the reference to 'Christ Jesu our alone saviour
and redeemer', which surely indicates a *private* scepticism about solifidianism, the central doctrine of Protestantism. Despite this, his thorough
conformism – which must have involved the *public* propagation of solifidian ideas – had the effect of converting members of his congregation to a
religion of sermons, reformed services and catechism. As Byford argues,
they came to identify themselves as Protestants, even if their brand of
Protestantism would not have satisfied proponents of more radical
reform.[103]

Ian Green's study of catechism has done a great deal to focus our
attention on post-Reformation ministers who were moderate in their
attitudes, sensitive to the capacities of their parishioners, and willing to
proceed gently in the task of persuasion. He writes,

> It is...possible that the relatively calm, uncontentious nature of cat-
> echetical teaching which most authors adopted was actually more
> typical of what happened in a great many parishes which were situated
> some distance from the capital and the universities – in other words a
> lower-key and perhaps less well-informed but not necessarily insincere

commitment to conveying the basics, combined with a due performance of the annual round of ceremonies and the rites of passage which parishioners expected and demanded.[104]

It could be added that such clergymen stand more happily in a ministerial tradition that pre-dated the Reformation than in one that commenced with the zeal of the Elizabethan puritans.

The problem of establishing what people thought of their clergy in the sixteenth century has generated a controversial and polarised historiographical debate. On the one hand, Dickens has sought to bring scholarly credit to an old Protestant prejudice, namely that the people of late-medieval England were thoroughly disenchanted with their priests, and were therefore more than ready to accept the Reformation when it came. He refers to the 'widely diffused anticlericalism of the age' and thinks in terms of a gathering movement towards lay emancipation from clerical control. Within his account, anticlericalism functions as a spur to reform on what might be called a German model. At the opposite extreme, Haigh has portrayed anticlericalism as a consequence, rather than a cause, of the English Reformation. Late-medieval priests, he insists, were widely loved. Although he catalogues the criticisms expressed in tithe disputes, complaints about mortuary exactions, parliamentary debates, humanist writing and Lollard comment, Haigh nevertheless feels able to conclude that they did not amount to much. Elizabethan Protestant ministers, in contrast, were resented and despised. From their raised and intimidating pulpits, they served up doctrines which few could understand. Both physically and metaphorically, they preached over the heads of their parishioners. They stirred up hostilities with their inflated standards and ceaseless campaigning. They sought to eradicate traditional sociability, and drove people to look back nostalgically on the days when the priest had been just one of the lads.[105]

There is little to recommend either side of this debate, except perhaps its entertainment value. Dickens's book takes small account, even in its second edition, of all the evidence that late-medieval parishioners were investing heavily and enthusiastically in their clergy. Haigh's work adopts a blinkered view of post-Reformation ministry, failing for example to understand that education does not inevitably lead to an inability to communicate, that not all Protestants were puritans, and that the preaching of predestination was not widespread in ordinary parishes. He also applies very different standards to evidence from either end of the century, treating a handful of late-medieval parochial disputes between laypeople and clergy as insignificant, but a comparable number of Elizabethan cases as a veritable landslide.[106]

A more measured assessment of the evidence suggests that levels of popular anticlericalism were roughly similar in 1500 and 1600, though a somewhat heightened sense of disillusionment may well have accompanied the rapid changes of the 1540s and 1550s. There are clear signals that some people resented their clergy throughout the century, and we do not need to drain all the colour from the picture in order to set such signals into a more plausible perspective. In the late-medieval period, problems might arise from the tension between two very different lay perceptions of the priest: as, on the one hand, a figure of immense sacramental power and, on the other, an ordinary human, complete with the defects and desires of the species.[107] The second of these perceptions, naturally, was still there in 1600, but the former may have been replaced by that of the minister as a somewhat intimidating, university-trained preacher. The pedestal had been moved, but life on top of it was still something of a balancing act, and problems still arose.

Dissatisfied layfolk of the late-medieval period included the Londoners who in 1513 or 1514 brought a case in the court of Star Chamber complaining in great detail about the many fees and dues that they were required to pay to their clergy. In 1529, the inhabitants of one Devon parish took this grievance a stage further, and reportedly buried their priest alive when he tried to insist upon the payment of a mortuary. Whiting argues that anticlerical incidents grew more common from the 1530s onwards, as a direct consequence of the disruptions of reform. He speaks of 'a substantial erosion of popular respect for the clergy'. Certainly, there were many individual clerics in this period who were not held in the highest regard, as indicated by the insults that flew their way: 'knave', 'Whore-monger', and 'maggot-carrier', for example. In Marian London, an order had to be issued to stop servants from throwing crab-apples at passing priests, apparently a common recreation. In the early 1560s, the churchwardens of Wickwar penned a less than glowing review of their recent clergymen: 'some of them were liars, some drunkards and blasphemers, some borrowers of horse and money and ride away with all'.[108]

Records of the later Elizabethan and Jacobean decades provide a continuing supply of anticlerical moments, and historians have often interpreted increasing documentation as increasing incidence. In the 1590s, Gilbert Wolward of West Wratting (Cambridgeshire) challenged his vicar: 'Are you a minister that shoulde be a man of peace? You are more meete to make an uproar and to set men togither by the eares.' A little later, in Ely, a parishioner told his curate 'that he had noe more Creditt than his dogge'. One Wiltshire man told his vicar that 'when [he] died...he thought he should meet him riding on a black bull'. Less cryptically, another villager declared all ministers 'to be naught'. As Martin Ingram points out, however, 'such cases trickled into the courts ...in very small numbers indeed, and seem often to have resulted from particular tensions existing between the abuser and the minister concerned'. Precisely the same observation can be made of most of the outbursts against late-medieval clergy. They are not evidence of widespread popular anticlericalism, and should be treated with caution.[109]

As Swanson has observed, many complaints of this sort can even be viewed as 'pro-clerical', in that they reflected high popular expectations about the behaviour of the priesthood.[110] The targets were individuals who failed to meet these expectations, and the underlying perspective was quite a positive one. The man who denounced the ministry in its totality was very unusual (and in a very bad mood). Before concluding, we should also look in more detail at other evidence of supportive attitudes towards the clergy. One useful measurement is the level of recruitment: if the laity felt positive about the clergy, they were more likely to seek to join their ranks. There is general agreement that late-medieval ordinations were at a healthy level, though there were proportionately fewer in the south than in the midlands and the north. From the 1520s, however, there are signs of a very serious decline in all dioceses.[111] The early Elizabethan church was short of suitably reconstructed clergymen, and had to rely on traditionalists more extensively than its leaders would have wished. By the end of the century, however, it seems that the difficulties were easing as ordinations and opportunities came together once again. Certainly, bishops felt able to raise the standards of knowledge they required from prospective clergymen, and a university degree became increasingly necessary. During the early seventeenth century, the universities were producing at least as many ministers as the church could absorb, implying that clerical careers were popular once again. Supply and demand seem both to have been increasing – surely the sign of a buoyant clerical economy.[112]

Testamentary bequests made by laypeople to their clergy suggest a similar pattern, though late-medieval levels of giving were definitely not matched by Elizabethan parishioners. Approximately one in three testators of the early sixteenth century made bequests to those in religious orders (monks, nuns and friars), though there is once again a high degree of geographical variation. The secular clergy (priests and chaplains) attracted much more generosity, and roughly two out of every three testators recorded bequests in one form or another. This generosity began to evaporate rapidly in the 1530s, and did not pick up significantly during the latter part of the century. It is probable that fewer than one in five Elizabethan testators made bequests to their parish clergy, and Whiting sets the proportion as low as one in thirty for the will-makers of Devon and Cornwall during the 1560s.[113]

Certain qualifications need to be made before the evidence is accepted as a reflection of plummeting esteem for the clergy. First, several of the forms of giving that had brought money and goods to late-medieval priests were no longer encouraged, nor even permissible. Chantries and memorial Masses were things of the past. Secondly, local administrative systems were changing in such a way that religious provision was being supported less through one-off 'voluntary' gifts than through regular and carefully-organised rates. Regimes, for better or worse, were becoming more bureaucratic, and people may well have felt that their religious obligations were fulfilled in other ways. Thirdly, and despite the last point, a modest up-turn in voluntary giving to the clergy has been detected during the early decades of the seventeenth century, though the reliability of the relevant statistics is notoriously difficult to assess.[114]

Occasionally, ordinary people also expressed an active support for their clergy through petitioning or even rebellion. Religious risings rarely, if ever, recruited a majority of adults within a region, but they do nevertheless reveal that substantial numbers felt strongly enough to take action. Attachment to traditionalist priests was revealed, for example, in the western rising of 1549, and to a lesser extent in the rebellion of the northern earls in 1569. But the most conspicuous episode had occurred thirty years earlier, during the 'Pilgrimage of Grace'. This major rebellion demonstrated, amongst other things, the important role played by local monasteries in the lives of many English laypeople up until the point of their dissolution under Henry VIII, particularly in the north. Religious houses were valued as centres for charity, pilgrimage and sermons. Some time later, the residents of Pontefract were reported to be in 'great misery' as a result of the local abbey's demise. They were deeply saddened to see 'the holy sanctuaries of God so pitifully defiled and spoiled'. Equally revealing, however, was the example of the Yorkshireman who participated in the despoiling of the abbey at Roche, despite his professed lack of hostility to the religious orders. He asked his critical son, 'What should I do? Might I not as well as others have profit of the spoil of the abbey? For I did see all would away; and therefore I did as others did.' He may not have despised the abbey, but he clearly had no profound and unshakeable devotion to it. According to Whiting, the monasteries were dissolved 'against only limited resistance, and with extensive acquiescence or co-operation'.[115]

Reformist clergy received major collective support even less frequently, but there were certainly elements of it in the East Anglian disturbances of 1549 and Wyatt's rebellion in 1554. In view of the disruptive atmosphere that prevailed in these decades, it is hardly surprising that popular loyalty to the post-Reformation clergy took some time to develop. By the 1640s, however, there were numerous cases in which local parishioners vigorously resisted the expulsion of their established ministers by the forces of parliamentary puritanism. By this date, it seems, popular support for the reformed (but not too reformed) clergy of the church of England was quite extensive. Unfortunately, however, turbulent times had returned again.

In all likelihood, the majority of parishioners – both before and after the Reformation – were content with the services offered by their clergy. Many of these services changed quite radically, and a new model of a 'godly', educated, preaching ministry had come into existence. Other aspects of the vocation, however, remained largely the same. Perhaps people lost some faith in the priesthood, or ministry, during the decades of maximum turbulence. And it would be a mistake, at either end of the century, to portray the populace as deeply or universally enamoured of their vicars. There was some resentment, some indifference and some hostility; but, overall, there was considerable and enduring warmth. Without it, the sparks and the splinters that flew during these difficult decades would surely have been more damaging and overwhelming than they actually were. Sixteenth-century people were in the habit of taking their lead from local figures of authority, amongst whom the parish clergy figured prominently. This is not to say that they were blindly obedient – for they were quite capable of partial and even somewhat subversive compliance – but that they were basically receptive to the advice of trusted leaders. In this respect, the response of the majority of England's clergy to the Reformation was crucial. In the main, they too followed their leaders and implemented changes that clearly had the potential to tear society apart. The popular compliance emphasised so strongly by Robert Whiting was orchestrated, if often with some reluctance, by the clergy. They were an ambivalent but vital source of stability, and their example helped to make the English Reformation the strange and stripy creature that it was.

3

LAYFOLK ALONGSIDE THE CHURCH

The laity also revealed their religious sensibilities in ways that were connected a little less directly with the church. The line dividing one set of attitudes or actions from another is an arbitrary one, for the borders between 'inside' and 'alongside', or 'compulsory' and 'voluntary', are not marked by any clear fences. People could pass freely across them without realising that they were entering another zone. Nevertheless, these distinctions are useful in bringing some structure to the material, and in focusing our minds upon the blend of 'have to' and 'want to' ingredients that constituted early-modern popular religion.

Extra-liturgical Festivity

The rich calendrical cycle of the late-medieval church involved the laity not only in special church services, but in a wide range of festive activities that linked the sacred and the secular. These were concentrated in the period from Christmas to Midsummer, and have recently been described in detail by Ronald Hutton.[1] High points included the Christmas festival, during which houses were decorated with holly, ivy and broom. The merriment in a locality at this time might include the staging of plays about the nativity (or a variety of other subjects), the antics of 'maskers' dressed in festive disguises, or the election of a 'Lord of Misrule' to preside over the celebrations. In some places a wassail cup was carried around the parish, and drinks were offered in return for contributions to church or civic funds. The cup could also be used to 'wassail' the fruit trees, with the aim of coaxing them into lavish productivity in the coming year. The singing and playing of carols seems to have been very widespread, and Duffy has argued that the presence within the texts of snippets from the Advent and Christmas church services demonstrates 'a widespread lay familiarity with those parts of the liturgy'.[2]

Later in the year, Shrove Tuesday was another festive highlight, just before the rigours of Lent. People everywhere feasted and indulged in a wide variety of local sports, many of which involved the torture of animals. The names speak for themselves, and suggest that poultry were particularly unlucky: 'cockthreshing', 'cockfighting' and 'tilting at the cock'. Badgers, bulls and bears could also find themselves in trouble. Easter Day was a time for feasting (on specially blessed eggs, amongst other things) and the decoration of houses with fresh flowers and rushes. 'Hocktide', at the start of the second week after Easter, saw some interesting gender games in which women tied up men (or vice versa) before releasing them for a fee, which went to the parish. This was not the only occasion upon which women played a prominent and vital role in local fund-raising, though it was probably the most exciting. St George's day on 23 April was a rather more masculine affair, but it too could be of considerable economic importance to the parish. At Bassingbourn (Cambridgeshire) during the early sixteenth century, the village play about St George was advertised in no fewer than twenty-seven neighbouring settlements as part of a fund-raising drive.[3]

At some point during the weeks after May Day, many parishes held their 'church ales', occasions upon which fund-raising and festivity danced hand in hand. These, according to Hutton, were celebrations of summer and of community, and they often provided the churchwardens with their single most substantial source of income. Church ales were rarely annual events in an individual parish, but were organised on occasion, usually when the parish church needed a rush of funds for some particular project. They were generally held either in the church itself, or in a separate hall if the parish was lucky enough to possess one. The staple ingredients of this localised festivity included a variety of 'May games', hired musicians, morris dancing, floral decoration, the crowning of mock-kings or queens (sometimes Robin Hood and Maid Marian), processions and theatrical entertainments. It seems that the youth of the parish frequently took the lead in the organisation of such performances. Many parishes erected maypoles, and all participants expected ample food and drink. Sometimes, a number of local parishes might combine in order to stage a bigger, better ale, and one such group in Henrician Suffolk provided a menu of beer, milk, bread, cream, eggs, honey, spices, veal and mutton. In 1498, three Staffordshire parishes appointed a festive Robin Hood figure to gather funds at a local fair.

Individual parishes also held feasts to celebrate the dedication of the local church to its patron saint. These were concentrated in summer and early autumn, and involved a variety of practices. Robert Whiting offers us a glimpse of patronal festivities in the west country. At Braunton, a feast on Easter Monday reminded parishioners of their debt to St Brannoc. The inhabitants of Halberton arranged games and revels on the day of the Assumption of the Virgin Mary, patron of their church. These days were also marked, of course, by special church services, and the line between the sacred and the secular seems impossible to draw.[4]

The other great occasion for set-piece entertainments in late-medieval England was Corpus Christi Day, which fell in June on a date determined by that of Easter. In addition to the special liturgical processions of this day, parishioners in communities great and small might also have the opportunity to participate in what Miri Rubin calls 'a dense array of social activities', chief amongst them being the dramatic productions that have made the feast of Corpus Christi famous.[5] These ranged from the single plays staged in many small communities, to the complex cycles that were put on in a handful of major centres like Coventry, Chester and York. The latter were usually organised by the urban craft guilds, and have been called by Hutton 'arguably the most truly popular theatrical achievements of all time'. In many places, substantial sums were spent on costumes, special effects (such as earthquakes), and mobile stages complete with changing-rooms. The subject matter varied somewhat, but 'the essence of the play cycles was the presentation in simple, colourful and dramatic form of the scriptural narrative, ranging from the Old Testament stories to the nativity, the missionary life of Christ, his passion, resurrection and ascension'. Legendary material relating to the lives of the saints was also regularly included. Characters appearing in the play at Ashburton included international mega-stars like Christ, Herod, and the devil, along-side more local celebrities such as St Rumon of Tavistock. In Coventry, the accounts contain pithy records of the actors' fees: 'to God 16d'. The fundamental purpose was, then, always religious, and Duffy sees the plays as impressive evidence that the laity were concerned to teach themselves about the basics of Christian belief. They did so through a canny mixture of doctrine, sensation and humour, designed to entertain and educate at the same time. In the pewterers' play at York, for example, the story of the nativity was told, but Joseph featured as an aged cuckold who had lost out to a more potent force![6] For Hutton, these productions presented 'a triumphant review of Christian belief at the end of the "ritual half " of the year'.

Midsummer, skilfully accommodated by the church as the feast of St John the Baptist, was, in Hutton's words, the 'zenith of foliage, flowers and daylight'. People built bonfires, decorated their doors with foliage, and burned lamps before their houses. There were hospitality tables set up by the rich, morris dancing and pageants. Not all parishes were sufficiently resourceful to provide 'a serpent which spat fireballs', but it seems that a majority of parishes marked the date in some special way. The remainder of the year, though certainly not without its festive customs, was noticeably quieter and more restrained.

The functions of all this festivity were as varied as its forms. The church ale at Plymouth was held 'for the honour of God and for the increasing of the benefits of the church of St. Andrew'.[7] Fund-raising was indeed a central concern, and the various practices outlined above took their place alongside rates, collections, rents, burial fees, and bequests of lands, goods or cash in maintaining the solvency of the local church. Extra-liturgical festivities were also designed for the religious instruction of the populace, and most of the period's Corpus Christi plays were presumably written by clerics. They were not, however, staged by clerics, and the dramatic performances were just one of the opportunities available for members of the laity to express their religious instincts in a positive, creative and stimulating manner. The festivities absorbed and channelled lay spiritual energy, and provided an important balance within a religious system that gave the priesthood such a powerful role.

Plays, ales and feasts were also about the construction and affirmation of the Christian community. They brought people together, sometimes reminding them of their place within an unequal hierarchy, sometimes encouraging a sense of underlying equality, and sometimes inverting the established order in such a way as to give temporary power to the generally disadvantaged. A Marxist interpretation would view many of these festivities as a skilful elite strategy to control popular discontent by allowing it a harmless outlet. Certainly, there is something of this in the image of Robin Hood walking round a local fair with his collecting box! Even the physical abuse of animals can be portrayed as an element of the affirmation of community, since it gave expression to the fundamental divide that has nearly always separated humans from beasts within Christian thinking. It may seem peculiar to treat such seemingly secular pastimes as cock-fighting and stoolball as aspects of popular religion, but there are certain justifications. 'Holy day' activities, however secular they look, involved the special marking of God's time, and the distinguishing of it from ordinary time. In an admittedly loose sense, therefore, festive pastimes celebrated the sacred, and re-built the community of God's people, even if the majority of God's people were not necessarily fully conscious of it. Festivities were indeed 'for the honour of God'. In another sense again, the festivities aimed to bring prosperity and protection to the earthly community, by enlisting divine or animistic power through rituals such as that of 'wassailing' the fruit trees. It seems clear that the dividing line between the two forms of power was left deliberately vague, and it is also possible to see customs like that of the Midsummer bonfire as a means by which the official church sought to contain popular instincts that were rooted in a pagan past.

Recent writers have presented these festive traditions as 'popular' in both the main senses of the word. They were often shaped by lay energy, and the great feast of Corpus Christi was in fact a late-medieval development that owed much to the needs and demands of the people. Quite how extensive 'the people' were in this case, it is difficult to say. Certainly, we should remember that the shapers of festivities that were often costly before they were lucrative were likely to have been the wealthier members of society. In 1537, one Herefordshire man bequeathed a brass pot to the parish for use in church ales, 'and any busnesse of the churche'. But not everybody had a brass pot, let alone one to spare. For the attitudes of people closer to the bottom of the heap, we have very little direct evidence. Indirect evidence, however, leads us towards a positive conclusion. Whiting mentions archaeological evidence of open-air amphitheatres in the west country with the capacity to accommodate an audience of 2000 people at late-medieval religious plays. The Coventry plays were said to attract a 'very great confluence of people thither from far and near'. Of course, in some of the practices there must have been a certain sense of social duty, but it appears to have been reduced to a minimum by the colour, entertainment and creative scope that characterised so many of them.[8]

Before our eyes brim with tears for this lost world, a few minor qualifications should be made. In the first place, as Hutton has emphasised, not everything happened everywhere. In other words, a specific parish would not have maintained all the customs listed above, but would have practised a selection of them. Many places, furthermore, could not have afforded the spectacle that was possible in prosperous urban centres, and their festivities would have been much less lavish.

Secondly, we might wonder just how effective performances like the miracle plays were in disseminating religious knowledge. Their evident popularity is no guarantee of their educational impact, and – as any Tory politician will tell you – it is possible to stretch the 'learning can be fun' argument too far. Presumably, there came a point at which the bawdry became confused with the piety in the minds of uneducated observers. Elizabethan reformers made this objection with force, and it should not be dismissed out of hand. In the mid-seventeenth century, one aged Lancashire man told a shocked Yorkshire divine that the only thing he could recall about Jesus Christ was a vague image of 'a man on a tree', with blood that 'ran down'. This image came not from the sermons of Protestant ministers, but from a Corpus Christi play that he had watched many decades before. The case has been used by Duffy to demonstrate 'the enormous didactic and imaginative effectiveness of the religious plays of the late Middle Ages: once seen, never forgotten'.[9] This seems excessive, and it is difficult to regard this old man as a shining example of the educational power of late-medieval festivity. Like many a modern movie-goer, he remembered some of the special effects, but did he have the faintest idea what the film had really been about?

Thirdly, we may wonder whether the public celebration of communal oneness was ever quite as seamless as historians occasionally seem to imply. In pre-Reformation society, as in post-Reformation society, 'community' was a construct in need of continual repair if the most dangerous human tendencies were to be held in check. And sometimes, the cracks showed clearly. Duffy quotes one Jacobean conservative's deeply nostalgic account of late-medieval festivity, which includes the observation, 'And in all these bonefires, some of the friends and more civil poor neighbours were called in, and sat at the board with my grandfather.'[10] The words 'more civil' slip past unnoticed, yet they contain the unmistakable hint of social exclusiveness. Hospitality, it seems, was for one's friends and a few of the nicest poor folk. Duffy's 'holy neighbourliness' may not have extended to everyone. The tensions within the system are also suggested by the anxiety with which the local authorities sometimes regarded some of the inversionary rituals of popular festivity. In 1509, for example, the city fathers of Exeter banned the staging of Robin Hood plays because of the threat they were felt to pose to local order. It is important to note that this attitude was already present before the Reformation brought to it a new intensity.

During the sixteenth century, England's festive culture underwent major changes. Protestants of the first generation were willing to use some of the traditional vocabulary of festivity in their campaign against the old faith, and they wrote plays every bit as scurrilous as some of those they aimed to replace. In one bible play, Infidelitie invites Mary Magdalene to play upon his recorder: 'Truely you have not sene a more goodlie pipe, it is so bigge that your hand can it not gripe.'[11] Early Protestants were, however, suspicious of anything that seemed to imply an over-enthusiastic adoration of the saints, and of customs which appeared to treat the church precincts as a playground. During the reign of Edward VI, therefore, many of the old festivities were under some form of attack. Hutton describes, for example, how the dissolution of the religious guilds in 1547 put an end to most of the processions that had, in the past, marked the feasts of St George and Corpus Christi. Church ales also became far less frequent. Under Mary, the old customs were allowed to return, though not all of them did so with quite the richness of days gone by. The repeated reversals of official policy during the mid-century must have created serious confusion over the permissibility of various festive forms. This confusion persisted into Elizabeth's reign, but the conservative ethos of the majority of parishes ensured the survival of church ales, popular drama and many of the old recreations, for a time at least. Hutton describes the first Elizabethan decade as 'a notable time for old-fashioned merry-making'.[12]

In the last three decades of the century, however, the connection between traditional festivities and the church was becoming steadily weaker, as the powerful popular energies within English culture were suppressed or redirected. Officially-organised church ales, Hocktide games and festive collections all became far less frequent (though by no means non-existent), as local administrative regimes came to rely increasingly on compulsory rates and rents for their funds. Such devices certainly were not new, but they were definitely becoming more dominant. Hutton, interestingly, sees this as evidence that 'a cultural pendulum' was swinging back from colourful voluntarism towards the compulsion that had prevailed before 1450, rather than as a direct consequence of Protestantism. Perhaps, as Martin Ingram suggests, the heightened compulsory element bred a more minimalist approach to religious observance amongst the majority of people.[13] It could be added, however, that the levying of rates aimed to place parochial finances on a surer footing than had prevailed in the past, and one that was appropriate in a period which saw a significant expansion in the duties fulfilled by local government.

It would be wrong, in any case, to argue that the festive marking of religious time simply came to an end. In fact, it was often the case that the old rituals and practices were driven out of the church, but allowed to persist in non-ecclesiastical settings. Most reformers seem to have accepted this as a workable compromise. 'The result', says Hutton, 'was not so much an episode in the history of resistance to the Reformation as a part of the process of acceptance of it, easing the transformation of a Catholic to a Protestant society.'[14] There is no doubt that a wide array of popular customs survived into the seventeenth century, where they eventually met (and overcame) the wrath of Cromwell. These survivals included Hocktide and May games, Candlemas carols, festive decorations on Palm Sunday, wassailing, Christmas 'masking', marking bread loaves with the sign of the cross, and sports on Shrove Tuesday. Parishioners very occasionally reported one another to the church courts for the festive lighting of bon-fires, or morris dancing, or participation in unseemly Christmas games, but it seems certain that the vast majority of such incidents were widely tolerated.

Comparable 'migrations' of festive customs can be observed in some of the alternative dates promoted by Protestants for celebration, most notably the accession day of Elizabeth I (17 November). By 1590, the city of Oxford was not unusual in marking this day with music and fireworks. A generation later, as David Cressy has shown, 'bonfires and bells' were employed in celebration of a series of dates with distinctly Protestant associations (November 5th, for example). In addition, the residents of post-Reformation England enjoyed religious festivity of a sort in the official practice of 'carting' sexual offenders through the streets while basins were struck loudly before them. Religious reform, official policy and folk culture could all meet happily in public on such occasions. Perhaps we need to understand, with Mark Byford, that 'Given the right conditions, Protestantism could flourish because of, rather than in spite of, popular values.'[15]

Some of the great medieval play cycles survived into the 1570s, often with texts that had been modified to make them a little more acceptable to Protestants, but the flower of English religious drama was quite definitely withering from this point onwards. The major plays at Coventry, York, Chester and Wakefield had all come to an end by 1580, and were replaced by more secular pageants. Village drama underwent a similar decline. This was of immense cultural significance, not least because it may have been one of the changes that inaugurated, paradoxically, a great age of English secular drama. As one flower withered, so another grew. Lowering our cultural sights somewhat, it could also be argued that the popular religious energies expressed through late-medieval drama were to some extent re-channelled rather than completely obliterated in the late sixteenth and seventeenth centuries. There are some significant parallels to be drawn between the old plays, with their emphasis on Scripture stories and morality, and some of the new forms of cheap print that developed during the early-modern period. One of the best-selling ballads of the age was a simple tale of the life of Christ, and numerous printed songs provided snappy guides to upright moral living.

Another aspect of the late sixteenth and early seventeenth-century changes was the emergence of stricter attitudes towards observance of the Sabbath. The traditional, irregular pattern of feasting and fasting was gradually superseded (though never completely) by a new and more rhythmic pattern of days of work and days of rest. By the 1620s, most people seem to have abstained from non-essential work on Sundays, though many still regarded the hours between and after church services as a time for making merry. Common recreations included dancing, ball-sports, and patronage of the local alehouse. Conflict over the validity of these practices could be intense by this date, and has been portrayed as one of the causes of the civil wars. Certainly, there were real bones of contention here, though Ingram has argued persuasively that the attitudes of the majority towards common recreations were more flexible and accommodating than the most striking incidents might suggest. Most prosecutions, it seems, were directed at those whose antics caused them to be absent from church or involved the violation of church premises. The individuals who, in 1621, held a cockfight in the chancel of Newton Tony church could hardly expect that their enterprise would be overlooked. Similarly, the men who played football in the churchyard during service time at Great Baddow in 1598 were pushing their luck, and had little just cause for complaint when the preacher emerged to confiscate their ball. It is likely, however, that a great many less provocative recreations were practised without fear of prosecution. In Carlton (Cambridgeshire), for example, games of football took place in the churchyard, but were only reported when the participants knocked a pregnant woman to the ground in their single-minded excitement.[16]

We have, then, clear evidence that England's festive culture was changing markedly in the sixteenth century. Some of this reveals straightforward decline, and some of it suggests that old impulses found new outlets. Other evidence again implies that in many places the changes, though highly significant, were not particularly violent or abrupt. Extra-liturgical customs which were no longer permitted were asked to move elsewhere, or were left to fade with the generation of people to whom they were most familiar. In some places, the changes were sudden, and accompanied by bitter conflict; but in more places, arguably, their profoundly unsettling potential was eased by a slow process of implementation.

It is time now to look in more detail at the energies that drove these developments. The most famous critics of popular festivity in the sixteenth century were, of course, the puritans – those men and women who, by 1580, had come to feel with a sometimes frightening intensity that the Elizabethan church was only partly reformed, and that it retained far too many reminders of an evil popish past. The puritans, a 'militant tendency' rather than a party, comprised a small minority of the laity and a some-what larger minority of the clergy, but their influence upon English religious culture was out of all proportion to their numbers. Their pub-lished works bore angry titles such as *A Dialogue agaynst Light, Lewde, and Lascivious Dauncing*, and reminded readers 'what destruction fel upon Sodome and Gomora for their sinnes'. Several historians, including Ronald Hutton and Keith Wrightson, have seen in puritanism the main force behind the simplification of English festivity in the sixteenth century. For them, the leading lights in the campaign against traditional festivities were the self-styled 'godly' campaigners in the localities or the press, rather than the bishops or the Privy Council, whose attitudes were more accom-modating.[17]

This argument can be substantiated by reference to a number of fierce local disputes that rocked English towns and villages in the period. In 1589, for example, a holy alliance of evangelicals in Banbury (Oxfordshire) attempted to ban wakes, church ales, May games, and so on. The Privy Council intervened on the side of the opposition conservatives, who presumably felt themselves to be equally holy (after their own fashion), but the town nevertheless developed into one of England's noted puritan centres. With sufficient drive, zealous minorities could achieve a great deal, and Wrightson's account of the 'reformation of manners' in Terling (Essex) is another classic case of puritanism in the ascendant.

But zealous or not, the puritans in most communities were so thin on the ground that they can hardly take all the credit for a partial transforma-tion of English culture. Ingram, writing on Wiltshire, finds little evidence of puritan domination or of a concerted and energetic campaign against traditional festivities. For him, the rates that replaced church ales 'reflected the growing bureaucratisation of parochial finances and generally owed very little or nothing to puritan ideology'. And though there clearly was contention on the issue of Sunday and holiday recreations, 'the principle of leaving well alone in fact represented the majority opinion, even among the upper ranks and the middling sort'. The authorities usually adopted a reasonably mild and flexible attitude to popular festivities, and only grew more aggressive when the services or premises of the church were infringed in some way. It may well have been widely understood that popular games and festive rituals served important functions in holding communities together and providing opportunities for the release of pent-up energies. In the early seventeenth century, this attitude was articulated in print with increasing frequency, as two very different conceptions of community stared at one another with increasing mutual defiance. In 1633, the Bishop of Bath and Wells explained that feasts and church ales were important 'for the civilizing of people, for their lawful recreations, for the composing of differences by occasion of the meeting of friends, for the increase of love and amity, as being feasts of charity, for relief of the poor, the richer sort keeping then in a manner open house, and for many other reasons'. It sounds as if traditionalism was reasserting itself in forthright style, and Hutton argues that in the period between Elizabethan puritanism and the civil wars, customary festivity did indeed enjoy something of a renaissance.[18]

The friction between these two sets of attitudes is of very considerable significance. It helps to explain how so much traditional festivity was lost, but also how a good proportion of it was preserved in one form or another. It assists us in the problem of explaining how the Elizabethan Reformation was comparatively non-violent, but it also reveals within that Reformation a dangerous tension that would be (partially) resolved only through civil war, half a century later.

Yet it does not fully explain the pattern of change, and other factors must also be drawn into the account. There were some powerful non-religious reasons for the simplification and enhanced surveillance of festivity. The price inflation and population increase of the second half of the sixteenth century created various interrelated stresses within English society. People had less money to spend, and – even without puritanism – may have had little choice but to reduce their investment in plays, pageants and the like. One later commentator went so far as to attribute the decline of church ales to 'popular prejudice'. Even in the more stable economic conditions of today, we spend less on Easter eggs in times of recession, though we might crave the chocolate more than usual. As early as 1540, the burgesses of Wallingford had ended their Hocktide festivities because of the 'sumptuous costs'.[19] Rapid demographic expansion inevitably bred an intensified anxiety concerning the maintenance of good order, and this too motivated the shapers of local and national policy to view festive gatherings of people as potential sources of trouble. For both these reasons, fund-raising systems which relied upon the orderly collection of compulsory rates looked like a more sensible option than an irregular programme of ales, plays and rituals. Religious reformation and bureaucratic 'rationalisation' proceeded in tandem, but the first was not by any means the only cause of the second. To a degree, popular compliance with the process of reform was built upon this confluence of Protestant priorities and economic conditions.

Puritanism, in its vehemently hostile attitude to common recreations, was an extreme response to the Elizabethan atmosphere. As one contemporary joke had it, puritans considered a game of bowls on Sunday to be just as wicked as an act of adultery on Monday. For the majority, factors encouraging a reduction of festivity were balanced by a sense of need. To zealots, most games and pastimes seemed unforgivably 'heathenish' and wicked, but for people in general they served an important function in reaffirming the bonds (and, it has to be said, the fractures) within their communities. Popular attachment to traditional festivity was undoubtedly strong. Its purpose was to 're-create' society and its myriad components in a fascinating and vital way. Although puritan critics would never have conceded it, this ambitious exercise was not unrelated to the Christian objective of reifying community through shared liturgical performances. In a sense, Sunday sports may have been a loosely affiliated feature of orthodox religion, rather than its terrible antithesis. A majority of England's governors, one suspects, understood the importance of festivity well enough, and were content not to push too hard. For this reason, a significant number of the old recreations still had a place, even if they were often moved from their traditional surroundings, and were watched somewhat more closely than before. Once again, we see evidence of a process of negotiation and compromise beneath the more familiar story of puritanically motivated imposition.

Attitudes to the Church Courts

The policing of holiday recreations was not in the hands of any professional force, but was instead the responsibility of the local inhabitants themselves. Most particularly, this involved the vicar and the church officers, who received enquiries from, and sent information to, the diocesan authorities. But people in general were expected to pass on to their representatives any rumours of immoral conduct within the neighbourhood. The institutions which sifted and acted upon such evidence were the ecclesiastical courts. They formed a vast web of justice covering the entire country, and extending into a great many spheres of local behaviour. In the words of Martin Ingram, they occupied, 'at least in theory, a place of the utmost importance in the social fabric'.[20] The courts were a crucial point of contact between parishioners and the institutional church, and the documentation they generated provides us with extremely important and colourful evidence regarding the attitudes of people to that church, and to the main moral and religious issues of the day.

Ecclesiastical justice, based on canon law, was administered either in special courtrooms in the major provincial centres, or in local churches and even inns when the courts went out on 'visitation'. At such times, the churchwardens of every parish were expected to provide formal 'bills of presentment', written or dictated in response to pre-circulated questions. These questions, or 'visitation articles', identified the matters about which the judges wished to hear. The local officers could also make additional, voluntary presentments at any time of the year. Information was carried to and fro by the courts' 'apparitors', 'a familiar sight as they strode or rode about the countryside'. The courts could bring prosecutions for a huge range of offences, including simony, the neglect of church buildings, refusal of fees, heresy, idolatry, absenteeism, fornication and adultery. These were 'office causes', similar in form to modern criminal proceedings. The courts also heard 'instance causes', in which one party sued another for offences such as defamation or breach of contract. Civil litigation in secular justice provides a rough analogy.

The principal punishments available to the courts as they sought to reform the offenders were admonition, public penance, and excommunication. Admonition – 'a simple reproof from the judge' – was the least severe. Penance required a public apology, and sometimes that the culprit dress in a symbolic white sheet in order to deliver it. Penance could, however, be commuted into a money payment for local 'pious uses', at the discretion of the judge. Excommunication, a still more serious matter, ordered that the individual be excluded from all the church's ministrations and sometimes from civil society as well. In addition, all those who became subject to an investigation were required to pay the court's fees, and this amounted in effect to an extra form of punishment.

The conspicuous changes of the sixteenth century made remarkably little difference to the institutional and constitutional framework of the church courts. Collinson has identified this as a significant area of continuity for the English population. The structure of ecclesiastical justice still stood, and stood still: 'In this forum, which touched most English men and women sooner or later, it could indeed be said that the Reformation did not happen to any marked extent.'[21] It was a continuity that made England distinctive within Protestant Europe.

Historiographically, the church courts used to have a negative reputation, and were widely neglected as a result. When considered, they were portrayed as inefficient, corrupt and unpopular. This attitude is now changing rapidly, and the old picture of ecclesiastical justice (presented, for example, by Christopher Hill) has recently been revised in two slightly different ways. Some historians (for example, Haigh, Houlbrooke and Whiting) have found the courts in the late-medieval period to have been impressive and valued institutions, but have argued that their status was substantially undermined during the Reformation. Others, headed by Martin Ingram, have extended the positive analysis into the decades between 1570 and 1640, arguing that, under the circumstances, the church courts continued to perform 'remarkably well'. In several areas of conduct, notably religious observance and sexual activity, they even managed in this period to effect a gradual, unspectacular, but cumulatively substantial improvement of standards. Levels of corruption and inefficiency were well within acceptable contemporary parameters.

Ingram's interpretation is easily the most convincing on offer, and it is worth dwelling for a while on his account of the tone of ecclesiastical justice in practice. The system he describes was impressively flexible, and sensitive to the grassroots circumstances within which it operated. Other scholars have sometimes treated the courts' reliance upon local reporting, and the consequent and undeniable under-presenting of offences, as a shortcoming. Churchwardens were ordinary people, moral policemen for a year, and they inevitably let many offences slip through the net. Within Ingram's interpretation, however, this circumstance is portrayed more as a strength than a weakness. He points out that canon law required potential litigants to settle their differences out of court if possible, and that it demanded the provision of information on *notorious* cases only. The diocesan authorities understood that their requests for information would receive a selective response from the localities, and in practice they accepted the right of parishioners to draw the line between the trivial and the serious. The process of compurgation, in which an individual could be cleared of suspicion by sworn statements of trust from other locals, epitomised this understanding. Effectively, it was possible, within limits, 'for communities to construct their own disciplinary agendas'. The court's judges are portrayed, in the main, as men of common sense, who used their discretion wisely and carefully. Overall, Ingram finds evidence of a 'symbiosis between courts and communities', which was under threat only when militant puritan ministers rode into town, or when the Laudian reforms of the 1630s undermined the broad consensus.

The court books, which survive in their hundreds, therefore present us with evidence not of an oppressive, 'big brother' of a church, commanding people to spill the beans on the mildest misdemeanours of their neighbours; but instead of a process of negotiation which allowed parish representatives to decide which of the bishop's 'visitation articles' to respond to with greatest thoroughness. We can therefore learn something about parochial priorities in moral and religious matters. Many types of case – heresy, for example – are actually very isolated, even in parishes where heretics are known to have dwelt. The area of behaviour that emerges as being of the greatest concern, both before and after the Reformation, was sexual morality. Harper-Bill's analysis of the business of the Suffolk courts in 1499 reveals the dominance of sexual cases, and Ingram's table of offences in Wiltshire in 1585 does not look radically different.[22] Roughly one-third of visitation presentments involved fornication, bastardy, bigamy, unlawful separation, and so on. These presentments furnish us with an incredibly detailed catalogue of sexual misconduct, ranging from the extremely vague ('he is as lyke to have a wiefe in another place as not') to the highly specific ('before ii or iii honest women [he] did showe his pryvities at Downham').

The Reformation, not surprisingly, did make an impact on the nature of the business that came before the courts. At both ends of the sixteenth century, parish representatives brought cases concerning the physical neglect of the church, failure to attend services and to receive communion, the sowing of discord, and the withholding of dues, but these matters loomed larger under Elizabeth than they had done under Henry VII. The changes reflected social problems, religious tension and tighter standards in proportions that are impossible to calculate. They should perhaps be seen as shifts in the balance of a solid system, rather than as evidence of any profound transformation of the courts' role. Much business changed very little, and the records of ecclesiastical justice suggest a robust similarity in the common-sense concern of parishioners for the maintenance of moral order and outward respect for the church. The root of these emphases was an urge to build, maintain and enforce communal peace and stability. In Ingram's words, 'The demand for "peace", "love", "charity" and "quietness" among neighbours is a constant refrain in contem-

porary records.' The refrain was not rewritten as a result of the Reformation, and Dickens speaks of 'an uncanny sense of continuity across the
period of cataclysm'.[23]

Evidence of the courts' unpopularity is now being set into its proper
context. Of course, there is material indicating dislike for the courts'
operations, and there is more of it for the decades after 1550 than from
those before 1530. Puritans regarded the courts as an evil remnant of the
popish past, and an utterly inadequate forum for godly discipline. Common lawyers resented the jurisdiction of the church over matters which
they considered themselves better qualified to adjudicate. Some individuals, neither godly nor legally-trained, scoffed at the 'bawd court' or
the 'bum court', and spoke of its punishments with derision. In 1557, one
west countryman was heard to boast of his adulterous exploits, and to
dismiss the possible consequences as 'but a sheet matter'. In 1595, a
Stratford woman invited and received a sentence of excommunication
with the memorable courtroom ejaculation 'Goodes woondes, a plague
of God on you all, a fart of ons ars for you.' Several decades later, Edward
North of Sutton (Isle of Ely) was similarly dismissive of church discipline,
'sayeinge it is but a seaventeene pennie matter for any fault'.[24]

Nevertheless, historians are misguided if they argue either that this
evidence was representative of majority attitudes, or that it shows a
collapse in the status of the courts as a consequence of the Reformation.
One or both of these propositions feature in the work of Haigh, Whiting
and Houlbrooke. In fact, there are very good reasons for arguing that the
courts were widely respected, and that they retained that respect until the
latter part of the seventeenth century, and perhaps beyond. Their levels of
business were rising steadily from the second half of the sixteenth century,
indicating that the system was being widely used. Jim Sharpe calculates,
for example, that the work-load of the courts in the diocese of Chester
doubled between 1544 and 1594.[25] The instance machinery of the courts
was frequently called upon by people wishing to defend their reputations,
especially in sexual matters, against allegedly defamatory reports. When
people choose to make use of institutions, it is normally fair to deduce that
the services of those institutions are valued.

The majority, moreover, almost certainly feared the humiliation of
ecclesiastical punishment. Eric Carlson describes the ordeal of Elizabeth
Hoode, ordered 'to stand at the Bull Ring in Cambridge clothed in a white
sheet down to the ground, holding a white rod or wand in her hand and
having a paper written declaring her offence'. One such paper, composed
for a bigamist, read 'My filthy life I do detest / that I eight years have lived

in. / Alas two wives I have possessed, / The Lord forgive my foul sin.'
These were not merely the quaint punitive rituals of 'olde England', and in
1618 one Ely minister asked the court not to impose the full rigour of
penance against a local fornicator, on the grounds that the shame of it
would endanger his mother's health. On hearing of his conviction, she had
'swooned almost irrecoverably'.[26] Another index of respect for the courts
is the level of contumacy, or refusal to comply with their orders. Ingram
has revised the earlier, more negative, estimates of historians, and calculates that attendance rates ran at 75 per cent or higher in the period
between 1570 and 1640. By contemporary standards, this is an impressive
figure and certainly indicates a basically compliant populace. It is likely,
furthermore, that expressions of defiant hostility towards the courts represent the antithesis of mainstream attitudes, rather than their pithy encap-
sulation. Criminals do not, in general, hold courts of law in high esteem.
Why would they?

In conclusion, the system of ecclesiastical justice provided people with
an almost constant point of reference through the drama of sixteenth-
century change. The business of the courts expanded, and adjusted itself to
an altered religious environment, but it certainly did not experience any
fundamental transformation. Nor did levels of respect diminish significantly, and we can reasonably argue that the records provide more evidence of basically positive attitudes to the church, on both sides of the
mid-century disruptions. They also demonstrate, once again, that one of
the pillars of popular religion was the preservation of harmony, simultaneously spiritual and social, within the locality. This pillar was undoubtedly shaken during the sixteenth century, but its foundations proved
strong. It remained one of the key supports for the Christianity of the
majority, and its importance in helping society through a difficult period of
religious change is difficult to overestimate. As Andrew Brown has
observed, 'the appeal of enforcing moral behaviour... drew on values,
deeply embedded in Christian society, that did not depend for their
expression on precise theological doctrines'.[27]

Forms of Fellowship

In late-medieval England, the laity watched over their own moral and
religious conduct not only through the church courts, but through the
guilds or confraternities. These were voluntary fellowships, organised by

their lay members, and dedicated to some special spiritual personage or entity. Amongst these, the most popular were the Virgin Mary, the Holy Trinity, Corpus Christi and St John the Baptist. Guilds existed in their thousands, and, as we shall see, were affected far more directly than the church courts by the official Reformation. In recent years, the guilds have attracted considerable attention from historians of late-medieval religion, because of their role as a laypeoples' forum for the expression of popular religious concerns. It is appropriate, at the outset, to distinguish the spiritual guilds from the mainly urban craft guilds, which certainly had religious functions, but which existed primarily for the management and protection of a particular trade.

No two religious guilds were identical, yet they all had a great deal in common. Their primary function was to provide members with a measure of insurance against the pains of this world and, more particularly, of the next. Payment of the appropriate subscription fee guaranteed that an individual would receive a good burial, and that the ordeal of purgatory would be eased somewhat by intercessory Masses and prayers said regularly on behalf of all the guild's dead members. It was not even necessary to be alive at the time of joining, and the dead were enrolled at half-price in Stratford! Members who died away from home were sometimes brought back to the parish at the expense of the guild. The fulfilment of obligations to the dead required living members to hire the services of extra chaplains, and to take an active role in the maintenance and enhancement of the local church. The confraternities appointed special officers to keep the lights burning before relevant images, and the Guild of the Assumption in Leverington (Isle of Ely) was founded specifically to repair an image of the Virgin. Many church-building projects received support from the local guilds. Confraternities might retain their own choirs or organists, and the Holy Trinity guild in Coventry paid for the services of no fewer than thirteen full-time priests.[28]

The intercessory purpose was also expressed in the celebrations organised by each guild to honour its patron. At Bardwell (Suffolk), one guild marked the relevant saint's day with a procession to church, a special Mass, and a feast for one hundred and fifty members. On 23 April, the Guild of St George in Norwich honoured its patron with bells, chanting, candles, banners, a parade of members in red and white livery, an elaborate re-enactment of the confrontation between George and the dragon, and a lavish feast. Such feasts were held either in church property or, when the local guilds had sufficient wealth, in specially built guildhalls. Many of these can still be seen in the towns and villages of England. At

Baston (Lincolnshire), the female members of one guild danced together in a saint's day procession to the church, and the guild of St Martin in Stanford (Lincolnshire) arranged a bull-baiting event each year.[29]

Dead members may have had the most to gain from the guilds' activities, but the living could also hope for certain benefits. Some guilds ran schools or almshouses for members, and one even founded a Cambridge college (Corpus Christi). Many lent money to members to assist in their economic ventures, or gave them hand-outs of food or cash when they had suffered misfortune. Members could also rent portions of their confraternity's stock, a privilege which for those at Dullingham (Cambridgeshire) included the chance to make use of 'the bolokys of the gyld'.[30]

And with these opportunities went obligations. Many guilds recorded ordinances demanding that their members maintain certain standards of behaviour, and prescribing punishments for those who failed to do so. In general, these regulations reflected the corporate aspirations and the claims to respectability of the institution involved. Members of the Guild of the Assumption in Cambridge, for example, were forbidden to wander the streets at night (without good reason), to keep bad company, and to play at chess or dice. Any member of one London guild could find himself expelled if 'he lie too long in bed, is lazy, and loses his goods through foolishness'. Several guilds expressed concern over sexual misbehaviour. Many forbad members to take their interpersonal grievances to law until the guild had made an attempt at arbitration, and the Guild of the Blessed Virgin at Kingston-on-Hull ordered the ejection of any member found to be a 'lover of law-suits'. The preservation of 'unytye and love betwyne partyes' was an important priority, and several of the items in a guild document from late-medieval Wisbech emphasised the need for peace. Members of the Guild of the Holy Cross in Stratford held their annual feast in order that 'brotherly love shall be cherished among them, and evil-speaking be driven out; that peace shall always dwell among them, and true love be upheld'. Other guilds were empowered to enforce attendance at church on key holy days. The behaviour of members at their annual feast was also to be carefully regulated. Participants might be required to wear the distinctive hoods of their confraternity. Some guilds stipulated that no members were to attend barefoot, or to make excessive noise, or to steal one another's stools during the meal. One guild, perhaps concerned that the sobriety of the occasion might prove overwhelming, banned its members from falling asleep at the table.[31]

The day-to-day business of a typical guild was in the hands of a group of officers, elected from amongst the membership. The highest of these was the warden or master, who coordinated and directed the activities of a chamberlain, a steward and an almoner. The lesser officers were those appointed to maintain the guild's lights or images in church. In 1538, the confraternities in Spelsbury (Oxfordshire) provided a total of fourteen individuals with responsibility over specific lights.[32]

Guilds ranged in size from those with annual incomes of £1000 to those able to support only a fraction of the activities described above. They were also extremely widespread. The heaviest concentration may have been in the eastern counties (Norwich alone had twenty-one in the early sixteenth century), but they must have been familiar institutions in a large majority of English settlements. The counties of Northamptonshire, Cambridgeshire and Lincolnshire each had well over a hundred guilds. London had as many. Not all of the confraternities lasted more than a few decades, but for every guild that was lost a new one seems to have been founded. Numerically, these institutions certainly were not in decline in the late-medieval period. Rather the opposite.

Recent historians have been at pains to emphasise the openness of guild membership and the positive appeal of belonging. The tone of the writing implies that there was a place for virtually everyone in one or other of the confraternities existing in each locality. Of course, not everyone could join every guild, but specific confraternities existed to meet the needs of most social groups, whether these were based on occupation, gender or age. In St Neot (Cornwall), the 'wives of the western end of the parish' evidently had their own confraternity! Hanawalt and Mcree point out that nearly half of the names appearing on surviving membership lists belong to women, and argue that 'virtually everyone' belonged to one or more guilds in rural villages. Women regularly featured as holders of minor guild offices, and Scarisbrick makes a minor heroine out of the 'Joan Belcher' who looked after a Trinity light in Spelsbury (Oxfordshire). For him, rural guilds in particular were places where 'rich and far-from-rich, male and female, layman and cleric could meet and rub shoulders as nowhere else'. In Ludlow, a grand and impressive total of 1176 people joined the main guild between 1505 and 1509.[33]

The confraternities did not, however, cater for everyone, and a measure of exclusivity was undoubtedly part of their appeal. Some urban guilds, like that of St Mary in Cambridge, excluded the vast bulk of the population by charging entrance fees of ten shillings. Hanawalt and Mcree admit that many ordinary labourers would not have been able to afford even the most humble of subscriptions, let alone substantial sums like this one. Even Christopher Haigh, who is disposed to be as positive about the guilds as possible, could only come up with a figure of 10 per cent for guild membership in late-medieval London. This seems surprisingly low. A few guilds restricted membership numbers to twelve or even fewer, and many foundation documents spoke of the poor in such a way as to demonstrate that they were unfortunate outsiders, deserving of charity, and certainly not cherished brethren. Occasionally, guilds excluded specific occupational groups – bakers and priests, for example – from membership, and one confraternity could find no place for local mayors and bailiffs, 'unless . . . of humble, good and honest conversation'.[34]

Occasionally, there are also hints of pressure being applied to people in order to encourage membership. At Tydd St Giles (Isle of Ely) in 1464, it was reported to the church courts that 'Richard Odam and Thomas Hunston promised to be members of the gild of St. John the Baptist before a year had elapsed and have not become so.' Not all late-medieval people were anxious to belong to guilds, and Andrew Brown has observed that even the wealthier guilds could find it burdensome to meet their obligations to the dead. Moreover, the motives for some of those who did join may not have been quite as positive as is often implied. Attempts are currently being made to remove the fear of purgatorial suffering from the spectrum of motivations, but one suspects that, for many people, it was an all-too prominent preoccupation. Alongside an unquestionably positive pull towards guild membership, there were therefore a number of more negative elements, and there were even some good reasons for avoiding participation in the culture of confraternities. This mixture helps to explain why the percentage of testators registering bequests to the local guilds ranged from 57 in Devon and Cornwall to a mere 2 in the archdeaconry of Buckingham.[35]

Another debatable feature of the confraternities was their relationship to the greater structures of church and state. Clearly, there was potential for friction. The guilds were, after all, run by the laity, and their members sometimes resided outside the boundaries of the parish. Did they, therefore, pose a threat to the established order? Some evidence might imply that they did. Confraternities, at times, certainly attracted the suspicion of leading governors. In 1388, for example, a major enquiry into the activities of English guilds had been ordered by the government of Richard II. And individual parish priests were not always grateful for the existence of guild chaplains: in 1444, the peace of Henley-on-Thames was broken by a row between them. Overall, however, recent scholars have argued convincingly that the guilds were complementary to, rather than subversive of, the dominant institutions. Their activities added greatly to the richness of local church interiors and of the liturgical round. The Guild of the Assumption in Pampisford (Cambridgeshire) existed to provide funds 'for the use and repair of the church which is in poor condition'. Other guilds regularly donated surplus funds to the local church. The guild chaplains were not, in general, rivals of the parish priests. Instead, they often served as trusted assistants. Duffy calls one such chaplain a 'linchpin of parochial life', and describes his multiple roles as recorder of the churchwardens' accounts and director of the village play about St George. In Gervase Rosser's view, the late-medieval guilds made possible a flexible response to the problems caused for local worship by demographic contraction. The parish, being of a more fixed identity, was less able to adjust effectively. In other words, guilds and parishes worked together for the good of the community.[36]

The guilds therefore fulfilled a variety of important and valuable functions. Most fundamentally, they provided a substantial proportion of the population with assistance along the hard road towards salvation. They also eased the pressures of earthly existence, and offered people a sense of belonging. Guilds generally operated in support of parochial worship, and did their bit to promote rectitude and social harmony. Alongside these positive factors, however, we should also note that many were excluded from guild membership, that a few (at least) felt pressured into joining, and that some found the burdens of confraternal duties rather onerous. Not everyone, therefore, was beating at the guildhall doors, hoping for admission, and some of those on the inside must have been there primarily because they feared the spiritual consequences of staying out.

It is only by being aware of these less pleasing possibilities that we can hope to understand the final chapter in the history of the guilds. They were dissolved by statute in 1547, and Edward VI's government set about the business of confiscating their assets. In the next few years, the guilds faded from existence with a rapidity that Susan Brigden has described as 'mysterious'. In fact, there are signs that the system of guilds was already in decline from the 1520s onwards. Guilds featured less frequently in the charitable giving of testators. It seems that approximately one in ten wills included a bequest to the guilds in the late Henrician years. Whiting argues that in Devon and Cornwall, parishioners became more reluctant to hold guild offices from 1530 onwards. He also shows how several local guilds were cutting their expenditure on memorial Masses in the mid-1530s. Under Queen Mary, guilds became legal once again, but only a tiny proportion of them were re-founded.[37]

It is not easy to explain these findings. The pro-Catholic scholars have attempted to do so with almost exclusive reference to non-spiritual factors.

They see the mid-century decline in guild fortunes as a result of difficult economic conditions, or of understandable anxieties about government intentions in a period of seemingly rudderless change. People were naturally reluctant to invest in institutions that looked likely to fall under the axe. We might add that the thoroughness of the Edwardian campaign against the guilds made their revival under Mary considerably more difficult than it would otherwise have been.

These arguments, though clearly relevant, seem somewhat feeble when set against evidence seen by the same scholars as overwhelming proof of the power and popularity of the guilds, just a few years earlier. With stakes as high as the salvation of souls, might we not expect some vigorous signs of commitment? There are, admittedly, some appealing examples of parishioners plotting to conceal guild property and goods from the hungry eye of the state. One London guild obtained a royal licence to alienate its assets to a member, just before the act of dissolution, then leased them back from him a few days later.[38] Apart from such cases, however, there is astonishingly little evidence to suggest that people stood up in defence of the institutions they seem formerly to have loved. It is difficult to avoid the conclusion that the late-medieval guilds may not have been quite as golden as we have been led to believe. Arguably, a substantial proportion of the population felt a certain sense of relief when the official denial of purgatory eased their obligations to former generations. Very few of these people were Protestants, and, if asked, the vast majority would have said that they preferred the old to the new. Nevertheless, we have to concede the possibility that their commitment to this aspect of Catholicism did not run quite as deep as most recent historians have argued. Without doing so, it is impossible to explain fully why so few people felt moved to dip into their pockets for the re-foundation of the religious guilds under Mary.

The most devout of late-medieval Christians found a more intense form of fellowship through pilgrimage. This was probably a minority pursuit, but amongst that minority, pilgrimage was an important devotional practice. The most ambitious journeyed to Jerusalem or Santiago, and the English Hospice in Rome provided shelter for thousands of pilgrims in the late fifteenth and early sixteenth centuries. Others made less exotic journeys to the wealth of shrines that existed on home soil. Some asked others to undertake pilgrimages on their behalf. Alice Cooke of Horstead, for example, left money in her will for a man to tour nine local shrines, including 'Our Lady of Rafham', 'St Parnell of Stratton' and 'St Leonard without Norwich'. For Duffy, the primary purpose of pilgrimage was 'to seek the holy, concretely embodied in a sacred place, a relic, or a specially

privileged image'. It was also a penitential good work, designed to earn
God's mercy, and many shrines carried papal indulgences. Pilgrims also
hoped for specific earthly favours, particularly a cure from disease or
suffering ('both Men and Beastes which had lost their Prevy partes, had
newe members again restored to them, by this [St] Walstane'). They
therefore carried symbolic wax offerings, which varied in relation to the
needs of the pilgrim and the healing speciality of the shrine to be visited.
Assorted visitors to one shrine in York are known to have left, amongst
other things, two cows, thirteen legs, four breasts and a fleet of model
ships.[39]

Pilgrims travelled in groups (or 'flocks', as one early reformer scornfully
put it), and cultivated a distinctive appearance. They often carried special
staffs, wore cockle-shell badges, and walked barefoot. As Chaucer knew,
there was close fellowship to be had in the company of pilgrims, and their
example formed an exuberant strain of piety within late-medieval popular
religion. But pilgrimage, like the guilds, succumbed a little too easily to the
Reformation attack which began in the 1530s.[40] Once again, the apparent
readiness with which most people acquiesced in the officially sponsored
demolition of their sacred shrines places a faint question mark over the
depth, if not the vivacity, of their devotion.

In the new world of Elizabethan Protestantism, there were still those
who formed bands to make religious journeys. These were the self-styled
'godly' or, in Patrick Collinson's words, 'the virtuoso minority whose
practice of religion was prodigious'. One of their most conspicuous activities was that of 'gadding to sermons', or travelling in groups away from
their home parishes in search of more zealous stimulation elsewhere. In
the 1580s, for example, people in St Albans noticed that 'many of this
gadding people came from farre and went home late, both yonge men and
yonge women together'. In Derbyshire, a group of gadders discussed the
sermon and sang psalms 'in their return home'. They did not travel great
distances, and were not called pilgrims. In fact, they regarded themselves
as the polar opposites of those misguided fellows of the past. Yet, in their
voluntarism and their urge to undertake communal journeys, the 'gadders'
exhibited impulses very similar to those which had motivated earlier
generations of godly travellers. One Elizabethan noticed the popularity
of sermons given by godly clergymen in London, and remarked, 'The
people resort unto them as in popery they were wont to run on pilgrimage.'[41]

It is never easy to decide what we should call these people. For most
contemporaries, the label 'puritan' – in common usage from the late

Elizabethan decades – meant rather more than 'committed Protestant'. It also implied a desire for further ecclesiological change, a nonconformist instinct, an extreme intensity of temperament and a gross insensitivity to the cultural norms of the majority. It was possible, therefore, to be a convinced Protestant without being a puritan. For this reason, the tendency of historians to conflate the two categories is somewhat unfortunate. Contemporary 'puritans' often did something comparable, speaking as if they alone were truly pious. One Jacobean rector criticised them for singling themselves out as 'brethren', 'as if none had brotherhood in Christ, none had interest in goodness, none made profession of the Gospel, but themselves'.[42] Once again, there is a danger that those whose piety was less conspicuous but not necessarily less impressive will be left out in the historiographical cold. Clearly, those contemporaries whose piety went beyond the ordinary must have covered a spectrum from the quiet and completely conformist at one end, to the loud and partially nonconformist at the other. The problem, as ever, is that the former, though probably much more numerous, bequeathed far fewer sources to posterity. Their 'godliness' is therefore much more difficult to investigate.

Unfortunately, there are no obvious solutions to these terminological difficulties, and most historians end up using all the available terms interchangeably, and hoping for the best. It may be helpful in the following account to employ 'the godly' as an umbrella term for all those of unusual Protestant commitment, while reserving 'puritan' for the most militant amongst them. Keith Wrightson, usefully, has defined a 'puritan' as 'a godly activist'. Perhaps the dividing line between 'godliness' and 'puritanism' can be located in the association of the latter with an urge to campaign vigorously for the reform of wider society. Many of the 'godly', arguably, were more moderate in their interactive instincts. As William Hunt has remarked, 'A Puritan who minds his business is a contradiction in terms.'[43]

By all accounts, including their own, the puritans were a rare breed. This was a theological truth as well as a demographic one, for they evidently believed that something like 95 per cent of the population were predestined to eternal damnation. Admittedly, they came to dominate local affairs in a substantial number of communities, most of which were urban settlements such as Northampton, Banbury, Bury St Edmunds and, somewhat later, Dorchester. Puritans were more numerous in London, the midlands, the south-east and East Anglia than they were elsewhere, though there were definite pockets in Somerset, Cheshire and Lancashire. It was certainly possible for villages, as well as towns, to fall under the puritan spell, and Terling in Essex is a famous example. But it seems that rural England, in general, encountered 'godly activists' more as isolated cliques than as substantial local gatherings. In Wiltshire, Martin Ingram could find no examples of communities dominated by puritanism in the manner of Terling. Even in Northamptonshire, studied by William Sheils, it seems that less than one in five of the clergy at any one time were puritans. Presumably, the proportion amongst the laity was much lower. When the puritan author Arthur Dent commented that the elect 'walke very thinly in the streets', he apparently did so with good reason.[44]

There has been some heated debate regarding the social status of those most commonly drawn to puritanism. Keith Wrightson has tended to argue that its values appealed most strongly to local elites, those members of the 'middling sort' who were increasingly dominant within parish government. Margaret Spufford, with partial support from Martin Ingram and Patrick Collinson, has disputed this, insisting that committed religiosity was a force ignorant of social boundaries.[45] This dispute will clearly not be resolved in a synthetic paragraph. It can be suggested, however, that 'puritanism' as defined above – a militant social creed as well as a code of piety – was more likely to develop in those members of the wider 'godly' who found themselves in positions of local power. For this reason, 'puritanism' may have displayed a significant social bias, while 'godliness' was more evenly distributed. Having said this, there were militant Protestants on all levels, and none of our boundaries – social or religious – are secure.

The Elizabethan godly were characterised by a wide variety of attitudes and activities, many of which invite comparison or contrast with those of earlier pilgrims and guild members. The puritans exhibited an uncompromising intensity, which sometimes led them to baptise their offspring with specially invented names. At Warbleton in Sussex, Elizabethan babies were welcomed into the church bearing names like Sure-Hope, Fear-not and Sorry-for-Sin. The puritans held their theological beliefs with similar zeal, and adopted the Calvinist doctrine of election far more enthusiastically than the population at large ever did. Predestinarian theology interacted with a heightened consciousness of human depravity to generate a state of mind that was rarely happy. The minister and author Arthur Dent said that members of the elect were like people who had been strapped fast to an enormously high church steeple: they were perfectly safe, but terrified when they looked down. The puritans' fundamentalist reading of the Bible treated it as the absolute, infallible guide to godly living, and they often knew their Scripture with a thoroughness that would have shamed some of the clergy. In Collinson's words, 'All non-scriptural doctrine and practice, all non-scriptural art, amounted to lies, false religion.'[46]

The godly were similarly obsessed with sermons, and 'gadding' across the countryside was just one expression of this. In 1588, a yeoman from Feering (Essex) provided in his will for sixty sermons to be given in his locality following his death. Committed Protestants regularly pooled their resources in order to found special 'lectureships'. These were held by invited preachers, whose sermons augmented the ministrations of the allegedly inadequate ordinary clergy. To the puritans, a minister who could not preach well was no minister at all, and Collinson describes a lively transfer market which has something in common with the world of modern premiership football. The town of Yarmouth, in the mid-Elizabethan period, had its talent scouts and its shrewd awareness of the power of money. In 1578, a salary of £30 was promised to a particular preacher, 'if he will come hither'. A few years later, one of the town bailiffs journeyed fully fifty miles to negotiate for the release of Bartimaeus Andrews from his duties in a country parish.[47]

Puritan activism took several forms. It led the grassroots version of the parliamentary campaign for further ecclesiastical and liturgical reform. This campaign, in its various European versions, is now being termed the 'second Reformation'. In England, the alliance of zealous magistrates, ministers and local lay groups was its backbone. Puritans regarded the church as 'but halfly forward and more than halfly backward'. They objected, in particular, to the clerical surplice, the sign of the cross in baptism, the marriage ring, and the unreformed structure of the church courts. Lay puritans naturally supported those members of the clergy who made stands against such 'abuses', and sometimes made stands of their own against those who did not. Ingram mentions the example of a Wiltshire weaver who, at Easter in 1603, criticised the Prayer Book and Homilies, arguing 'that there would be no edification for the people in them, and that the unpreaching minister could not rightly, and had not the power to administer the sacraments'. Not all of the godly were so militant, however, and Richardson gives us the example of a Lancashire woman who modified her attitude to kneeling for the communion in order to avoid being denied the sacrament.[48]

The puritans' campaigning zeal also had a moral or social dimension, and schools like Oakham and Uppingham are a surviving reminder of the pronounced educational impulse within early-modern godliness. In the twentieth century, 'puritanism' has achieved common usage as a label applied to those who seem to oppose all forms of pleasure. It is possible to exaggerate this feature of puritanism in the sixteenth-century context, but the zealots of Banbury, Northampton and numerous other towns were justly renowned for their desire to create a society that was pure from head to foot. Such groups turned their critical attention to an array of local habits, from football to fornication and from archery to adultery. They were not, of course, the only people to regard the reform of such abuses as a matter of urgency, but puritans set about the task with a measure of fire and fury that marked them as distinctive. Perhaps we have an example of a more moderate member of the godly in the Kent schoolmaster who owned a Bible (at a time when very few did so), but who had been known to allow dancing in his house on the Sabbath. Collinson uses the case for a different and equally plausible purpose, to imply that the Sunday recreations demonstrate the insincerity of this man's godliness.[49]

The inward dimension of the puritan urge to confront the wicked ways of the world was a deep desire for spiritual fellowship. This expressed itself in several ways, including intermarriage. Within a locality, the godly regularly met for edification and a sense of togetherness. These meetings ranged widely in size. In the 1580s, for example, one parishioner from Aythrop Roding (Essex) invited just ten of his more godly 'kindred and neighbours' to join him one Sunday evening, where they communed in a programme of doctrinal discussion, readings from Foxe's *Book of Martyrs*, and food. Other gatherings, like the clerical–lay 'exercises' and 'prophesyings' of the 1570s, were on a bigger scale and required more careful preparation. And at Southam (Warwickshire), a godly event in 1596 attracted 'many hundreds' from the surrounding area for a day of fasting, sermons and, to conclude, a shared meal. Collinson has recently pinpointed these occasions as the centrepiece of puritan culture. By the early seventeenth century, it was common for those attending such gatherings to receive communion, and Arnold Hunt has warned us not to underestimate the importance of the sacraments to England's puritans. This advanced Protestant piety also had a household dimension, and the larger homes of yeomen and gentry, with their servants and labourers, could amount to godly commonwealths in miniature.[50]

Group discipline was a fundamental principle within all these forms of fellowship, and it found one of its most advanced expressions in the 'covenant'. This was an agreement made between a minister and his most favoured parishioners, binding them all to a life of zealous piety. Collinson mentions the example of the Essex minister who, in 1588, formed a covenant with a mere twenty of his parishioners. These people were reported to 'as farre exceed the common sort of them that professe the Gospell as the common professors do exceed them in religion which know not the Gospell'. In this 'interesting three-tiered analysis', we can see the dangers for historians of assuming that 'godliness' and 'puritanism' were co-terminous. In truth, the zealots were an elite within the wider body of 'professors of the Gospel'.[51]

It is hardly surprising, given such attitudes, that the puritans were one of the least popular of Elizabethan cultural groups. Their habit of practising some measure at least of social separatism can hardly have endeared them. Their activism could create communities that were 'scandalously divided'. A satirical and stereotypical 'stage puritan' evolved, and London theatre-goers came to know the godly activists as licentious, holier-than-thou, hypocrites. Ordinary people in rural villages sometimes poured scorn on the puritans in their midst. One man from Margaretting (Essex) penned a libellous verse which was not exactly elegant, but which made its point: 'Gowers the Puritane sayth that the signe of the Crosse ys the marke of the beast / But his understandinge ys grosse; and he's a knave at the least.' The puritans did not consider themselves widely loved, and one fictional convert commented sadly, 'how deadly the wicked hate the righteous'.[52]

The godly in general were not, of course, disliked with the same bitterness. It is a possibility rarely countenanced that the sober fellowship of moderate Protestants may actually have impressed many contemporaries, yet there are occasional suggestions that this was the case. One seventeenth-century author, no friend of the puritans, argued that the increasing emphasis placed by committed Protestants on personal morality and Sabbatarian observance from the 1590s onwards actually had the effect of winning widespread popular sympathy: 'the piety of the persons being a fair way to perswade the world of the truth of their opinions'.[53] The author's point reveals a perspective on the religious sensibilities of ordinary Elizabethans which has little in common with that adopted by many social historians of religion. Could it be that a substantial proportion of the population found advanced Protestant piety impressive, even if they felt unable to display it themselves?

Perhaps it was the dignified example of Protestantism's more moderate souls that made possible the emergence, in the seventeenth century, of a genuinely Protestant strand within popular culture, based around the Bible, sermons, and personal discipline. Certainly, the godly had by this date made considerable, if never complete, inroads into the traditionalist culture of the early Elizabethan majority. The dreams of an earlier generation had hardly been realised in full, and the activism of the 1570s and 1580s had given way to a somewhat quieter, more personal and domestic set of aspirations. Yet the impact of the godly upon their society is not to be underestimated, even if they themselves felt more defeated than victorious.

The godly, like the guilds before them, related to state and church in ways that were sometimes complicated. The term 'puritan' was popularly associated with disobedience and subversion. Archbishop Whitgift was also intensely suspicious of puritan activities, particularly the experiments with Presbyterian-style ecclesiology that marked the 1580s, and he campaigned vigorously for declarations of loyal conformity from the parochial clergy. The complexity is in the established fact that the majority of puritans opposed the notion of ecclesiastical separation, and that they did so with a zeal that was characteristic, if in this case a little surprising. Collinson, in his recent work, has emphasised the factors which bound the puritans to the established church, rather than those which suggest that separatism was their logical destination. Most puritans believed, for example, that the Church of England exhibited the fundamental signs of a true church. Their obsession with sermons, and their never-ending interest in the reform of society as a whole, also had the effect of anchoring them to the establishment. And, despite the hostility of Whitgift, many puritans lived under the jurisdiction of more tolerant bishops, and were allowed a degree of latitude in practice. For these reasons, their professions of basic loyalty can be regarded as sincere.[54] As we shall see, however, the sectarian option was certainly not eschewed completely.

It may at first seem unlikely that the fellowship of the later sixteenth-century godly had much in common with that of pre-Reformation guild members and pilgrims. Certainly, the general atmosphere was infinitely more complicated, tense and stressful under Elizabeth I than it had been in the early years of Henry VIII's reign. Guilds, it is true, were much more widespread than godly conventicles, and they were obviously less interested in campaigning for religious change in society at large. Theologically, the two forms of fellowship were worlds apart. Nevertheless, there are several significant areas for comparison, and it can be argued that Protestant godliness absorbed and re-expressed many of the spiritual impulses that had made the guilds such a lively feature of late-medieval religion. We can see similarities in the quest for fellowship through special gatherings, the emphasis upon moral conduct and its enforcement, the urge to recruit (and to some extent control) additional clergymen, interest in education, and the essential voluntarism. These were all amongst the defining characteristics of both types of association. As Gervase Rosser puts it, 'the two forms of association ... shared common ground in the psychological and social needs, unanswered by the parish, to which they responded'.[55]

It is also intriguing that guilds and Protestant godliness tended to flourish in the same areas (especially eastern England), though the connection is difficult to establish in concrete terms. It is much too simplistic to regard the guilds as a straightforward seedbed for voluntary Protestantism, since their *raison d'être* was so fundamentally conservative. But perhaps we can suggest that the vibrant energy of one eventually flowed into and boosted that of the other. In more general terms, Tanner has argued that the Protestant godliness found in Elizabethan Norwich was, to some extent at least, the natural culmination of the city's developing lay piety in the late-medieval period.[56]

Of course, the fellowship of the godly conventicle was not the only setting within which the displaced energy of the late-medieval guilds could express itself in the post-Reformation era. Some of it, arguably, was channelled into the church courts, which provided parishioners with the opportunity to regulate one another's moral conduct. The guilds had fulfilled this role in their time, and it seems possible that their demise was one factor in the increasing business of the Elizabethan ecclesiastical courts. Parish officers were also increasingly busy, and Alldridge has argued that new opportunities for public service in Chester compensated in full for the end of the guilds.[57]

We might also speculate about the role of the post-Reformation household as a focus for corporate instincts that had previously revealed themselves amongst guild-members and pilgrims. The godly household was not, of course, a creation of the Reformation, and there is a school of thought which argues that Protestantism made little difference to family life. Duffy, Haigh and others have demonstrated that late-medieval Christians were well aware of the importance of the household within religious life. One Warwickshire manuscript of the early fifteenth century contains instructions written by a cleric to a wealthy layman concerning his pious habits. He is advised to implement a life-dominating schedule of godly thoughts, sayings, readings, prayers and gestures. He is, for example, to remind himself constantly of his own worthlessness by saying 'Woe is me. Welawey.' He must avoid all 'dances, buckler-play, dicing, wrestling, and the like'. And at dinner, he is expected to make a secret sign of the cross on the table, using five breadcrumbs. The ideal of the godly household was clearly well-established in the late-medieval period.[58]

It seems likely, however, that the social, economic and religious changes of the sixteenth century did make a difference, and generated amongst religious authors an interest in the household that was simultaneously more intense and more wide-ranging. The resultant literature has been trawled repeatedly by historians of domestic relations. Interest in the godly family was already growing stronger in the early sixteenth century, when Whitford's famous *Werke for Householders* appeared, but it accelerated dramatically in and after the Elizabethan decades. 'If ever we would have the church of God to continue among us,' Richard Greenham told his readers, 'we must bring it into our households and nourish it in our families.' Those who would listen were reminded constantly of their duty to promote reformed godliness through the family, called by one catechist 'the lowest place of the church'. They were asked to enforce an endless round of prayer, catechism, Bible-reading, exhortation and psalm-singing.

The godly household of the early seventeenth century had much in common with its pre-Reformation ancestor, but there are strong suggestions that the place of the family within religious culture more generally had been heightened. The upsurge in writing about the relationship between husbands and wives was one sign of this. Patricia Crawford sees the powerful emphasis upon the role of the wife within the Protestant household as partial compensation for the demise of inspiring female role models like the Virgin Mary and the saints. Anthony Fletcher concludes a recent review of the contemporary literature by saying that post-Reformation writings were distinctive in 'their force and coherence rather than their total originality'.[59]

Much of the evidence, as usual, relates to the wealthiest and most godly of households, and it is virtually impossible to assess the levels of religious fellowship that prevailed amongst the majority. Duffy regards humble householders with a commitment to domestic godliness in the late-medieval period as fairly representative. By the mid-seventeenth century, Tessa Watt argues, a thriving market for cheap religious print existed amongst 'honest householders' on all social levels. The distinctly partial presence of cleanly Protestant theology in many of these publications certainly indicates that the purchasers were not puritans. Whether or not these historians are right, it seems possible that a post-Reformation intensification of emphasis upon religious fellowship within the household may have some connection with the demise of traditional corporate institutions like the guilds.

In some towns, it appears that participation in civic government was yet another outlet for older religious impulses. In late-medieval Wisbech (Isle of Ely), the local guilds were bustling and popular. In 1549, shortly after their dissolution, the town became a corporation, by royal charter, and took over much of the guilds' property. The records of Wisbech's civic government under Elizabeth overflow with the language of fellowship, and the settling of disputes between individual inhabitants was an important feature of its work. In numerous cases, arbitrators were appointed, and subsequent orders issued 'that the forsayd parties shalbe lovers and fryndes hereafter And where as either of them have offended the other Any kynde of wyes by wordes that they shall forgyff frelye the same from the bottome of their hartes'. Such reconciliatory interventions are clearly reminiscent of those made by the late-medieval guilds. In this case, it sounds rather as if the guilds had merged in order to form the corporation, and in 1567 the good men of Wisbech were still praying for the soul of Edward VI! The guilds were no more, but purgatory lived on.[60]

The episode tells us a number of things. It suggests that theological confusion was widespread: even the more educated of Wisbech residents were unaware that praying for the soul of a dead Protestant monarch during the reign of a live one, and making an official record of the gesture, was not a good idea. But the corporate records also provide evidence of the resourceful way in which English people found outlets for impulses which had been denied their traditional forms of expression. This was a creative response to official, unsought Reformation, and it helps to explain the gradual, quiet transfer of religious allegiance that took place in most communities during Elizabeth's reign. By the end of the century, Wisbech was a mainly Protestant town (though it also had its share of Catholics, Familists and separatists). In conclusion, it seems that a strong popular instinct for some form of religious fellowship 'alongside the church' survived the Reformation intact, and found expression in a variety of contexts. During the sixteenth century, this instinct thrived (with certain reservations), then suffered acute dislocation, then finally settled into new patterns. It 're-formed' within a reformed religious culture. That culture was more tense, more complicated and more fragmented, but its roots drew some of their sustenance from the rich soils of the medieval past.

Testaments of Faith

Historians, understandably desperate for direct and statistically presentable evidence on popular religion, have often turned to wills. These exist in large numbers for the sixteenth century (especially towards its close), and the vast majority open with a preamble in which the testator bequeaths his or her soul to God. W. K. Jordan, with extreme and unwarranted optimism, called wills 'completely honest documents' and 'mirrors of men's souls'.[61] Without going this far, we should at least note that the recording of these religious preambles in their thousands does provide further evidence of a broad familiarity with the basic Christian doctrines amongst a substantial proportion of the population. More ambitiously, the 'dedicatory clauses' of early-modern wills have been counted, classified and contested by scholars in the hope of establishing how enthusiastically the people of England received the new theological emphases of the Reformation. Early exponents of this technique believed that Catholic and Protestant wills could be distinguished with reasonable confidence, and they established a system of classification which has been applied in various guises by subsequent scholars. Testators who left their souls not only to God but also to the Virgin Mary and the saints (often 'the holy company of heaven') were counted as Catholics, especially if they also requested memorial Masses and prayers. Those who omitted Mary, the saints and the Masses, preferring instead to state a reliance for salvation on their faith in Jesus Christ, were registered as Protestants. In between these two types, historians identified various 'neutral' categories, in which were placed wills of seemingly indeterminate spiritual affiliation. Some analysts made further distinctions, but these three main types dominated most interpretations.

The broad trends uncovered by this exercise are reasonably clear but, as we shall see, not necessarily as helpful as they seem. They must be presented here in fairly general, non-statistical terms, for the simple reason that no two scholars have used precisely the same categories. It would therefore be misleading to calculate synthetic averages. Wills of the traditional type were all but universal in the first two decades of the century. They remained comfortably in the majority in virtually all areas until the reign of Edward VI. From about 1540, however, traditional wills were in an unspectacular but definite decline. At the same time, the proportion of neutral wills rose noticeably, and that of Protestant wills increased slightly. Under Edward VI, traditional wills declined more rapidly, losing their overall majority between 1550 and 1553. Once again, however, it was neutral wills rather than clearly Protestant ones that made up most of the difference. In most areas, neutral wills became the largest of the three main groups, and often exceeded 50% in the last years of the reign. During Mary's reign, traditional wills rose again, but rarely did they achieve proportional levels to match those of the pre-1530 period. They topped the table in most regions, but did not always rise above 50%. Neutral wills remained a very substantial grouping, while the proportion of Protestant wills shrank dramatically, usually to well under 10%. When Elizabeth came to the throne, the proportion of traditional wills collapsed, their leading position being taken by the neutrals. Only in the last two decades of the century (and the first few of the next) did decisively Protestant wills become significantly more widespread. Throughout the period, scholars have also noted the existence of 'mixed' preambles, which seem to combine elements of Protestant and Catholic forms.[62]

Within these trends, major regional differences have been noted. In general, testators from south-eastern counties moved somewhat more swiftly towards neutral and Protestant preambles than did will-makers from elsewhere. In the dioceses of Durham and York, for example, the percentage of traditional wills dropped from 93 in 1520–33 to 80 in 1534–46; but in Suffolk, it fell from 88 to 55 in the same period. In some towns, such as Sandwich (Kent), traditional wills had already dropped as low as 20% by 1540–1. In the very different city of York, however, they stood at 96% at this date. One-fifth of the wills written in Marian London were Protestant, but only one-twentieth of those written in Devon and Corn-wall. Parallel discrepancies can be identified in all decades of the century, except perhaps the first two.[63]

The fact that contemporaries themselves sometimes looked to will pre-ambles for evidence of the beliefs held by specific individuals is often held to encourage confidence in the basic methodology. Certainly, the results look clear and useful at first sight, but historians have become steadily more aware of difficulties and dangers. Most testators were sick, and called upon others to write their wills for them. It therefore seems possible that the beliefs expressed in the preambles were not those of the will-makers themselves, but those of their scribes. The influence of the local clergy has been identified as another powerful but inestimable factor. Some testators even made use of printed formularies, from which model preambles could be copied. Others, known from supplementary evidence to have been deeply religious, made brief and seemingly disinterested preambles. We begin to wonder whether the average testator (or scribe) actually put any thought at all into the composition of the dedicatory clause. Historians, furthermore, have often reminded each other that only a disproportion-ately old and wealthy minority of the population made wills, though this minority was expanding sharply during the century.

More recently, Eamon Duffy has expressed misgivings of a far more acute and forceful nature. He takes issue with proponents of the largely consensual argument that a move away from traditional forms indicates a

decline in traditional religion. Duffy points out, quite rightly, that those
who dropped the saints (like so many hot potatoes) when ordered to do so
were revealing a basic level of common sense, rather than a receptiveness
to new theologies. We cannot, therefore, deduce a widespread acceptance
of Protestantism from the Edwardian and Elizabethan collapses in traditional will preambles. Duffy's second main complaint is still more fundamental. He argues that many of the signs of Protestantism discovered by
previous commentators in wills of the period were, in truth, nothing of the
sort. He reminds fellow researchers – and they do need reminding – that
Catholics believed in Jesus Christ too, so that testators who emphasised
His role in their salvation were not necessarily Protestants. To illustrate
this important point, Duffy provides examples of testators who combined
Christo-centric preambles with traditional requests for Masses or for the
prayers of the saints. Where earlier scholars had seen popular theological
confusion in such examples, Duffy finds orthodox Catholic commitment.
Similarly, he argues (and proves) that references to predestination or
election in will preambles were not necessarily signals of Protestantism.[64]

These are important points, and historians must now revise their categories in the light of them. The damage may not, however, be quite as
devastating as Duffy intends. Certainly, wills indicating a basic awareness
of the role of Christ in salvation should never be classified as Protestant. It
should be noted, however, that such wills were extremely rare in late-
medieval England, a fact that is concealed by Duffy's decision not to
present his evidence statistically. Peter Heath found that only 8 out of
315 testators from Hull mentioned Christ in their preambles, and that
only one of these did so in a manner that could be described as Christo-
centric.[65] And Duffy's analysis is more questionable in its insistence that
testators expressing trust 'only' in Christ, or in Christ 'alone', were as likely
to be Catholic as Protestant. Admittedly, one or two of his examples
support this assertion, but the majority do not. The preambles he quotes
are, in the main, Christo-centric without actually being solifidian. In other
words, they leave out the word 'only' and refer to the (subordinate) part
played by Mary and the saints in helping humans to reach heaven.

It can easily be demonstrated that, in the context of the mid-sixteenth
century, the word 'only' carried huge force, and was widely considered to
express reformist attitudes when used in association with faith in Christ. In
1543, for example, pressure from conservatives led to an alteration in a
draft of 'the King's Book', an official publication on matters of faith. One
statement was revised in order to make clear that faith justified 'neither
only nor alone'. This insertion – a clear attempt to distance officialdom

from Protestantism – seems to indicate that the leading theologians of the day would not have accepted the proposition that solifidianism was a Catholic doctrine too. In 1554, the conservative Marian Bishop Edmund Bonner issued visitation articles which specifically asked for information on parishioners who had spoken favourably of justification by faith alone. It seems unlikely that he intended to congratulate them with a friendly pat on the back. Bonner's like-minded colleague Bishop Gardiner poured scorn on Protestants for believing that salvation 'needs no works at all, but only belief, only, only, nothing else'. Finally, we have already acquainted ourselves with the traditionalist clergyman who, during Elizabeth's reign, deliberately omitted the expression 'Christ Jesu our alone saviour and redeemer' from the preamble to his will.[66]

If traditionalists of this calibre considered 'only' to be a Protestant buzzword, then we should do the same. The implication for historians is that the vast majority of explicitly solifidian preambles can still be counted as Protestant, though merely Christo-centric ones cannot. There will, very occasionally, be exceptions, but if we are looking for a clear and statistical probability, then we have found one. Mid-century testators (or their scribes) were far more likely to have absorbed the idea of salvation by faith in Christ 'alone' from Protestant teachings than from anywhere else. In mid-century Gloucester, wills using words like 'only' frequently contained other, unequivocal signs of Protestant commitment; but the occasions upon which they included obviously traditionalist references were rare.[67] Of course, none of this solves our other interpretative difficulties, for we can still not be certain that a Protestant dedicatory clause reveals the existence of a dedicated Protestant testator.

It would clearly be wrong to ignore completely the minute percentage of individual testators who *did* combine unmistakable solifidianism with unquestionably traditionalist expressions or bequests. If we do not accept Duffy's argument that such testators were orthodox and uncontradictory Catholics, then what alternative interpretation is available? Three possibilities can be suggested. First, it seems likely that a proportion of these mixed preambles reflect a measure of popular confusion about the options that were acceptable at any particular time. One Somerset testator, writing five years into the very Protestant reign of Edward VI, requested a dirge for his soul 'if it shall stand with the king's proceedings'. He clearly had very little understanding of the key theological debates of the day. Many others, throughout the middle decades of the century, qualified their religious bequests with similar clauses. Secondly, there may have been a tendency amongst ordinary testators and scribes to blend the elements of rival theologies into a mixture that seemed satisfying, or at least service-able. In the middle of Edward's reign, a Wakefield testator left his soul to God and the saints, but asked specifically for burial according to the (Protestant) 'common book of service'. Arguably, such people were reveal-ing a reluctance to accept the 'either/or' choices with which theologians on both sides presented them, opting instead for a 'pick 'n' mix' approach. A striking example of this occurred in the will of a yeoman from Eye (Suffolk), written in 1557. He used a controversial and thoroughly solifi-dian preamble, which is known to have been circulating amongst com-mitted Protestants at the time, but he added a clause asking his executors to dispose of any unbequeathed goods for 'the welth of my sowle whereas is most nede', His solifidianism had not eclipsed his belief in purgatory, though strictly speaking it should have done. Thirdly, those recording mixed preambles may deliberately have been hedging their bets at a time when the tone of royal religion sometimes seemed to change with the weather.[68]

Counting clauses will probably remain a popular pastime amongst historians, and it is not without its value. Despite numerous problems, the percentage game does tell us something about popular religion in the period of the Reformation. Above all, the people of sixteenth-century England emerge as pragmatists, who were ready in most circumstances to toe the official line for the sake of a quiet life. The exceptions prove the rule. Nevertheless, we can deduce that the theological instincts of the majority were basically conservative, particularly away from the south-eastern counties. Testators did not swing from reliance on Christ, Mary and the saints to reliance on Christ alone with a huge collective sigh of relief. Instead, they adopted neutral expressions in their wills, or emphas-ised Christ without adding the crucial word 'only'.

This tendency was exemplified superbly in the case of Geffrey Toms of Stoke Lacy (Herefordshire): in 1559, with religious uncertainty at a peak, he made two wills, identical in all respects except that one opened with a fully traditional dedicatory clause, while the other opted for a Christo-centric (but not solifidian) form. His executors were presumably intended to present for probate the document that seemed least likely to cause a stir.[69] This testator, surely, was a Catholic who wished to make a theo-logically honest, but uncontroversial, will. Yet the common readiness to make the necessary adjustments may, just possibly, indicate a certain superficiality of commitment to the old faith, particularly in the late Henrician period, when the saints were losing testamentary ground long before they had been banned. Clearly, they were already under official suspicion, but that is not necessarily a justification for the abandonment of old and trusted friends.

Overall, will preambles confirm that the English Reformation succeeded not because it had majority support at its inception, but because most people responded with a blend of compliance, caution, flexibility and creativity, thus allowing a religion that was more Protestant than Catholic to evolve across at least two generations. Ingram has called this a process of 'Protestant drift'.[70]

Popular pragmatism deserves to be treated quite positively. It reflects more than a secular instinct for protection of one's property, though the existence of this motive can hardly be denied. Most people did not wish to risk the smooth passage of their worldly estates by inserting officially unacceptable clauses into the religious preambles of their wills. They therefore swam with the tide. It can also be argued, however, that the flexible response of many people to the pressures of the period reveals a deeper awareness of the religious duty to work for communal harmony. This alternative, and more important, spiritual dimension of will-making can be summarised under the heading 'charity'. It provides us with another of those profound but underestimated continuities which, for mid-century people, linked the past and the future. Of course, the officially-acceptable beliefs surrounding death changed more dramatically than almost any other branch of theology. The denial of purgatory was an extraordinarily significant act. It is interesting, therefore, that so many traditional preoccupations and actions in the face of death survived intact, even if their theological foundations had been altered.

The duties fulfilled through will-making are a clear example. Testators rarely tell us precisely why they made their wills, but we can pick up occasional hints. One testator in seventeenth-century Cambridgeshire made his will 'because there should be no controversy after my death for my goods and for the maintenance of love and peace in the world'. This too was surely the goal of Margaret Atkinson who, in her will of 1544, asked that a posthumous feast of bread, ale, bacon, mutton and rabbits be provided for her neighbours, 'desiring all the parish, as well rich as poor, to take part thereof, and a table to be set in the middle of the church with everything necessary thereto'. In 1572, an innholder from Saffron Walden also gave his reasons: he wished to set an example to others, so that they 'may learne to be redy...When god shall call them'; he also hoped to ensure that, on his deathbed, he would not be troubled by worldly things, 'the wch at that tyme might perhappes withdrawe my mynde & godlye zeale to depart well and Chrystyanlye'; finally, he aimed 'to establish a direct order in the distribucion of such worldly goodes and riches as God hath lent me for the better quietnesse of my posteritie & succession'. The testator's dedicatory clause was abrupt and colourless by comparison: 'I bequeath my soul to Almighty God.'[71]

Other examples suggest that will-making was a time for people to restore ill-gotten goods and to make amends for any wrongs done to neighbours, thereby ensuring that death could be faced in a state of charity. It was a time for the affirmation of communal bonds under the eyes of God, before and after the Reformation. In a changing religious world, it gradually became less acceptable to stage a feast on church premises, but the desire to promote peace did not evaporate. Of course, these were all ideals, and many a dying parishioner failed to achieve them. In 1626, George Wilson of Wisbech wrote a will 'whereof I doe dispose of that little wch god hath lent me'. He did not sound happy, and, very unusually, did not commend his soul to God. Despite such examples, the ideals continued to occupy a place in most English minds. The model testator sought communal and personal peace, discharged his or her duties as a steward of God's goods, and prepared to die 'Chrystyanlye'. In 1561, one ailing Londoner – a Catholic who had also shown an interest in Protestantism – gathered his friends around him, and said 'masters, I cannot tell of what religion you be that be here, nor I care not, for I speak to tell you the truth, and to accuse mine adversary the Devil'. Despite all the tensions of the times, there were important points of contact between Protestants and Catholics.[72]

'Charity' is more familiar today in its specific association with acts of giving to the unfortunate. This was a vital aspect of will-making in the early-modern period, and the official theological grounds for charity were partially transformed during the sixteenth century. Most importantly, late-medieval people believed that 'good works' could improve their prospects of salvation and help to shorten their time in purgatory. They were taught that works alone were insufficient, but that they *could* help, if executed in the right spirit. In contrast, the Protestant orthodoxy was that an individual's good works had no direct influence over his or her spiritual future. They were not efficacious. Instead, they were the fruits of a faithful spirit – an important sign of a saved soul, but no more than that. Yet even at the refined level of theological discussion, the contrast is not always quite so profound. Charitable acts, for Protestants and Catholics alike, also glorified God, set an example to others, and helped to bind the community. Furthermore, Ian Green and Susan Brigden have both noted that Protestant writers, in their wish to promote charity, sometimes implied

that good works could, after all, be efficacious. Henry Brinklow, for
example, argued that the 'reward of everlasting life' would come 'to
them which, to their power, have provided to do for the widow and
fatherless'.[73] At the grassroots level, it seems even more likely that the
differences became blurred.

Economic historians have long debated the nature of early-modern
trends in charitable giving, and the sparks have flown freely in clashes
over the distorting effects of inflation, population increase and shifts in
social structure. Of course, not all (or even most) charity was the result of
wills, but testamentary bequests provide us with the fullest and most
quantifiable evidence we have. One pattern at least is clear enough.
Post-Reformation charity was more heavily concentrated on so-called
'secular' causes (poverty, education, roads and so forth) than late-medieval
charity had been. According to the calculations of W. K. Jordan, for
example, only 13% of charitable giving was devoted to the poor in the
six decades before 1540; under Elizabeth I, this had risen to 39%.
'Religious' giving (principally to the church and the clergy) entered a
corresponding decline as a proportion of all charitable provision recorded
in wills. Between 1480 and 1540, more than half of the charitable cake
went to religious causes; in the last four decades of the century, the figure
had fallen to a mere 7%. This stark decline in the religious portion of
charity was, however, reversed in the first few decades of the seventeenth
century, when the figure rose to almost 18%.[74]

The problem of establishing whether levels of charitable giving
increased or decreased as a whole is much more difficult, and different
methods of calculation yield different results. Jordan's triumphant writing
on the 'staggering' increase in generosity during the century after the
Reformation was possible only because he chose not to adjust his figures
in order to account for the period's high levels of inflation. Subsequently,
other scholars have attempted the necessary compensations, but no consensus has emerged.[75] Our 'best guess' may well be that 'secular' charity
did increase in real, and even *per capita* terms, between 1540 and 1650, but
that it did so quite modestly. If, however, the 'religious' portion of charity
were to be included in the calculations, it seems extremely unlikely that
pre-Reformation levels of giving would be matched in real, let alone *per
capita*, terms by those of the seventeenth century.

It is not easy to assess the significance of these trends. Society was
experiencing various changes that were not generated by religion, and
testamentary gifts therefore came to be made within a very different wider
context. By 1600, levels of poverty were higher than they had been in

1500, and the bureaucratisation of local government meant that parishioners were increasingly likely to be making regular and formal contributions to poor relief in the form of compulsory rates. The big religious changes also altered the charitable context significantly. The dissolution of the monasteries and the guilds, for example, removed institutions which had played a significant role in the provision of charity. On the other hand, the pressure this change placed on private pockets must have been lessened somewhat by the simplification of church services and equipment. Put crudely, Protestant churches were cheaper to run.

Despite such changes, certain conclusions can be drawn. For a variety of reasons, philanthropists great and small came to place the church lower down their list of priorities in the course of the sixteenth century. The dislocations attendant upon the changes of 1530–70 must have had some part to play in this, but they shared the stage with other factors. For one thing, Protestantism in its first, reactive phase fiercely condemned older patterns of giving, and urged testators to concentrate upon causes such as poverty. To a degree, therefore, a decline in religious giving was motivated by obedience. The growth of reliance on compulsory rates must also have reduced the likelihood of voluntary contributions to the local church. Furthermore, there were socio-economic reasons for the shifting pattern of generosity. The intensification of poverty during the sixteenth century would, of itself, have attracted philanthropic attention. In this respect, it is interesting that Protestant priorities worked along the grain of contemporary attitudes. Presumably, this was another of the factors which helped people slowly to accept the religious changes of the period. Having said this, Scarisbrick may well be right to assert that the old system could, in time, have adjusted to the new economic pressures, had it been given the chance.[76] The process of transition must also have been eased by the fact that, except in the case of the church, the officially recommended targets of philanthropic endeavour had not changed significantly. The religious world was not what it had been, but Christians were still urged to divert funds towards the poor, the sick, prisoners, roads and bridges.

It would be an error to regard the changing charitable priorities as clear evidence of that interminable process known as 'secularisation', though they may unknowingly have opened a door to the modern habit of distinguishing between religious and non-religious matters. Jordan's use of the word 'secular' in reference to causes such as poverty is in some ways misleading, because it seems to imply that only gifts to the church were spiritually motivated. In fact, his understanding of the situation was far less crude than the short-hand implies. The limits of the process were, in any case, revealed when testators turned their benevolent eyes back to the church in the decades from 1600. This important and sharp reversal may well represent a diminution in the sense of dislocation that must have characterised the early Elizabethan decades. An older instinct was reasserting itself in a more modest form, and church leaders clearly felt increasingly confident about urging generosity to the local ecclesiastical fabric. The situation was, however, far more fragile than it had been in the late-medieval period, and a sizeable portion of the renewed religious giving aimed not to beautify church buildings, but to fill them with puritan lecturers who hated the very idea. The balance was to be severely disrupted in the 1630s, when these rival objectives came into sharper conflict. The tensions thrown up by the Reformation were no thing of the past.

Piety in Print

In 1586, William Rushbrigg of Emneth (Norfolk) made a charity-packed will with a thoroughly 'neutral' dedicatory clause. Interestingly, this godly testator also bequeathed to his cousin 'one pair of spectacles, one service book, and another booke callyd the Sick mans salve'. This work, by Thomas Becon, was one of the period's most celebrated guides to Christian responsibilities in the face of death, and Rushbrigg's testament seems to demonstrate its practical impact on at least one yeoman. He had bought it, read it, absorbed its teachings, and now he was passing it on.[77] Unfortunately, we are very rarely able to pinpoint such encounters, and the extent to which laypeople in the period spent their spare time reading pious literature is a matter of educated guesswork.

The first problem is to establish what proportion of the population had the ability to read. None of the available records allows us to tackle the question in a direct and statistical manner. Attention has therefore focused on the ability of contemporaries to sign their names, which can be measured rather more precisely. This technique, employed by David Cressy, reveals a pattern of low and only gradually improving literacy in the sixteenth century. Cressy estimates that in 1500, 10% of men and 1% of women were able to write. By 1550, the figures had risen to 18% and 3% respectively. At the end of the century, writing skills were possessed by roughly 27% of men and 9% of women. He also discovers that the ability to write was closely related to social and occupational status in the early-modern period as a whole. Three main clusters are identified: clergy/

gentlemen, who were usually 30% ahead of tradesmen/craftsmen/ yeo-men, who themselves led husbandmen/labourers/women by approx-imately 40%.[78]

At first, these figures may seem to suggest that the reading of godly literature was a pastime available only to a narrow elite. This would, however, be a crude and insensitive deduction. An important article by Margaret Spufford has demonstrated the probability that a far higher proportion of the population could read than could sign their names. In schools of the period, reading was taught first, and pupils progressed to writing only at the age of seven or eight. This was also the time at which many grew strong enough to make some useful contribution to the family economy. As a result, a large number of children from humbler back-grounds may have left school with some basic degree of reading ability, but no writing skills. Counting their signatures in order to produce statist-ics on 'literacy' may, therefore, be a seriously misleading exercise. In early Jacobean Ely, the 'divers honest poore men & woemen that teache poore children' could certainly read, but one wonders whether they could write.[79]

Other factors also brighten the pessimistic picture somewhat. Elementary education was certainly much more widespread than was once thought, as the above quotation suggests. Moreover, people who live within predom-inantly oral/aural cultures will tend to treat texts as matter for reading aloud to others. They will also tend to have powerful memories. To Elizabethans, the modern habit of silent, solo absorption in a book would have looked like just one of the interactive options, and a rather anti-social one at that. It is extremely likely, therefore, that literature reached the illiterate with a fluidity that seems alien today. Of course, those who could read were best placed to enjoy and absorb the contents of books; but those who could not had their opportunities too. One catechism, printed in 1587, was designed for the 'ruder sort of people' who, if unable to read, could memorise it after hearing it read by others. Even further back in time, a copy of a late-medieval prayer to St Walstan, a Norfolk favourite, was aimed at those who 'be unlearnd nor can not read nor spell'. It was clearly envisaged that such people would gain access to it through recitation and commitment to memory. Not all of the evidence encourages optimism, however. In 1538, for example, all parishes were ordered to acquire a Bible, but the rector of Hastingleigh (Kent) did not really see the point, 'for we have but one that can read it and but sixteen householders'.[80]

There is no doubt that levels of literacy were rising steadily in the sixteenth century, and the quantity of reading matter provided by

London's printing presses was expanding to meet (and manipulate) the demand. By 1600, their output was much more substantial than it had been in 1500, though the most impressive surges still lay ahead. Throughout the period, a high proportion of printed matter was explicitly religious in content, even if that proportion contracted somewhat as publishers identified and exploited a market for more 'secular' forms of print. In the fifteenth century, most printed matter was specifically religious. By 1640, Tessa Watt calculates that the proportion had dropped to 42 per cent.[81] This was still a very substantial figure, and it should always be remembered that the distinction between religious and secular literature was far from clear. Spiritual and moral messages were widely strewn through works which have not been classified as religious.

In the first decades of the Reformation, Protestants and Catholics displayed different attitudes to vernacular literature. Not surprisingly, the contrasts emerged most passionately in disagreements over the wisdom of opening the Bible to the people. For Protestants, the publishing of Scripture was as fundamental a feature of their enterprise as justification by faith alone. William Tyndale became the foremost Biblical scholar of his age 'because I had perceived by experience how that it was impossible to establish the lay people in any truth except the Scripture were plainly laid before their eyes in their mother tongue, that they might see the process, order and meaning of the text'. In 1549, Philip Nichols of Totnes, a lesser known reformer, spoke of the great book's power to expose the falsehoods of priests: 'the public knowledge of the Bible and holy scriptures hath confounded trumpery, and hath opened to the eyes of the world all their deceitful doctrine'. Mid-century Protestants told dramatic tales of their experiences of personal conversion following exposure to the Bible. They scorned what they saw as the reactionary ignorance of the opposition, joking about traditionalist priests who suspected that only heresy could lurk in any book called the 'New' Testament. In the early decades, Protestants were willing to make use of all other available forms of literature in order to get the message across. From the early 1580s onwards, however, the puritans amongst them grew bitterly suspicious of printed texts which were anything but deeply and exclusively pious. The 'merry jests' of cheap print kept people from the Scriptures: they were 'devised by the divel' and 'Printed in hel'. The puritans had come to realise that texts could exert a negative power too.[82]

Catholic commentators were much less anxious about non-religious literature, but more suspicious, from the start, of direct contact between laypeople and the Scriptures. Particularly in the early decades of the

Reformation, they saw the Bible as something that was best published only through the filter of priestly interpretation. Protestants were ridiculed as 'twopenny book men', and attempts were made to restrict popular access to Scripture. An act of 1543 banned women, apprentices, artisans, servants, husbandmen and labourers from reading the Bible, thus restricting access to the wealthiest tenth of the population. One Henrician vicar told his flock he hoped the king would remove 'that disease from you which is the Testament'. Suspicions could run the other way too, as when an enterprising west country yeoman decided to steal his parson's reformist tracts in 1554.[83] For committed Catholics, the desire to restrict lay access to the Bible was motivated primarily by a fear that its contents could be misunderstood and misused, to the peril of thousands of souls. As time passed, however, this attitude relaxed somewhat, and Mary's government seems to have been a little less anxious than Henry's about the dangers of Bible-reading.

Of course, pious texts – the Scriptures included – had for a long time occupied an important place in traditionalist spirituality, but their positive power for the laity consisted more in their role as 'channels of blessing' than as sources of religious information. Gospel extracts could protect people against all manner of injuries. Many late-medieval texts and pictures also carried with them papal indulgences, which promised purgatorial remission to those who meditated on them: 'To them that before thys ymage of pyte devoutly say fyve Pater noster fyve Aveys & a Crede pytously beholdyng these armes of Christ's passyon ar graunted 32,755 yeres of pardon.'[84] Books could thus be sacred and powerful objects in themselves, though their benefits were only promised (officially) to those who meditated in a suitably pious and devoted spirit.

Throughout the century, leading Christians of both breeds saw the need to make available to the laity a range of printed aids to devotion. In the late-medieval period, the pious layperson could choose from a varied menu: primers (collections of prayers, psalms, and extracts from the liturgy); books of miraculous legends, usually concerning the saints; and works providing material on the Mass, moral living, godly death, pilgrimage, the calendar and various other matters. A high and increasing proportion of this literature was in English, though even Duffy concedes that the lack of vernacular Bibles was a notable omission. By the end of the century, the menu had shifted in several ways: Bibles were no longer in short supply, but works on the saints and pilgrimage were; metrical psalms, Books of Common Prayer, sermons and anti-Catholic polemic were all important categories; chapbooks and single-sheet ballads on religious subjects were produced in larger numbers; and the printing of reformed catechisms was already a big business. As Margaret Spufford has argued, many of the most basic educational publications, such as hornbooks and ABCs, aimed to teach reading through the medium of essential Christian doctrine.[85] In this sense, they too were religious literature. Alongside these options, Elizabethans seeking piety in print could still acquire primers and a variety of handbooks on 'practical divinity', death, and so on.

Such publications also covered a considerable price range, starting with ballads at a penny or less. Tessa Watt has argued convincingly that by the early seventeenth century, many of the cheapest forms of religious literature would have been within the economic grasp of a substantial proportion of the population, at least when times were reasonably good. Logically, this must have been considerably less true a hundred years earlier, before publishers began to make the most of ballads, chapbooks, hornbooks, cheap primers, catechisms and ABCs. Duffy, however, clearly believes that printed materials were already circulating widely on all social levels.[86]

We simply cannot know what proportion of the population experienced meaningful contact with religious print in its various forms. The optimism of Duffy and Watt is not to everyone's taste, though their work makes it increasingly difficult to argue that popular religion and print had little to do with one another. Several of the signs, particularly from the Elizabethan period onwards, seem to indicate that they were actually quite well acquainted. The annals of early Protestantism, for example, introduce us to numerous lowly individuals – weavers, glovers and labourers – who located the moment of their conversion in encounters with piety in print. In 1546, one humble man added to the flyleaf of a book he had just bought a sad little note regretting the government's decision to ban ordinary folk from reading the Bible. He even identified himself for us: 'Writ by Robert Williams, keeping sheep upon Saintbury Hill'.[87]

Print runs and the frequency of new editions provide another useful indicator, and it is clear that by the early seventeenth century, cheap Bibles, catechisms and religious ballads were all selling well. In 1585, such texts already occupied most of the shelf-space in the store-room of a Shrewsbury printer: his 2500 volumes included Prayer Books, catechisms, psalters, Bibles, sermons, devotional works, alongside historical romances and cookery books. In 1627, a Gloucestershire shoemaker, who also happened to keep exceedingly helpful records, made a list of his books: it included two Bibles, a Testament, three psalters and two catechisms, as well as more secular material. It has also been observed that the language of the Bible 'seeped into, and eventually saturated, religious mentality' during the early-modern period as a whole. Shakespeare was not, as far as we can tell, a man of unusual piety, yet his plays 'resound with echoes of the Bible'. Watt, it seems, may well be right to argue that 'a core of "honest householders"... at all social levels' provided publishers with a broad, non-elite, non-puritan market for cheap religious literature.[88]

The content of the cheaper forms of sixteenth-century print – ballads, chapbooks, hornbooks, primers and catechisms – can therefore tell us a great deal about the nature of popular religion. Some recent writing on early-modern European culture has been extremely pessimistic concerning the capacity of the sources to answer the questions that historians wish to ask.[89] The root of the problem is that we cannot disentangle 'supply' and 'demand' factors. We cannot tell how much material was 'popular' in the sense that the people actively wanted it, and how much was 'popular' in the sense that it was created 'for' the people by writers, publishers and censors who were not 'of ' the people. The sensible option is to acknowledge the problem, to understand that popular literature is a fascinating blend of both these possibilities, and to get on with the job in hand. Fortunately, this is precisely what other scholars have done, and their work makes possible the following broad comments.

Not surprisingly, the more accessible forms of print bore the imprint of the Reformation in a variety of ways. Across the century, the polemical content increased, the use of Latin all-but disappeared, and a higher emphasis came to be placed on faith in Christ. The saints and the Virgin Mary, so prominent in late-medieval literature, faded from view. From the 1580s, the most unequivocally Protestant of writers and publishers were also reducing their use of visual imagery, having become increasingly suspicious of pictures as an aid to devotion. Others were searching for pictorial alternatives to the traditional representations of Christ, Mary and the saints. It is also clear that providence, an interpretative system which explained the delights and disasters of life with reference to God's direct intervention in human affairs, enjoyed considerable appeal in the marketplace by the close of the century. The murder pamphlets analysed by Peter Lake were 'drenched in the language of divine providence and justice'. In the words of one author, the world was 'a theatre of God's judgements'.[90] Anti-Catholicism was also highly marketable by the early seventeenth century. These shifts all suggest that elements of the Protestant message were penetrating even the lower reaches of society, and proving reasonably 'popular'.

The evidence does not, however, suggest anything that could be described as a clean break. The process of change was in fact considerably more flexible, gradual and partial than might be imagined, and there is little to suggest that a zealous Protestant establishment took control of the printing presses and imposed its ideas upon a powerless populace. Commercial publishers and religious educators in both confessional camps all had to proceed with caution and subtlety if their differing ambitions – pecuniary and didactic, respectively – were to be realised. There are many signs of this flexible and somewhat untidy reality. The authors of early Protestant primers, for example, regularly mixed traditionalist and reformist elements. Marian authors, in turn, drew on features of the Protestant programme, particularly its emphasis on Christ's passion and on the Bible. Catholic primers might even include prayers written by leading Protestants. Best-selling late-medieval texts such as *The Kalendar of Shepherds* – a fascinating mixture of religious, astrological, calendrical and medical material – continued to be printed throughout the century. Some of the most popular Elizabethan works of 'practical divinity' were actually Protestant versions of Catholic texts. A different type of best-seller, Thomas Tusser's *Five Hundred Points of Good Husbandry*, included a section on religion which, in Byford's words, was 'full of doctrine and moral advice in areas almost wholly outside Reformation controversy'. And at least one printer did not see, or mind, the contradiction of working successively for Catholic and Protestant regimes.[91]

It seems likely that many Protestant writers accepted the practical necessity of retaining certain links with the past if they were to communicate effectively with a broadly traditionalist population. Commercial publishers, for their part, also sensed that naked Protestantism would not make them rich. In practice, therefore, printed Protestantism in its cheapest forms was rarely unadulterated. This theme has been explored most comprehensively in Tessa Watt's *Cheap Print and Popular Piety, 1550–1640*. She does find some evidence of thorough-going Protestantism, but the main thrust of her argument is that the religion of the majority was a 'patchwork of beliefs', old and new. Watt attempts to identify the most commercially successful of religious ballads, and she finds in them 'a fragmentary reception of Protestant doctrine'. Protestantism appears in references to justification by faith and the urgent need for repentance, in admiration for the Marian martyrs, and in the replacement of the saints by characters from the Old Testament. The commercial success of metrical psalms reinforces the impression that Protestantism could be popular. Alongside such features, however, Watt finds plentiful evidence of older priorities. In the most successful ballads and chapbooks, 'handy rules for social behaviour' were prominent. It might be added that the obvious interest in 'neybourhed, love and trew dealyng' often incorporated an apparent connection between virtuous acts and heavenly rewards. Even in ballads about Christ, Watt argues, a popular taste for the miraculous rather than the theological clearly lingers. And even in celebrations of the Marian martyrs, there are hints of a kind of reformed saint-worship. A substantial quantity of highly traditional imagery survives in the accompanying woodcuts, and indeed in the texts themselves. A pervasive fear of death and personal judgement remains prominent, and in ballads on such themes, 'old and new beliefs rubbed elbows without apparent sense of contradiction'.

Watt's presentation of the Reformation as it affected a majority of the population is distinctive, important and convincing. She alerts us to the existence of a substantial body of Protestant opinion that lacked the near-hysterical, iconophobic fervour of puritanism. She warns us against the ready acceptance of confrontational models for the process by which most English people came to identify themselves as Protestants. Conflict, though present and significant, was merely one side of a coin. Watt draws attention to 'areas of consensus and gradual integration', 'areas of culture where these conflicts were either resolved or unarticulated'. She reads her ballads and chapbooks as 'the products of a dialogue between Protestant norms and traditional practices'. Through this dialogue, traditional piety underwent 'a gradual modification' and emerged as 'distinctively 'post-Reformation', but not thoroughly Protestant'. Popular culture absorbed the new without necessarily abandoning the old, and without necessarily resolving the resultant contradictions. Watt's work is of immense value in helping us to understand how and why the English population gradually accepted a Reformation for which the overwhelming majority of them had not asked. In a sense, they came to think of themselves as being thoroughly Protestant precisely because they were often allowed, in reality, not to be.[92]

Of course, this 'flexible Reformation' was not quite the happy, negotiated settlement it might have been. Its partiality and gradualism contributed to the alienation of a powerful puritan minority, whose existence was simultaneously a strength and a weakness of the 'reformed' Church of England. In many of their writings, not surprisingly, we find a somewhat jaundiced corroboration of the portrayal of popular piety outlined above. The fictional, 'ordinary bloke' of printed puritan dialogues was warm in his Christian commitment, but content with the basics of conformist devotion, and reluctant to relinquish his common-sense feeling that those who did well in their lifetimes would also do well afterwards. Almost certainly, these writers substantially exaggerated the ignorance of the majority, and they did not acknowledge that the more zealous piety of a minority of humble citizens had its roots, partially at least, in the low-key warmth of the majority. Yet, with these qualifications in mind, their characterisation may not have been hopelessly wide of the mark.[93]

'Magical' Religion

In 1971, Keith Thomas published one of the masterpieces of recent historiography under the title *Religion and the Decline of Magic*. This work opened the eyes and minds of historians to the fact that early-modern people did not, by any means, draw all of their beliefs directly from the church's deep well. Even officially approved ideas and objects were often put to uses which orthodox theologians would not have liked. Thomas spoke of 'the debris of many different systems of thought', and argued that religion and magic, though closely entangled, were 'essentially different' or 'rival' systems of explanation in contemporary perception. The principal distinction of religion was that it provided a comprehensive interpretation of existence, where 'magic' (with the exception of astrology) aimed only to deal with specific, localised problems. This work has been criticised both for over- and under-estimating the power of 'magic', but everyone agrees that it greatly expanded the horizons of early-modern religious historians.[94]

Thomas's 'alternative' modes of explanation, further investigated by others, formed an enormous variety of beliefs and practices. We are introduced to the woman who, in 1543, dropped a holy candle upon the excrement of her enemy Elizabeth Celsay, in the belief that this ritual would split her buttocks open. Cursing took several forms, and could easily lead on to accusations of witchcraft against the individual involved (usually a woman). Archaeological investigations have uncovered a number of sixteenth-century 'witch bottles' containing human hair, fingernails or urine. These were apparently used by the victims of witchcraft in a counter-magical attempt to neutralise the danger. Techniques for charming and healing were also numerous. Scriptural phrases, such as 'not a bone of him shall be broken', could be used to cure toothache. One practitioner in Elizabethan Cambridgeshire protected a neighbour's pigs against disease by feeding them pieces of apple with 'certain letters' written upon them. Others burnt the urine-soaked hair of their clients; or asked them to place the bill of a white duck in their mouths while charms were recited; or anointed their gums with the brains of a hare. People went to astrologers, 'cunning men', 'wise women', 'charmers', 'blessers' and 'conjurors' for assistance with the full spectrum of human problems: illness, lost property, courtship, childbirth, and even lack of musical ability. The man who wore a charm provided by Anne Bodenham was told that 'he need not fear what money he owed, for no bailiff could take hold or meddle with him'. Other channels of supernatural aid or information were available through ghosts, ancient prophecies, dreams, and fairies.[95]

During the sixteenth century, it seems that such beliefs were widely distributed both in geographical and in social terms. Exotic healing and cursing rituals were not the exclusive preserve of primitive peasants in Europe's most remote regions. Instead, they also had a place in the worldview of monarchs and magistrates. The touch of a king or queen was believed to heal scrofula, a condition of the lymph glands. In 1586, an official list of the queen's worst enemies included several individuals whose troubling powers were clearly supernatural: Bertles 'the great devil', the 'old witch of Ramsbury', 'Maude Twagood enchantresse', and Christopher Watt 'sorcerer', for example. In the same year, an immensely learned friend of Archbishop Whitgift gave him, by will, 'my best ring of gold called Annulus Driandri with certen hoopes in it to knowe whenn the sonn is in any signe'. Cunning men, women and astrologers were all reported to be widespread, and commonly consulted by rich and poor alike. In 1549, one suspected sorcerer reckoned 'there be within England above five hundred conjurers as he thinketh'. This was probably a substantial underestimate. In 1561, it was said by Francis Coxe that the common people were reluctant to undertake any journey without first consulting an astrologer or an almanac. Six decades later, Robert Burton believed there were 'cunning men, wizards, and white witches, as they call them, in every village'. Not all historians, however, are willing to accept the accuracy of such evidence. Martin Ingram has sounded a more sceptical note, arguing on the basis of Wiltshire's church court records that 'in late Elizabethan and early Stuart times witchcraft and magical practices were not of major concern either to the ecclesiastical authorities or to the majority of the people'.[96]

Official attitudes to 'magic' did not remain constant during the period of the Reformation. In late-medieval England, its status is best described as ambivalent. On numerous occasions, churchmen of the period expressed their doubts about the nature of popular healing, charming and cursing, which often seemed to stray beyond the bounds of theological orthodoxy. A late fifteenth-century manual for priests insisted that those who made, used or promoted strange invocations without approval 'synnen ryght grevously'. St William himself registered his disapproval of magical pursuits when he appeared before a 'cunning woman' and forbad her to approach his shrine in Norwich. The fact that she had journeyed from Cambridgeshire on pilgrimage did not deflect his anger.[97]

On the other hand, the validity of these practices in the eyes of the populace was closely related to the church's performance of strikingly similar, and often closely related, rituals. Many church ceremonies involving holy water, salt, candles, crosses and repetitive invocations were considered by perfectly orthodox theologians to have immense protective power. For Duffy, the popular appropriation of some of these techniques was 'not paganism, but lay Christianity'. An awareness of this sharing of concepts bred a more flexible treatment of popular 'magic' by the church's spokesmen. Even the priest's manual, quoted above, went on to say that if 'symple people' used unorthodox charms, they should 'by ignoraunce...be excused'. It is not surprising, therefore, that members of the priesthood sometimes stepped over the line between the sacred and the sorcerous. In 1551, for example, a traditionalist Gloucester priest performed a ritual involving a key and a holy book in order to help in the identification of a criminal.[98] It seems that most of the clergy accepted and understood the supernatural culture of their parishioners, and operated within it. This may well be the explanation for the infrequency of late-medieval court cases concerning sorcery, witchcraft and so on. These were features of a basically consensual system of understanding, and harmful attempts to draw on supernatural power could be dealt with without recourse to the higher (earthly) authorities.

The Protestant reformers attacked this consensus, and attempted to impose a far clearer and more rigorous distinction between acceptable 'religion' and unacceptable 'magic'. Many of the rituals of the old church were placed in the latter category, and purged from the Prayer Book. In 1559, the Elizabethan injunctions banned the use of 'charms, sorcery, enchantments, invocations, circles, witchcrafts, soothsaying or any such like crafts or imaginations invented by the devil'.[99] This ruling was all part and parcel of the broader campaign to destroy the credibility of traditional religion by exposing its alleged superstition, obsession with the material artefacts of devotion, false claims to dispense divine power, ignorance of Scripture, cosy tolerance of pagan accretions, and general failure of principle. Within this scheme of things, the essential popularity of traditional religion was neither here nor there. People, whether they liked it or not, simply had to learn about the unacceptability of beliefs or behaviour which implied either that God's power could be easily coerced, or, worse still, that there were other sources of power. Protestants did not deny the possibility that God would, at times, allow divine power to express itself in evil, negative ways. They did not therefore dispute the existence of witch-craft and possession by spirits. They did, however, seek to undermine comprehensively the possibility that humans could, by performing certain actions, channel God's power to their defence. Many such actions were made illegal by statute in 1542, 1563 and 1604. Instead, the vagaries of fortune were to be understood in terms of divine providence, a scheme by which God intervened directly in human affairs – punishing the wicked, warning the morally dubious, and rewarding the good. People were taught that they could, through prayer, ask God for assistance, but there could be no guarantees that He would respond favourably.

It would be mistaken, however, to suppose that all of the grey areas had been whitewashed or papered over. The Elizabethan Church of England retained hints of the old 'magic' in incantatory prayers for protection, Rogationtide perambulations, and the very notion of sacred space. In puritan eyes, this list could be extended to include, amongst other things, the baptismal sign of the cross, the churching of women, and the wedding ring. The most vehement of Protestants might condemn all such 'abuses', but others held attitudes that were somewhat more moderate and flexible. With regard to witchcraft, for example, the godly doctrine that a pact between the practitioner and the devil lay at the heart of all cases was never fully enshrined in the parliamentary statutes enacted to facilitate prosecution. The Elizabethan authorities were equivocal in their attitude to astrology, condemning it on paper but not hounding its devotees in practice. We have already seen that Archbishop Whitgift possessed an astrological ring, and it could be added that the signs of the Zodiac are all noted in the 'Kalendar' of the 1559 Prayer Book. The ability of humans to manipulate God's power through cursing was also denied, but exceptions were made for those who found themselves in a state of extreme despera-tion. The church retained a few cursing rituals of its own. Even after decades of reform, therefore, we still find isolated cases in which clergy-men dabbled in suspicious activities. One Elizabethan vicar in Cambridgeshire was repeatedly accused of sorcery by his parishioners, and others were reported in the puritan surveys of the parish clergy. It seems likely that, well after the Reformation, many ordinary clergymen continued to regard the 'magical' tastes of their parishioners with a certain accommodating ambivalence.

Despite this, there is little doubt that the status of 'magic' shifted somewhat as a consequence of the Reformation. The changes, not surprisingly, made their mark on common practice in a number of different ways. It has been famously argued that the denial of counter-rituals led to a marked rise in the number of prosecutions for witchcraft. Thomas suggested that the Reformation, by reducing the power of people to respond to supernatural danger, left them feeling more vulnerable than they had ever felt before. The Elizabethan establishment continued to allow the possibility of witches, and provided new legal mechanisms by which victims could take action against their psychic persecutors. These mechanisms were widely preferred to the approved godly responses of prayer, repentance and fasting. The result was a surge in cases of witchcraft. According to Alan Macfarlane's estimates, 2000 people were tried for witchcraft in the period 1560–1706. The overwhelming majority were women, and roughly 300 were executed.[100] Thomas's analysis of trials on the Home Circuit (Essex, Hertfordshire, Kent, Surrey and Sussex) reveals a heavy concentration in the reign of Elizabeth I, especially during the 1580s and 1590s. A sharp decline began in the 1620s, interrupted only by a unique upsurge during the 1650s.

The Reformation attack on counter-magic was not, of course, the only cause of this increasing litigation. Historians have explored various features of the phenomenon. Feminist scholarship has sometimes portrayed the rising tide of cases as a complex attack by male-dominated authority on dependent or *in*dependent women. Jim Sharpe has argued, rather differently, that witchcraft accusations were made, as often as not, by women against other women. They therefore form one of the contexts within which female power was asserted and negotiated. Thomas and others have also explained the surge in prosecutions in terms of social tensions thrown up by the transition from personal to institutional charity. One standard pattern within witchcraft cases saw women being turned away by their neighbours when they came to beg milk, eggs or bread. The anger of the woman and the guilt of the neighbour might then interact to produce accusations of witchcraft. Malcolm Gaskill, however, has recently urged us to remember that this was just one of a range of possibilities, and not quite as typical a scenario as Thomas implied. By no means all of those accused of witchcraft were single, marginal and female.[101]

Another interpretative option would be to treat witchcraft accusations within the context of state formation, though this possibility has not yet been developed for the English evidence. Through the parliamentary statutes of 1563 and 1604, the state came to police the supernatural. By doing so, it invited the population to fight their battles through its machinery, and thus to validate its right to rule. Others again have been less impressed by the evidence. It has been remarked that this was not really a 'witch craze' in the continental sense at all. Indeed, a high proportion of the known cases were in Essex, and Ingram has argued that an awareness of witchcraft was probably 'only marginal to most peoples' lives'. Nevertheless, sources such as the casebooks occasionally kept by doctors make it difficult to deny that large numbers of Elizabethans on all social levels experienced intense anxiety at some point in their lives. In the will of one Essex gentleman, written in 1602–3, a sum of money was bequeathed to the local poor on condition 'that none [who] be suspected or detected in the devilish art of sorcery or witchcraft have any part'.[102]

The increasing popularity of the doctrine of divine providence represents a more positive effect of the reformers' attitude to medieval magic. It was, in many ways, a highly suitable alternative because, as Alexandra Walsham has observed, it catered for a popular obsession with the spectacular and supernatural. The authors of cheap print regularly interpreted strange occurrences as divine warnings against sin, irreligion and Catholicism. Events receiving this treatment included 'sliding of grounds, removing of highways, mighty floods by great abundance of rain, fearful lightnings and thunders, great fire from heaven, sudden earthquakes, strange and deformed children born, great dearth of corn, mighty plagues and pestilence'. Gaskill shows that deponents in murder cases regularly worked within the same frame of reference. They drew attention to peculiar happenings as providential indications of the suspect's guilt. Horses threw escaping murderers, and corpses bled at a killer's touch. In the sixteenth and seventeenth centuries, such unsettling events were often regarded as powerful condemnatory evidence. The language of providentialism runs through contemporary diaries and even wills. It is arguable that providence, which the Reformation boosted but did not create, became in the seventeenth century a powerful magnet for the population's instinctive interests in the supernatural. If so, then it was a major Protestant success.[103]

It is more difficult to establish whether the Protestant assault on magic led to a decrease in the readiness with which people resorted to wise women and conjurors. The dominant work would seem to suggest that it did not. Thomas has argued that cunning men and wise women remained popular, and were only prosecuted when their activities caused harm or involved clear fraud. When the church abandoned its protective rituals, they even 'appeared increasingly attractive'. Reginald Scot, a celebrated Elizabethan sceptic, agreed, and suggested that wise women had taken over the place formerly occupied by the saints in peoples' hearts. There is plentiful anecdotal evidence to indicate the survival into the seventeenth century of pre-Reformation protective gestures and invocations. Thomas has also argued that the common people retained their taste for charms and curses right through into the nineteenth century, long after intellectual changes amongst the most highly educated social groups had led to a rise in scepticism, and consequently, 'the decline of magic'. 'Even in modern times,' he tells us, 'gratings from the statues of saints on Exeter Cathedral have been employed in rural Devonshire to keep away disease from cattle and pigs.'[104]

Nevertheless, there are signs that majority attitudes may already have been changing in the early-modern period. It would certainly be possible to read the pattern of church court prosecutions in this manner. They rose under Elizabeth, perhaps reflecting a growing acceptance of the illegitimacy of magical consultations, then fell away under James, perhaps suggesting that a new, more Protestant equilibrium had been achieved. One Elizabethan case reveals an amusing reversal of the expected clerical–lay relationship. A vicar in Kent lost his voice when trying to perform his liturgical duties, and immediately suspected supernatural foul play; but his no-nonsense parishioners, less ready to cry 'sorcery', reckoned that he was suffering from 'the French pox'. In the seventeenth century, conjuring and sorcery came to be associated particularly with remote areas of Catholic survival, and even a fairly humble Lancashire apprentice could write of surviving charms as if they belonged to a different world. The content of cheap print, interestingly, does not suggest a great deal of interest in fairies, witches and protective rituals, though astrology was selling incredibly well. Intriguing glimmers of popular scepticism concerning the supernatural are revealed in pamphlet accounts of witchcraft cases, though this subject has not been systematically investigated.[105]

Overall, it seems most plausible to argue that the majority of people very gradually became less ready to seek supernatural aid, even if they did not necessarily reject the possibility of such aid absolutely and on principle. This process began with the Reformation, and was not complete two centuries later (perhaps it will never be complete). By the later seventeenth century, however, those for whom 'magical' explanations and remedies represented a significant feature of daily life and thought may have formed only a small minority of the population. Astrology, a more 'respectable' system, seems to have been an exception. In London at this date, the official bills of mortality regularly attributed sudden deaths to 'planet'. As early as 1606, however, one practitioner complained that most people viewed astrology merely as an entertaining recreation.[106] Whether or not he was right, it can be suggested that the combination of astrology and providence was, by the age of Charles II, sufficient to satisfy the needs of most people for a supernatural element in their lives 'alongside the church'. The countryside still had its white witches and fortune-tellers, but they may have been in the slow process of losing the cultural centrality they had once enjoyed.

Beliefs of a 'magical' variety did, then, have an important place within early-modern popular religion. We may be more dubious about Thomas's argument that magic and religion should be understood as alternative or 'rival' systems of explanation. It seems possible that this emphasis was included primarily because it seemed to add weight to another somewhat doubtful proposition, namely that a substantial proportion of the population lived and died without knowledge of, or interest in, the basics of the Christian faith. Earlier in the work, Thomas had warned, with more justification, that the two systems should not, in fact, be seen as 'opposed' to one another. It is perhaps difficult to imagine a situation in which 'rivals' are not to some extent 'opposed'.[107]

Numerous examples, several of them drawn from Thomas's own work, indicate clearly that, in the eyes of many people, the distinction between religion and magic had little meaning, whatever the theologians might have said. Late-medieval laypeople sometimes copied out approved prayers and strange charms without perceiving any contradiction. Healers regularly made use of liturgical prayers in their work. An Elizabethan mother was given a roasted cat, surely a 'magical' gift of some sort, to celebrate her participation in the official 'churching' ceremony. Booksellers stocked godly and astrological texts, probably on the same shelves, and individual customers purchased both. The authors of almanacs included liturgical information, and insisted that God lay behind the astral movements which they interpreted. The Elizabethan preacher George Gifford claimed to know of two churchwardens who had consulted the local cunning man concerning the location of a mislaid communion cup. He also alleged that ordinary people saw, or thought they saw, the hand of God in the talents of cunning women. And one wise woman from Barnsley went as far as to tell her clients that she had been 'allowed to charm by the Bishop of Gloucester', a rather unlikely claim.[108] In the light of such examples, Thomas's alternative 'magical' culture looks instead like one part of a syncretic blend that was dominated by more orthodox Christianity.

For people throughout the sixteenth century, 'magic' was just one of a wide variety of ways in which official religion was complemented or appropriated. There emerges, overall, a picture of a population whose response to an unrequested Reformation was resourceful, flexible and pragmatic, rather than dogmatic or defiant. The Reformation, amongst the bulk of English people, was a messy affair, a result of complex, unspoken negotiations as much as of fierce confrontations. There were plenty of tensions, of course, but there is also compelling evidence of a common readiness to shift very gradually towards new norms and assumptions. Old instincts were redirected along fresh avenues, and found ways to express themselves once more. This process was greatly aided by the various continuities – direct and indirect – that we have noted. The syncretic blend that constituted popular piety had many ingredients which, when mixed in different proportions according to taste, enabled English people of all sorts, and on both sides of the Reformation divide, to fortify, supplement or modify the religious brew offered to them by the church.

4

LAYFOLK BEYOND THE CHURCH

The spiritual expectations of most sixteenth-century English people seem to have been met quite effectively by the religious opportunities that were available within and alongside the church. No theoretically comprehensive institution, however, can please all of the people all of the time, and a period of significant change presents a particularly challenging atmosphere within which to operate. The Reformation century, not surprisingly, had its share of individuals and groups who preferred to seek spiritual fulfilment beyond the church. They were always a small minority, but their importance in the religious history of the period is indisputable.

In any age, a society's dissenters, nonconformists and deviants deserve attention for a number of reasons. Their numerical extent can serve as a very rough guide to general levels of satisfaction with the *status quo*. Their attitudes and activities also help to establish the parameters of the normal, providing the majority with something 'other' against which to define themselves. In many instances, however, dissenters are not completely 'other': instead, their extraordinary zeal has some at least of its roots in the more modest commitment of the majority, against which it eventually turns. Deviants are often insiders who have chosen to step outside, and they sometimes frighten or fascinate us precisely because we know we could have been like them. Paradoxically, we may find ourselves envying their devotion or determination. In a sense, dissent is a kind of mirror, showing society to itself from a vantage point that does not flatter. It therefore forces the allies of orthodoxy into a continual round of self-consciousness, self-examination and self-justification. It is for this reason that nonconformists always exert a disproportionate influence on society. Minorities make news.

They also make, or cause others to make, a remarkable quantity of documentation. This, in itself, attracts historians, who need to be constantly aware of the often extreme bias that finds expression in the sources. Nonconformists either write their own stories, or watch unwillingly as those stories are written by their fiercest critics. Their recorded history is therefore generated at the extremes of perception. Patrick Collinson has spoken warily of the 'engaged history' of the denominational tradition. In the mid-seventeenth century, Richard Overton had his critical eyes upon tale-tellers from the opposite camp: 'Who writ the history of the Anabaptists but their enemies?'[1]

The sixteenth-century English church, in its various guises, faced a chorus of criticism from dissenting groups of all shapes and sizes. The late-medieval Lollards objected to many of the beliefs and practices that would later provoke the hostility of the early Protestants. During the middle decades of the century, small numbers of Anabaptists, Freewillers and Arians found fault successively with the Henrician, Edwardian and Marian churches. Under Mary, the most conspicuous dissenters were, of course, the men and women who refused to relinquish the Protestant convictions that they had held legitimately in the previous reign. The Elizabethan church provoked principled objection from both sides, and had to meet the threat posed by Catholics of various shades and by Protestant separatists like the Brownists and Barrowists. There were also some more obscure and exotic forms of dissent, such as that developed by the mystical Family of Love, whose members believed that a Dutch merchant called 'HN' was the new messiah. The followers of one home-grown visionary declared him King of Europe in the unlikely setting of Oundle, Northamptonshire. To this catalogue we should also add the isolated individuals who, throughout the century, pop up in the records with strange and unexpected opinions in their heads. In 1584, for example, one Hereford man exclaimed, 'What passe I for my soule? Let me have money ynough – I care not whether God or the dyvel have my soule.' Other mavericks doubted the truth of Scripture, denied the Trinity, saw heaven and hell as states of mind, and declared a readiness to trade all the world's religions for a jug of beer.[2]

In sixteenth-century England, religious objectors attempted to solve their casuistical problems in a number of ways. Some, like the Catholic recusants under Elizabeth, were nonconformists in a clear and physical sense. They refused bodily attendance at the services of the established church, and they faced the consequences. Others, like the 'church papists' of the same reign, adopted a more pragmatic stance. They elected to avoid worldly punishment by operating a policy of minimalist obedience. Physically, they came to church, but while there they attempted to keep their spiritual and emotional distance. One priest advised that no man should attend an official church service, 'except he at his coming in his heart exempt himself from this service and all that is partaker of it'.[3] In effect, these were two different definitions of nonconformity, the one outward and the other inward. The friction between them caused heated discussions within many of the century's dissenting minorities.

The Distribution of Dissent

It simply is not possible to establish with any certainty what proportion of the population placed itself 'beyond the church', whether physically or spiritually, at any one time. We are heavily reliant upon contemporary persecutors, the activities of whom were sporadic and selective to a degree which we cannot determine. Nor can we know the ratio of separatists to pragmatic conformists within dissent as a whole. Historians therefore interpret similar material in different ways, and it is no surprise that their emphases often reflect their denominational affinities. Dickens and Scarisbrick both use the adjectives 'widespread' and 'tenacious', but the objects of their celebratory interest are Marian Protestantism and Elizabethan Catholicism respectively. Each sees the other form of dissent as unpopular and limited.[4] Reliable figures are therefore hard to come by, but a couple of observations are indisputable: committed nonconformists were more numerous and varied in 1600 than they had been a century earlier; but despite this change, dissenters were still very heavily outnumbered by their conformist contemporaries.

A chronological survey of the century suggests the following patterns. In national terms, late-medieval Lollards were statistically insignificant, though in particular localities they could amount to a forceful presence. Henrician Protestants were also very thin on the ground, though their numbers were increasing steadily. Some five hundred suspects were, for example, arrested following the conservative Six Articles of 1539. Thomas More warned that 'in every ale house, in every tavern, in every barge, ... as few as they may be a man shall find some'. Mid-century Anabaptists, Freewillers and other radicals were far fewer, and concentrated in a handful of locations. In 1549, the Protestant Latimer was alarmed by reports of a town inhabited by 500 Anabaptists, and Joan

Bocher of Kent, who was burnt for heresy in 1550, claimed that 1000 others belonged to her sect. Both individuals were probably exaggerating, though their reasons for doing so were very different.[5]

Committed Protestant dissenters were a famous and conspicuous group during the reign of Mary, and their numbers were significantly higher than they had been a decade earlier. We know the names of a couple of thousand devoted Protestants, but it is impossible to tell whether they represent a substantial portion of the iceberg or merely its tip. The same can be said of the Catholic recusants in the reigns of Elizabeth and James. A government survey of 1603 identified 8590 recusants, but an indeterminate number of 'church papists' was not included in the sums. Bossy attempts to make the necessary allowances, and produces an estimate of 30,000–40,000 for the total Catholic community. Adherents of the old faith therefore comprised approximately 1 per cent of the national population.[6] During the same period, Protestant separatism must have been running at a much lower level, and the Family of Love seems to have attracted considerably fewer than a thousand members. If something like ninety-eight of every hundred individuals chose not to reject the religion by law established, then the official church was performing surprisingly well. Of course, nonconformist ideas may have had a considerable impact beyond the ranks of the fully committed. In late Henrician Yorkshire, one man neglected to make his annual confession, 'saying the cause moving him to the same was that there was a saying in the country that a man might lift up his heart and confess himself to God Almighty'.[7] We cannot necessarily measure the influence of 'a saying in the country' by counting martyrs and militants.

The geographical profile of dissent is somewhat easier to reconstruct, though generalisations become harder to substantiate when they are extended into the seventeenth century. Very broadly, it can be said that earlier Protestant nonconformity and the various forms of radicalism from Lollardy to Familism were concentrated in the south and east of the country. Lollard cells were at their most numerous in Essex, part of the Kentish Weald, Middlesex, and the Chilterns in Buckinghamshire. There were also Lollards in Oxfordshire, Bristol, Coventry, Northampton and Leicester. A high proportion of the Henrician and Marian Protestants were found in Kent, Essex, Middlesex, the Thames valley and East Anglia. Colchester, for example, was regarded by reformers in the 1550s as 'like unto a city upon a hill'. This was not a purely topographical observation, for it was also like 'a candle upon a candlestick', spreading light in the darkness.[8] The areas most commonly associated with Anabaptism were

London, Kent and Essex. Freewill established a footing in the same counties. Protestant separatism under Elizabeth was much more likely to be encountered in Norfolk, Suffolk, Essex and Kent than further west or north. The explanation for this general pattern can probably be found in a combination of factors: proximity to continental influences; a better supply of Protestant preachers; higher literacy levels; and more advanced economic networks, which provided ready-made channels for the dissemination of new ideas. We should also mention the more vigorous official investigations that seem to have occurred in the counties closer to London, and that may make the pattern look clearer than it actually was. Some of the same factors help to explain why, even within the southern and eastern counties, Protestant forms of dissent developed most readily in towns (a Europe-wide correlation), and in rural areas characterised by dispersed settlement and proto-industry. The link between the cloth trade and radical dissent has been noted many times.[9]

We must, however, avoid crude assumptions about socio-religious processes that depended intimately upon the energies and peculiarities of individual human beings. People's beliefs were not dictated to them by their environment, and A. G. Dickens proved the point by calling one of his works *Lollards and Protestants in the Diocese of York*. The northern towns of Beverley, Halifax and Hull were home to established Protestant minorities well before the reign of Elizabeth. Lollard opinions were occasionally reported in Herefordshire, a very conservative county. There were fears of Anabaptism in the dioceses of Gloucester and Worcester. The majority of people in 'dissenting areas' were not, moreover, dissenters. Even in Henrician Amersham (Buckinghamshire) and Elizabethan Balsham (Cambridgeshire), where Lollards and Familists seem to us to have dominated the respective scenes, nonconformity did not enjoy a numerical majority. Early Protestantism may have made most of its headway in the south and east, but counties such as Sussex and Hampshire were little affected.

Elizabethan Catholicism was a complicated case. In the 1560s, the deepest resources of traditionalist feeling were in the north and west, and it was to be many decades before the new faith seemed secure. In 1570, the conservative province of York seemed to Archbishop Grindal like 'another church, rather than a member of the reste'. Seven years later, well over half of the recusants identified by the government were in this geographical zone. As late as 1620, Catholic worship was still the norm in some parts of Lancashire. This county, however, proved to be distinctive in its resilience and defiance. Some have spoken of the general but gradual contraction of Catholicism in the north, using handsome late twentieth-century words such as 'leakage' and 'shrinkage'. Certainly, by the mid-seventeenth century there were surprisingly few recusants in the south-west, Wales, Cheshire and the far north-west. Haigh blames this upon the continentally-trained missionary priests, who allegedly failed to give such areas adequate attention in the decades after 1580. Although the number of separated recusants seems to have risen everywhere in this period, it is likely that many church papists were being gradually absorbed into the established church. Alternatively, a once healthy piety was degenerating into 'crude superstition', for want of contact with priests. Catholicism was steadily becoming a distinct sect, rather than a system of observances and beliefs with the capacity to win widespread allegiance. The missionary priests, according to Haigh, spent a disproportionate amount of their time in the soft south, nurturing pockets of Catholicism in generally less conservative counties. In Northamptonshire, Hampshire and Herefordshire, Catholics formed a significant minority. In counties such as Cambridgeshire and Wiltshire, however, their numbers were extremely small. By 1600, therefore, there were recusants everywhere, though perhaps not as many as might have been expected, given the Elizabethan church's inauspicious inheritance.[10]

The relationship between social status and religious dissent is not easy to unravel. Anxious contemporaries often portrayed groups such as the Lollards, early Protestants, Brownists and Family of Love as lowly and vulgar. In 1551, Jean Veron reported that 'many of these Libertines and Anabaptists are running in hoker moker, among the symple and ignoraunte people'. Three decades later, Bishop Freke of Norwich reported that the Suffolk Brownists were drawn from 'the vulgar sort of people', and that they met together in droves, 'not without danger of some evil event'. Some historians have picked up this emphasis with an enthusiasm born out of various preconceptions, while others have proposed the alternative argument that attachment to such groups was easier for people who were literate and economically independent. Affiliation, it is suggested, was therefore strongly biased towards the urban middle ranks. Both lines of argument can be, and sometimes have been, overstated. Recent empirical research has tended to show that early-modern dissent was distributed right through the social hierarchy, with only a marginal imbalance towards the middle orders. Anecdotal evidence reinforces the suggestion, made in the previous chapter, that illiterates were not necessarily barred from meaningful contact with print. In Henrician London, for example, a Protestant bricklayer named John Harrydance carried the New Testament wherever he went, and admitted that 'he all these thirty years hath endeavoured himself to learn the Scripture, but he cannot write or read as he saith'. It is true that the very rich and the very poor were less frequently associated with dissent than those in between, but this was partly because the former were best placed to evade punishment while the latter were not always considered to be worth punishing. Urban artisans and craftsmen do appear to have played a slightly disproportionate role in the history of Protestant dissent, as do the wealthier members of rural society, but people from many other backgrounds also took important parts.[11]

Three unusual cases deserve separate mention. The Anabaptists always included a high proportion of foreign exiles, which complicates the picture somewhat. The Elizabethan Family of Love, in surprising contrast, appears to have drawn most of its members from the native population, but they were clearly clustered at the prosperous end of their local hierarchies. This unusual pattern has been explained in terms of their introverted mystical faith and their reluctance to evangelise. Familism rarely seems to have moved out of the relatively comfortable circles in which it first began to move during the 1550s and 1560s. Elizabethan Catholicism also presents a distinctive social profile, or has seemed to. Scarisbrick and Walsham have recently challenged an older consensus which argued that, by 1600, Catholicism was predominantly 'seigneurial', or dominated by the gentry and aristocracy. They cite examples of lowly Catholics who organised the celebration of Mass in their homes, or went to prison, or carried incriminating messages. Many recusants, Scarisbrick reports, were 'yeomen, labourers and mechanicals'.[12]

Nevertheless, it probably remains true that a majority of the more humble late-Elizabethan Catholics were affiliated in some way to one of the major households of the conservative gentry. In Linton (Cambridgeshire), virtually every one of the known Catholics was attached to the family of Master Ferdinand Paris. Diarmaid MacCulloch may be going too far in portraying Catholicism as 'the property of an embattled gentry minority, sheltering as best they could a few humbler folk', but this image has not yet been vandalised beyond recognition. MacCulloch's verdict is strikingly similar to that of the Elizabethan John Gerard, who described the Catholics of East Anglia in the early 1590s as 'mostly from the better classes; none, or hardly any, from the ordinary people'. Perhaps the work currently being undertaken on 'plebeian' Catholicism will help to resolve the matter. For now, we may conclude that Catholicism could and did appeal to people on all levels of society, but that its ability to fulfil its potential amongst those not lucky enough to be called 'gentle' was constrained by the difficult circumstances in which it existed.[13]

Most of the individuals who were investigated for heresy during the sixteenth century were men, and historians have occasionally jumped thoughtlessly to inappropriate conclusions. Haigh, for example, points out that only one in six of the Marian Protestant martyrs was female, and deduces that 'women had found less to attract them in a Bible-based religion'. He does not, however, use the fact that the comparable figure for Elizabethan Catholic martyrs was one in fifty to demonstrate the inherent unattractiveness of the old faith to women. In truth, we can be certain that women were highly active within all of the century's dissenting movements, even if the finger of the law pointed most often at the men. Female dissenters, as Patricia Crawford has said of the Catholics, displayed a commitment that was 'unobtrusive and constant'. Religious women in fact took advantage of a legal system which treated them as being of little consequence in order to find a sphere of conspicuous participation. In the 1520s, Alice Colins was 'a famous woman' amongst the Lollards of Burford (Oxfordshire), 'and had a good memory, and could recite much of the Scriptures, and other good books'. She was also active as a teacher of men. Marian church services were reportedly boycotted in one Suffolk parish by many parishioners, 'especially the women'.[14] Catholic wives under Elizabeth commonly 'kept the faith' at home, while their husbands avoided punishment but risked conversion by behaving as partly-conformist 'church papists'. Amongst Protestant dissenters too, the domestic household took on a very considerable significance, and the household was, of course, an arena within which women held important responsibilities. But not all female dissenters operated behind the scenes, and several, from Lollards to Catholic recusants, paid the ultimate sacrifice for their devotion.

Catholic and Protestant forms of dissent were probably equally attractive to men and women. They may not, however, have appealed equally to people young and old. Susan Brigden and A. G. Dickens have both presented early Protestantism as 'predominantly a movement among the young'. According to Dickens, Henrician and Marian Protestantism was received most enthusiastically by people in their mid-twenties. Foxe celebrated the heroism of Marian martyrs considerably younger than this, such as the Brentwood apprentice who went to the stake at the age of nineteen. As he prepared to die, sunshine burst forth through the clouds to illuminate a final godly gesture: he threw his psalm-book to his brother with the defiant exclamation, 'I am not afraid'. We also have a few suggestive anecdotes which pit idealistic young Protestants against their reactionary parents in fierce domestic confrontations. The Venetian ambassador who, in 1557, remarked that there were no English Catholics under the age of thirty-five was very obviously exaggerating, but he was probably identifying a genuine imbalance. Of course, there were plenty of aged Protestants and youthful Catholics too. John Fines has questioned the view that proto-Protestant dissent was a habit of the young, citing the fact that the Lollards of Coventry, investigated in 1511, had an average age of forty-two. We might remark, however, that they had presumably been younger once.[15]

Beliefs

Dissenters, by definition, were united in their belief that the established church provided an utterly inadequate forum within which to explore and develop their relationship with God. When they looked at the official church, they found not only weakness, as the puritans did, but wickedness. The intensity of their feelings was well illustrated by a young Lollard-Protestant who, in 1543, pronounced that the parish font 'is but a stinking tarn, and he had rather be christened in the running river than in the said tarn, standing stinking by half a year'.[16] The nub of much sixteenth-century nonconformity was found in one or both of the twin principles that no true church should admit the ungodly, and that no godly person should belong to an untrue church. As we have seen, however, the duty of separation was not perceived by all dissenters as something that necessarily required physical expression. For many Lollards, Familists and church papists, as well as some of the earlier Protestants, it was considered possible to attend church without truly being there.

Of course, the precise theological reasons for rejecting the official church varied widely. The sixteenth century provides a wonderful array of defiant men and women, overcoming their fear in order to make bold statements of belief before their accusers. The nature of this 'extracted' evidence is more problematic than many historians allow, and may often tell us as much about official paranoia as about dissenting theology. Nevertheless, it is virtually all we have, and historians tend to assume optimistically that, although the sources distort reality, they do not utterly misrepresent it. The alternative is to admit that there is no such thing as 'reality', and to find ourselves lowered slowly into the acid-bath of post-modernism. Historians, in general, are not quite ready for this.

Some of the most colourful contemporary statements of dissenting faith were taken from the Lollards. These 'heretics' traced their origins to John Wycliffe, the fourteenth-century academic who developed a comprehensive critique of the late-medieval church. By the early sixteenth century, Lollardy had lost its association with the Oxford schools, and Scarisbrick has argued that it had degenerated intellectually to become 'upland semi-paganism'. This extraordinarily prejudiced description has been roundly criticised, though Anne Hudson, in her superb book *The Premature Reformation*, charitably supposes that it derives merely from 'ignorance of the sources'.[17] Hudson presents us with a Lollardy that, even a century and a half after the death of its founder, was coherent and vigorous. She concedes that the intellectual foundations of some beliefs were no longer visible, but she sees the later Lollards as truly the heirs of Wycliffe.

Lollard cells did not all hold identical beliefs, and individuals within local groups often participated in intense debates concerning theological truth. Nevertheless, there clearly was a solid core of shared ideas. The extent to which these prefigured the concerns of Protestantism, particularly in its most zealous strains, is remarkable. Lollards criticised a wide range of orthodox doctrines and practices, including transubstantiation, confession before priests, the revering of images, the authority of the papacy, pilgrimage, the liturgical use of Latin, baptism, purgatory, prayers for the dead, and the observance of feast days. They regarded holy communion as a purely commemorative or figurative act, and they treated the Bible in English as the fundamental guide to Christian belief and behaviour. For Lollards, the Scriptures were 'the evident and supremely important centre of life'. The later followers of Wycliffe sometimes had high 'eschatological expectations', and they often expressed a belief in predestination. Fundamentally, they sought a direct, uncluttered and personal relationship with their maker. Neither Wycliffe nor his disciples, however, developed any systematic doctrine of salvation by faith alone, and this was almost the only central tenet of Protestantism that they did not anticipate. Hudson shows, however, that a few of the late fifteenth-century Lollards in Coventry were moving in that direction, three decades ahead of Luther.[18]

Late-medieval Lollards were masters and mistresses of the theological sound-bite, and no account of their beliefs should deny them the opportunity to speak for themselves. In their words, we hear the voices of otherwise unexceptional individuals, intent upon expressing their sense of the sacred through the earthy idiom of the everyday. These words convey a forceful impression of common-sense rational materialism, sometimes with a pantheist edge. One Lollard declared, 'hit wer as good offer a candell to a owll in the wode as to a image of our Lady'. The man who preferred to be baptised in a river rather than a font justified his opinion by saying that 'when God made the world, he hallowed both water and land'. In Herefordshire, John Cooke was reported to have asked a clerk, 'What availeth your babling and your singing at Matins?' He then answered his own question: 'By God's blood, no more worth than Tokyr's wife's cow to low, or else that my bitch should take Richard Tokyr's sow by the ear.' Another was alleged to have said 'that our Lady wold assone shyte as doo enny miracle'. With equal contempt, Elizabeth Sampson attacked the sexual reputation of a local image: 'Our Lady of Willesdon was a burnt arse elf and a burnt arse stock.' Others were slightly less offensive. One Lollard claimed that God could be seen more easily in the face of a beautiful woman than in the consecrated host. Another declared that if the local image of St Martin had any brains at all, it would vacate its cold and lofty place in order to sit by the fireside. Devoted laypeople also attracted some scorn, and one Lollard alleged that 'folks go on pilgrimage more for the green way than for any devotion'.[19]

Occasionally, historians discover individuals or incidents that undermine the general impression of coherent and consistent doctrine. Lollards were generally extremely hostile to saint worship and the common obsession with miracles, yet there are several cases in which they seem to have been generating cults of their own. One Lollard priest, burned in London in 1440, was regarded as a saint. Some, like John Stilman of London, saw Wycliffe in the same light. In 1494, when 'an old cankered heretic' called Joan Boughton went to the stake, she called upon the Blessed Virgin to intercede for her. On the following night, 'the more part of the asshys of that fyre that she was brent in were hadd awaye, and kepyd for a precious relyk in an erthyn pott'.[20]

It is not easy to interpret such examples. Should we place them to one side, as rare signs of inconsistency and confusion? Or were the participants, in their own minds, simply replacing bad cults with good ones? Or should we regard them as yet more evidence that, amongst the population of sixteenth-century England, absolute intellectual consistency was not as fundamental as we think it is to us? Perhaps ordinary people, even Lollards, cobbled together a satisfying religion from the various, and sometimes seemingly incompatible, components that came their way.

The first English Protestants drew inspiration from new writers and translators, but in many respects England's 'new-fangled heresies' were also an absorption and re-formulation of older, Lollard ideas. From the

1520s to the 1550s, Protestants at the grassroots level objected to the same features of the established church and used the same earthy language as the followers of Wycliffe had done. They also exhibited a similar pattern of theological variety around an essential core. This goes some way towards explaining Thomas More's seemingly incoherent view that Protestants were simultaneously a fraternity and a hotch-potch of individuals, no two of whom believed the same things. Transubstantiation was rejected, but not all Protestant dissenters went so far as to hold a purely commemorative view of the sacrament. In 1540, one London pinner considered the Mass to be 'a good thing', but 'not as men took it, very God'.[21] Similarly, there was a spectrum of opinion regarding the doctrine of predestination. If anything, Protestantism was identified even more closely than Lollardy with the vernacular Bible, particularly the New Testament as it was translated by William Tyndale. A much more conspicuous difference, however, was the new emphasis, taken from Luther, on justification by faith alone. As we have already seen, this doctrine was regarded by Protestants and Catholics alike as one of the chief diagnostic features of the reformist programme.

The Protestant separatists of Elizabeth's reign shared much theological ground with the dissenters of previous reigns, and were distinguished primarily by a more radical understanding of the ecclesiological implications of their beliefs. The Brownists in Bury St Edmunds (Suffolk) were drawn to certain lines from Revelation which seemed to justify their hostility to the established church: 'Therefore because thou art lukewarm and neither cold nor hot, it will come to pass I will spew thee out of my mouth.' In 1582, Thomas Gibbs was accused of having painted this quotation onto the walls of the local parish church. Amongst these most radical of Protestants there was also a tendency towards unusually intense millenarian and messianic feeling. In Northamptonshire, William Hackett (King of Europe) claimed to speak with the spirit of John the Baptist, and to receive visitations from angels. Hackett's links with the more respectable puritan godly of the county naturally caused the latter acute anxiety, as William Sheils has shown. Similar embarrassment must have been associated with Elizabethan radicals who, variously, claimed to be Peter, Eli and even Christ himself. Keith Thomas has spoken of 'a small army of pseudo-Messiahs'.[22]

This millenarian element was also a feature of those radicals who were labelled 'Anabaptists'.[23] This term, like many others, was bandied about quite freely in the sixteenth century. It implied a coherent and unified movement, but English Anabaptism seems to be better understood as a set of loosely associated groups and ideas. Anabaptists shared with less radical Protestants a rejection of transubstantiation and the traditional sacrament of the altar. More distinctively, they generally denied the necessity and validity of infant baptism, believing that children were not born in original sin and could therefore not be damned before they reached the years of discretion or accountability. Beyond this, however, they held one or more of an assortment of tenets. Some, like John Champneys, were antinomians, arguing that the true godly had in some sense conquered sin and moved beyond the moral laws that governed ordinary mortals. Others espoused the Arian heresy, refusing to accept the orthodox Trinitarian doctrine that God and Christ were equal. Several rejected the belief that Jesus had literally taken flesh of the Virgin Mary, and Joan Bocher went to the stake rather than bend on this point. Accusations of communistic doctrine were frequently levelled at the Anabaptists, but there is little evidence that this found physical expression in the lifestyles of the English brethren. Such charges were frequently inspired as much by news of the more extreme German Anabaptists as by actual events at home.

Anabaptists were also hostile to Protestant ideas about predestination. They adopted the more optimistic view that Christ had redeemed all of His followers, who then had free will to accept or reject His great offering. This suspicion of predestinarian ideas was the central characteristic of the Freewillers in Essex and Kent, who offended the otherwise very different governments of Edward VI and Mary. J. W. Martin has portrayed the Freewillers as a highly engaged but non-dogmatic spiritual discussion group, rather than a clearly organised sect. They revealed an obsession with the words of Scripture, and a mystical interest in interior religion. They were also quite intensely anti-academic, reportedly scorning the teachings of learned men whose ideas about double election (to heaven and hell) seemed to make God the author of human sin. These interests were also shared by the Elizabethan Family of Love, the sixteenth century's most coherent fellowship of mystics. They believed that HN, their Dutch founder, had been appointed as God's most recent agent on earth, to spread ideas about deification, resurrection and perfectability that would one day unite the world in glory. Those who joined could aspire to become 'illuminated' or 'godded with God'. In other words, they could attain a state of spiritual perfection in this life. For Protestants, this was an extreme heresy which effectively denied the role in human salvation of Jesus Christ, the only perfect man ever to have lived. His sacrifice had purchased for his followers the prospect of perfection, but only after physical death. The Familists, in truth, defy classification according to

the normal Protestant/Catholic scheme. They saw themselves as transcending all such divisions.[24]

The beliefs of the Elizabethan Catholics were, of course, fundamentally
the same as those of their pre-Reformation ancestors, though the pious
thoughts and actions of the recusants may have assumed a new degree of
intensity. In Haigh's view, this was a response to persecution and the
increasing availability of piety in print. For Bossy, it had more to do
with the influence of the continental Counter-Reformation movement,
brought to England by the zealous missionaries who arrived from 1574
onwards. Despite these factors, Catholicism remained undeniably the
same religion, and the importance of keeping faith with one's forebears
was expressly stated by several recusants. The Catholics of the later
sixteenth century demonstrate that the traditional world of saints, sacraments and sacred power had survived all the assaults of reformers, though
it was now a much smaller and more fragile world. D. M. Palliser has
found a handful of northern wills which, as late as the 1580s, referred
explicitly to the Virgin Mary, the saints and prayers for the dead. Such
wills were a tiny minority by this date, but many Catholics nursed a belief
that the good times would return before too long, when the old faith
expanded again to take its rightful place as the official religion of England.
In 1582, one particularly confident Yorkshire trader reportedly issued a
bill that was 'to be paid when mass shall be said by lawful authority'.
Others were 'waiting for a day'. Perhaps this optimistic view served a
spiritual and emotional function parallel to that of millenarian prophecy
among some of the radical Protestant dissenters.[25]

Behaviour

Sixteenth-century dissenters of all shades faced similar pressures,
and shared a basic vocabulary of responses. All groups existing 'beyond
the church' aimed to achieve consolidation and, in theory at least, expansion. They all, therefore, had to grapple with the same fundamental
question: how would it be possible to strike a balance between the goal
of survival, which suggested the wisdom of secretive quietness, and the
goal of numerical increase, which demanded more vigorous and aggressive
tactics? To put it another way, this was a matter of finding a compromise
between the needs of inward and outward growth. No two groups
approached this question in precisely the same way, but every single

group showed signs of a sometimes self-destructive confusion concerning the best way forward.

Consolidation was the easier of the two principal objectives, though the risks in all aspects of a dissenting existence were considerable. Within a locality, the cohesion and spiritual well-being of a dissenting group were promoted in gatherings of the faithful. The members met together when it seemed relatively safe to do so, in numbers ranging from under a dozen to over a hundred. Lollards came together in taverns, private houses, 'holkys and hyrnes' [huts and hideouts] where they read and discussed the Scriptures, heard sermons and distributed books. These sessions, often called 'conventicles and schools', could on occasion last throughout the night. The early Protestants met for similar purposes, and an Exeter schoolmaster of the 1530s held 'conferences' with 'such as he could learn and understand to be favourers of the gospel and zealous of God's true religion'. At this date, when the status of Protestantism was ambiguous, it was also possible for adherents to gather at the official sermons of reformist clergymen such as Thomas Bilney and Hugh Latimer. The Protestants of Marian England met together for edification, often holding services according to the order laid down in the second Edwardian Prayer Book. In London, they gathered in various locations – private homes, inns, out in the fields, and even aboard two ships at Billingsgate. There were also reports of Anabaptist conventicles under Henry VIII, and Freewill conferences under Edward VI. In 1584, one group with Brownist inclinations met in an inn and spoke their prayers with such enthusiasm that 'the noise might be hard to the furtherside of the streate'. The Family of Love, in contrast, seems to have arranged 'parlour meetings' that were as inconspicuous as possible. Their proceedings remain largely a mystery.[26]

All dissenters shared a need for collective worship in some form or another, and the Elizabethan Catholics were of course no exception. In fact, the centrality of the Mass may have combined with a high doctrine of priesthood to make them particularly reliant upon opportunities for such worship. The tense circumstances in which they lived meant that the Catholic community was 'reconstructed ... in a domestic rather than congregational form'. Typically, meetings were arranged, figuratively and sometimes literally, in the shade provided by a conservative gentry household. Those who attended to hear Mass celebrated by a chaplain or itinerant priest were often the servants and tenants of that household. There were, however, exceptions to this pattern. It was reported in 1584 that Miles Yare, the serving parson of a Suffolk parish, was in the habit of saying Mass in his own parlour for the benefit of local conservatives. Ten years later, a seminary priest admitted that he had said Mass in a 'poor man's house'. In parts of Lancashire at this date, according to Haigh, the supposedly reformed services of the Church of England in fact retained so many features of the Mass that Catholicism was still effectively the norm. Here and elsewhere, Masses might even be said by imprisoned priests, and one report from 1633 claimed that a London gaoler had been caught swinging the incense burner himself! But it seems likely, despite such examples, that for many ordinary traditionalists, structured contact with a priest was lamentably sporadic. Frequently, therefore, they failed to realise their potential for recusancy. Of course, it was perfectly possible for Catholics who had no regular dealings with the priesthood to preserve their faith through a self-imposed round of household prayers and rituals, but it was not easy and it did not necessarily come naturally. Many therefore became church papists, a breed whose Catholicism was inevitably more vulnerable, if not necessarily doomed.[27]

Dissenting groups also strengthened their collective identity through the mutual support that members offered to one another in a wide range of forms. These included refuge for travellers, financial loans, book-lending, testamentary bequests, and general spiritual encouragement. In the 1540s, London Protestants gave accommodation and protection to outlawed preachers like Thomas Garrett and Robert Barnes. Half a century later, the Catholics did the same for their priests. Poignantly, a Marian Protestant named Mrs Marler sent the convicted 'heretic' John Bradford a new shirt in which to be burnt. In 1589, one Brownist in Bury St Edmunds bequeathed 'a possnet, a smocke, a neckar chew, a bolster, an apron and two Cushens to Good wife tiller', the widow of a man who had died for his separatist faith.[28]

The challenge of maintaining group cohesion beyond an immediate locality was a serious one, especially at a time when the authorities aimed, rather hopefully, to keep tabs on travellers. Leading dissenters often responded creatively and bravely, making impressive use of books, trade links, support networks and deception in their efforts to hold their fellowships together. There is plentiful evidence, for example, of Lollard interconnection across wide geographical areas. In 1518, a witness testified that the suspect Thomas Man had 'been in divers places and countries in England, and had instructed very many, as at Amersham, at London, at Billericay, at Chelmsford, at Stratford-Langthorne, at Uxbridge, at Burnham, at Henley-on-Thames, in Suffolk and Norfolk, at Newbury and divers places more'. Such people – and Man was not alone – distributed heretical books, carried news, and helped to ensure that Lollardy was an organism rather than a random scattering of disconnected cells. Richard Davies has recently disputed this view, but the evidence assembled by Anne Hudson and others remains impressive.[29]

Comparable evidence of inter-communication exists for all of the century's dissenting groups. In the 1540s and 1550s, Henry Hart covered the ground amongst the Anabaptists and Freewillers, achieving the informal status of a leader but successfully avoiding arrest in the repeated investigations. A Marian Protestant activist from Essex, George Eagles, was 'commonly called Trudgeover', a nickname resonant of itineracy. Perhaps it was no coincidence that shoemakers featured so prominently amongst the dissenters of the period! Under Elizabeth, Catholic priests were reported to 'convey themselves secretly from one papistes house to another', often operating in disguise. The queen's Privy Council was also on the lookout for a woman known as Lucy, said to be a 'common messenger' among the Catholics. The 'illuminated elders' of the Family of Love, led by the remarkably elusive Christopher Vittels, performed a similarly cohesive role. They were indispensable in the building and maintenance of a closely-knit mystical community whose members in Cambridgeshire, Devon and London all knew of one another. The Family's elders concealed books about their persons, wrote coded letters, used false initials, administered funds, and carried advanced warning of impending investigations. An exasperated enemy remarked of Vittels, 'What travell he hath taken, howe he hath trudged from countrie to countrie... is very wel knowi'. But nobody in authority knew where Vittels was at any particular moment, nor where he might be heading next.[30]

The ability to evade or deflect the hostile attentions of others was also developed amongst non-itinerant dissenters. In one particularly desperate example from the 1550s, a Protestant seaman reportedly jumped into the Thames from the back of a house in order to avoid the government officials who had come to the front. He also managed to find a boat, in which he then conveyed the rest of his group to safety, using his shoes as oars. Some Marian Protestants moved to other regions in order to avoid investigation. Thomas Bowtell of Newport Pond (Essex), for example, had 'fledde for religion into Wiltshire' with all his 'gooddes and cattalles'. Others, more famously, went into exile on the continent. Edwardian and Elizabethan Catholics were adept at the concealment of sacred goods. Caches of images, relics and vessels were hidden in lofts, under floorboards and beneath the ground, ready for the glorious day upon which the old faith would become the official faith once more. In Long Melford (Suffolk), an undamaged image of the adoration of the Magi was discovered under the church floor in the nineteenth century.[31]

The most reliable tactic for avoiding the hostility of outsiders was to blend in with them, quietly and cooperatively. One of the surprising findings of recent research on early-modern dissent has been the extent to which nonconformists, from Lollards to Quakers, lived as integrated members of their wider communities. Hudson and Plumb have both found Lollards who held local church offices. Brown adds some early Protestant examples from the Salisbury diocese, while others have discovered churchwardens, questmen and parish clerks amongst the Family of Love and the church papists. Andrzej Bida presents the small Catholic community in Elizabethan Linton (Cambridgeshire) as a sub-section of a larger community, rather than as a self-isolating group. The names of the Catholics here and elsewhere were entered into the parish registers, demonstrating that they generally accepted the official rites of passage. William Fulwell, who had been excommunicated for recusancy in 1580, nevertheless included in his slightly later will a bequest to the local vicar. He also asked the churchwardens to supervise his charitable legacies, and stipulated that his gifts were to be given out in the south porch of the church. Members of the Family of Love in the same region were just as involved in village life. They witnessed wills, paid their church rates, helped to run the manorial courts, gave generously to the local poor, and held a variety of offices. And in Kent, one dissenting tallow chandler was considered by his neighbours 'a separatist from the Church of England', but 'yet in his dealings . . . an honest man'.[32]

Many groups attempted to survive, physically and spiritually, through a combination of integration, secrecy and compliance. Similar patterns have been found to characterise the behaviour of Protestants in Catholic Italy. There was another side to the coin, as we shall see, but most dissenters generally kept themselves quiet. Heretical texts were usually guarded as closely as possible, and hidden when danger threatened. One Marian Protestant sought to repel investigators by concealing hers in a dunghill, and another had his bricked into the fireplace. Lollards and later Familists used semi-coded labels, such as 'gud and honest' or 'loving friends', with which to refer to one another. They also attended their parish churches, as did many Marian Protestants and Elizabethan Catholics. Each of these groups conducted intense internal debates over the validity of such conformity. The militants in both Protestant and Catholic camps denounced their more compliant co-religionists as 'Mass gospellers' and 'church papists' respectively. An earlier Lollard declared, with a similar debate proceeding in his head, that he would rather burn his books than have his books burn him. One Elizabethan Catholic married a Protestant but reportedly kept his beliefs entirely secret from his wife and others until he lay on his deathbed. Lastly, there were representatives of most dissenting groups who argued that it was legitimate to tell lies, or at least to hide the truth, when confronted by persecutors. The Family of Love was famous for this Nicodemite tactic, but its members were by no means the century's only dissemblers.[33]

It is difficult to establish whether pragmatic self-protection was the only generator of nonconformist compliance (an interesting paradox). Certainly, the motives for church attendance were often negative. Outward conformity was a matter of tactical hypocrisy, designed to stifle 'the rumour of the pepull', as one Lollard put it. Church papists often thought of themselves as playing a strategic waiting game. They were concealed within the church, dormant until a new age dawned – the human equivalent of buried images. Yet it seems possible that, in practice at least, the battle-lines running through a thousand general congregations must gradually have lost some of their meaning. When dissenters went beyond mere attendance, to hold offices or remember the church in their wills, were they merely putting up a smoke screen, or were they also expressing a sense of positive attachment to the wider community?

Of course, we can hardly know. It seems, however, that we should consider the possibility that many ordinary dissenters worked according to a practical model in which different religious communities – the dissenting fellowship and the parish congregation – overlapped rather than collided. The choices being made were not always as stark and obvious as they may look to us. Amongst the Marian suspects, for example, Bonner found many more waverers and doubters than committed and defiant Protestants. This too must have contributed to, and reflected, a greater flexibility within local religious cultures than historians have been prepared to acknowledge. Members of the Family of Love, in particular, seemed to display a positive sense of commitment to their wider communities which cannot easily be described exclusively as hypocrisy, self-protection or fearful compliance. It *was* these things, but it was also more than them. Susan Brigden has touched on a similar point, remarking that during Mary's reign, 'It was not only fear which led the godly to conform, but perhaps an inclination not to oppose the clear will of the majority of the citizens.'[34]

Religious dissent did not necessarily, therefore, walk hand in hand with social radicalism, nor indeed with political disloyalty. Although scholars may often wish otherwise, a substantial majority of the century's dissenters was almost certainly politically acquiescent. The solidity with which the Elizabethan Catholics stood for their queen against the Spanish enemy in 1588 has often been seen as a key indicator of this, though Peter Holmes has questioned the consensual interpretation. Other dissenting groups also provided conspicuous evidence of loyalty. During Wyatt's rebellion against the Marian regime in 1554, for example, the queen's Gentlemen Pensioners guarded her against danger, despite the Protestant convictions of many of them. Half a century later, the Yeomen of the Guard, several of whom belonged to the Family of Love, performed with similar steadfastness when the Earl of Essex threatened the stability of Elizabeth's court. The public statements of the English Familists placed great emphasis upon their devoted loyalty. Of course, the loyalty of dissenters was no simple and pure thing, and there were some striking exceptions. Nevertheless, we should not assume its insincerity.[35]

Such policies were never likely to draw many additional members into the group, nor to satisfy the psychological need for a sense of being different, and it is time now to study the reverse side of this coin. The necessity of evasion, the responsibility of persuasion, and the instinct for distinction all pulled Lollards, Anabaptists and Elizabethan Catholics in different directions. Alongside the evidence of deliberate social integration, therefore, there are many cases in which dissenters distanced themselves from the rest, or made militant gestures. Within every dissenting fellowship and most dissenting psyches, the behavioural options of compliance and defiance coexisted uneasily.

Several of our groups balanced their positive attitude towards wider society with actions clearly reflecting an urge to be separate. This expressed itself in a wide variety of ways. Lollards, early Protestants and Elizabethan Catholics frequently intermarried, and within the Family of Love it seems to have amounted to a matter of strict policy. Margaret Dunch of Stuntney (Isle of Ely), for example, married three times within the Family, moving from county to county as she did so. Her children behaved in much the same way. Henry Marsh of Balsham, a member of the same fellowship, twice married co-religionists who were younger than him by decades rather than years. Throughout the century, dissenters tended to witness and supervise one another's wills, often to the exclusion of their neighbours. They also took in one another's children as servants, or acted as their godparents.[36]

Dissenters often cooperated in their economic activities. The Lollards of Amersham (Buckinghamshire) frequently did business together and operated as a powerful economic force. Familists were to behave in a very similar way, sometimes sharing privileged information in order to prosper at the expense of others. Members of the Freewill group in Essex and Kent were apparently obliged 'not to Salute a Synner or a man whome they knowe not'. Elizabethan Catholics too were sometimes instructed of their duty to separate socially from Protestants as far as was possible, and some of them presumably did so. In Collinson's view, however, the Protestant separatists of the late sixteenth century were, paradoxically, permitted a reasonable measure of normal social activity. For them, spiritual separation was the fundamental duty, leaving ordinary neighbourly interaction comparatively intact. For the non-separatist puritans, in contrast, spiritual separation was to be avoided, and the instinct for distinction expressed itself more acutely in social terms.[37]

On many occasions, an urge to evangelise, or at least to take action that bore clear witness to one's faith, also found expression. Recorded incidents range from the comparatively benign to the downright obnoxious, though it should be noted that the latter sort were inherently more likely to be written down for our benefit. In the early 1530s, for example, a Protestant schoolmaster in Exeter, perhaps consciously following Luther's example, posted a notice on the cathedral door: 'The pope is Antichrist, and we ought to worship God only and no saints.' In 1532, he was burnt for his efforts. Other early Protestants left books on the doorsteps of their neighbours under cover of darkness, or kept their hats on while in church. There were also iconoclastic outbursts. As Margaret Aston has shown, the Buckinghamshire Lollards were probably responsible for a vicious and highly destructive fire attack on Rickmansworth church in c.1522. Late in Mary's reign, two Hertfordshire Protestants defiantly threw their offertory candles into the rood loft, 'to the evell example' of those present. Setting an example was clearly part of the point. In other cases, Lollards or Protestants in London allegedly spat on conformist neighbours, sang 'heretical' ballads, performed mock ecclesiastical rites featuring dead cats, and concealed themselves in walls, from which they uttered mysterious anti-Catholic statements. The bravest of them were also exceptionally bold in the face of official investigation, often making defiant use of what Collinson calls 'prodigious biblical learning'.[38]

Other dissenting groups provided comparable examples. We have already encountered the Brownists who placed offensive Scriptural graffiti on the walls of the church in Bury St Edmunds. The refusal of separatists and recusants to attend their parish churches in Elizabeth's reign was a defiant stance in itself. Church papists turned up, but sometimes misbehaved deliberately during services. In 1588, Richard Walwyn of Much Marcle (Herefordshire) picked a fight concerning his pew, then went forth 'out of the church'. Interestingly, he had also refused to remove his hat. Evidently, elements of the vocabulary of ecclesiastical protest remained unchanged throughout the early-modern period, whether the protesters were Lollards, Catholics or Quakers. When Elizabethan recusants went on trial, they could be as stubborn and brave as their Protestant forebears. In 1601, when Anne Line was charged with protecting a priest from justice, she told her judges, 'My Lords, nothing grieves me but that I could not receive a thousand more.' She was hanged shortly afterwards. Members of the Family of Love were notoriously unheroic, but even they revealed a capacity to defy high-ranking accusers. In 1580, the Wisbech glover John Bourne went on a brief hunger-strike and cracked jokes at the expense of the local bishop and his learned companions. It should be noted, however, that he abandoned both tactics when the judges informed him that his fellow Familists had identified him as their leader.[39]

At the militant end of the behavioural spectrum, we find those cases in which a tiny minority of nonconformists became involved in rebellion and conspiracy. Those who participated in the Pilgrimage of Grace under Henry VIII cannot helpfully be treated as 'dissenters', but any account of nonconformist behaviour in the sixteenth century must pay brief attention to the Catholic risings of 1549 and 1569, the Protestant rebellion led by Sir Thomas Wyatt in 1554, and the series of plots directed at Elizabeth's regime in the 1580s by disaffected priests and their followers. There were other examples too, and even a few episodes of distinctly parochial plotting. One Elizabethan church papist, intent on obstructing the smooth running of the local liturgy, used his position as the local parish clerk in order to change the time shown by the church clock. It is possible to argue, as Holmes has done in the case of the Elizabethan Catholics, that most dissenters were far more subversive than they look, and that they would all have turned the clock back or forwards, given the opportunity. It is, nevertheless, difficult to avoid the impression that the vast majority of dissenters had no serious interest in taking part in militant uprisings. Of course, an instinct for such involvement must have existed within the make-up of many of them, but it was not an instinct upon which the majority were ever likely to act. By the early seventeenth century, even the missionary priests were softening their line and conceding that Catholic loyalism was there to stay. Walsham portrays this shift in attitude as a priestly response to pressure from the Catholic laity.[40]

Dissenting behaviour therefore covered a considerable range, and embodied a complex set of tensions – between integration and separation, loyalty and conspiracy, compliance and defiance, secrecy and evangelism, courage and common sense. Contemporaries can have found no easy pathway through this maze of motives, and the route for historians is scarcely more straightforward. It can be said, however, that each dissenting fellowship managed, through the spectrum of activities and attitudes, to maintain an impressive coherence and stubbornness. It is also a significant fact that dissenters, whether Catholic, Protestant or 'radical', responded to the same pressures in ways that did not diverge dramatically. There is some value, therefore, in treating them all as part of the same phenomenon. It might be observed, finally, that although dissenting activities quite successfully held the line against the pressures either to conform or to accept martyrdom, they generally failed to achieve conspicuous expansion. The Family of Love was an extreme case of this failure, but by no means a solitary one. It seems that, in all phases of the century, a combination of majority obedience and nonconformist compromise ensured that the numbers of those who stood 'beyond the church' remained very small. Most lay dissenters did not take upon themselves to evangelise, and most of their neighbours felt no urge to encourage a change of policy.

Continuities and Interconnections

There has long been a tendency amongst Protestant denominational historians to argue that the roots of the Congregationalist, Quaker and Baptist movements lay amongst the late-medieval Lollards. This is one example of a deep-rooted human instinct, present within most of us, to trace our descent from those whom we consider to have been admirable in the past. As such, it deserves somewhat sceptical assessment from other historians. Something similar can be said of the desire of Marxist historians such as Christopher Hill to discover a long-lived radical community of socio-religious nonconformists extending 'From Lollards to Levellers'. Much of the evidence for such continuities has been highly anecdotal and of indeterminate significance. More recently, however, an intriguing attempt has been made to place older assumptions about the 'descent of dissent' on a more solid and statistical footing. A small team of researchers, led by Margaret Spufford, has used the techniques of surname analysis and genealogy to argue that dissent did indeed pass in families and, apparently, also from the earliest fellowships of proto-Protestants to the great nonconformist denominations of the later seventeenth century. There are some forbidding obstacles to be surmounted in the interpretation of Spufford's findings, but the statistics themselves are compelling.

Spufford, aided by her husband Peter and by Nesta Evans, has looked in detail at the relationship between Lollardy and post-Restoration dissent in twenty-one parishes around Amersham (Buckinghamshire). They calculate that amongst the local population as a whole, 29 per cent of the surnames present in 1524–5 were still there in the 1660s. The rate of continuity found in the surnames connected with Lollardy was, however, much higher, standing at 90 per cent. This striking discrepancy cannot be explained by arguing that the Lollards were wealthy, and therefore more settled in their region. In fact, the survival rate of their surnames was twice that of even the wealthier members of the general population. Of the Lollard surnames still present in the 1660s, the overwhelming majority (nine out of ten) were connected with the Quakers or Baptists then thriving in the area. Overall, therefore, it is demonstrated that dissenting families were far more stable within this region than were other families, and that the descendants of Henrician Lollards were much more likely to be dissenters in the later seventeenth century than were the descendants of their more orthodox neighbours. These patterns demand explanation.[41]

It is an exciting likelihood that the abnormal stability of these families has something to do with their abnormal religion. No purely socio-economic factor can provide the answer, since the dissenters do not seem to have been significantly different in their composition from the rest of the population. It appears, therefore, that they stayed where they were because they were religious nonconformists. The most plausible reason for this lies in the pattern of external and internal relationships which dissenting fellowships developed as part of their programme for survival. Collinson, in his 'critical conclusion' to Spufford's book, has written of 'a benign double strategy of endogamous and exogamous integration'.[42] The importance of this strategy may well have meant that dissenters, paradoxically, were tied more closely into their localities than were other people. They had built support networks, and they had often established a tolerable *modus vivendi* with their conformist neighbours. Dissenters had therefore invested much in local life, and they had much to lose by abandoning it.

There are, however, some significant qualifications to be made, and it seems that Spufford and company have posed a set of interesting questions without fully answering them. Collinson, somewhat sceptical of the Chilterns as 'a kind of religious wildlife refuge', has drawn attention to the absence of any satisfactory investigation of what happened in the 150 years between Lollardy and Quakerism. The Spufford thesis is, as he argues, 'a mint with a hole'.[43] In particular, Collinson asks about the religious affiliations of Lollard descendants during the reigns of Elizabeth and James. Until we know whether the descent of dissent carried it through puritan partial conformity, or through something more radical, we cannot really be sure with what we are dealing. It should also be remembered that although some Lollard descendants emerged as Baptists and Quakers, the vast majority did not. The findings must be assessed with caution. Doubtless, we are all descended from nonconformists of one sort or another somewhere along the line, for we all have millions of ancestors. These roots may not, however, have any direct bearing on our own views, unless we choose to trace and highlight them. The issues will not be settled until the hole has been plugged and the community of religious historians has examined the Spufford case in detail. For now, we can only say with certainty that something strange and significant was going on.

It is certainly possible, at a more anecdotal level, to establish the existence of interconnections and continuities between groups of dissenters during the sixteenth century. Most obviously, there was a close relationship between the later Lollards and the first Protestants, and it is rarely if ever possible to draw a clear boundary line. As Dickens has argued, the Lollard tradition maintained a forceful presence within Protestantism for years. For many, it remained 'the basic, perhaps the predominant, element'. Fusion was slow, even after the appearance of Tyndale's New Testament in 1526, and many of those accused of heresy by the courts in the following decades were more strongly committed to the old Lollard beliefs than to Lutheran teaching on justification or the sacraments. Documented meetings between Lollards and Lutherans sometimes reveal a measure of tension which may, conceivably, have functioned as a barrier that was only semi-permeable. In 1527, for example, two Essex Lollards visited a Lutheran friar in London, with the intention of purchasing a copy of Tyndale's Testament. They showed him their old Lollard manuscript-Bible, which contained the books of the Evangelists and the epistles of Peter and Paul. These books, 'the said friar did little regard, and made a twit of it'. Pompously, he told them that their old manuscript was not to be compared with his new printed one, which 'is of more cleaner English'. The two visitors duly purchased their copy of Tyndale, but they may not have switched neatly from Lollardy to Lutheranism as they did so. It is interesting that a dozen Wycliffite texts were printed in the 1530s, alongside more clearly Lutheran works, suggesting that an older form of demand still retained its force.[44]

Nevertheless, the episode does also demonstrate the way in which Lollard affinities could generate a basic interest in, and enthusiasm for, the new Protestant texts and teachings. In Dickens's view, it was a potent blend with implications for the progress of the Reformation, and he speaks of 'a diffused but inveterate Lollardy revivified by contact with continental Protestantism'. Hudson presents several interesting examples suggesting how old Lollards became new Lutherans during the 1520s and 1530s. The most interesting case is that of Thomas Harding, a Buckinghamshire Lollard who had been investigated repeatedly during the first two decades of the century. In 1532, he was in trouble again, though the mini-library found beneath his floorboards was now dominated by the printed works of Tyndale. The doctrines to which he admitted at his trial included many 'longstanding Lollard views', but Harding also stated that faith alone was the root of salvation. 'What he learned from his new books', Hudson concludes, 'was largely a reinforcement of his earlier Lollard opinions; but the new emphases and explanations reveal that Harding was not too old nor too set in his ways to learn from Tyndale'.[45]

Other historians have attributed the precocious impact of Protestantism in particular regions, such as the area of Kent around Rye, to the earlier presence of Lollardy there. Indeed, there are powerful strains of Lollard self-expression in the words of the Rye Protestant Robert Wood, who said in the 1530s that official church services were 'of no more effect than the blething of a Cowe to here calff, and the calff ayen to the Cowe'.[46] Other locations in which similar overlap has been noted include Bristol, Coventry, Colchester, London, Suffolk, and the dioceses of Salisbury and York.

Continuities of ideas and personnel have also been found bridging the chronological gaps between Henrician Lollardy, Edwardian Anabaptism, Marian Freewill and Elizabethan Familism. It was a commonplace of anti-dissent writing that those involved with such groups were 'sick-brained', and likely to flit erratically from one foul heresy to another. Clearly, this was a slur, but there *were* personal connections between these radical fellowships. Joan Bocher, the maid of Kent, had a background in Lollardy, and came to be associated with mid-century Anabaptism. She must have known Henry Hart, who also appears to have had a role amongst the

Anabaptists of the 1530s. He was certainly a leading figure within the Freewill groups of the 1550s. In this capacity, he would have encountered a certain Master Lawrence of Tolleshunt Knights (Essex), whose probable relatives became members of the Family of Love during the reign of Elizabeth.[47] This was not, however, the only line of Familist ancestry. Other members of the fellowship had their origins in groups as diverse as the late-medieval priesthood, enthusiastic Catholic conformists, early Protestants, and even astrologers. The roots of radicalism grew in many directions.

By far the most animated debate over the presence of continuities within sixteenth-century dissent has focused on Catholicism, and particularly the foundations of the post-Reformation recusant tradition. John Bossy, as early as 1965, staked out a provocative and highly influential position. He argued that Elizabethan recusancy was in fact anything but 'traditional'. Instead, it was the creation of the seminary priests and Jesuit missionaries who began to arrive in England from 1574 and 1580 respectively. These men, though generally English by birth, had undergone training in William Allen's recently established seminary at Douai in the Netherlands. There, in Bossy's view, they had been exposed to new influences associated with the Counter-Reformation, and had been transformed into a new breed of English Catholic clergy. Men like Edmund Campion and Robert Parsons brought to England a religion which insisted on greater commitment, personal involvement and discipline from its adherents, who were expected to receive communion and make confession more regularly than ever before. Attendance at 'heretical' Protestant churches was fiercely condemned. The missionaries also built flexible and imaginative networks of communication through which the new word could be spread.

Meanwhile, according to Bossy, the older form of English Catholicism, which was more relaxed, ritual-centred and automatic, had withered in the harsh environment created by Elizabethan reform. The traditional Catholic community had admitted defeat, retreating into the households of conservative gentry or adopting the behaviour of the church papists. The missionaries therefore brought a new community into being, but it retained its vibrancy and boldness only for a short time. By the end of the century, disputes between the missionaries and the secular clergy (backed by most of the laity), particularly over the vexed issues of loyalty and conformity, had become intense and damaging. Ultimately, the missionaries were forced to modify their extremely demanding position, and English Catholicism lapsed once more into a state of quietism. 'Loyalty supplanted enterprise. The history of Elizabethan Catholicism is a progress from inertia to inertia in three generations.' Bossy's reading of the evidence is broadly shared by scholars such as Aveling and Dickens.[48]

It is not shared, however, by Christopher Haigh, who endeavours to turn the Bossy thesis on its head. For him, the surviving Marian priests, who never spent time in Douai, were much more important in the foundation of the post-Reformation Catholic community than Bossy would allow. They were active and committed, preventing the destruction of the old faith in the 1560s and 1570s despite their immense disadvantages. They helped to ensure that surviving Catholicism was coherent and robust, often remaining within the established church but catering for the preferences of traditionalists within the congregation. The growth of recusancy, in Haigh's view, had begun well before the missionaries arrived.

He is particularly critical of Bossy's portrayal of the mission priests, and argues that it owes too much to contemporary Jesuit propaganda, which, not surprisingly, presented them as heroes. For Haigh, the missionaries were a hedonistic and strategically inept group. They based themselves in the south and east of the country, despite the fact that most of the Catholics were in the north and west. They preferred the comforts and company associated with southern manor houses to the rigours of life amongst the poor of the northern uplands. At the same time, rather surprisingly, Haigh criticises the missionaries for actually seeking martyrdom, rather than concentrating on the spiritual welfare of their flock. Better to die a hero than a herdsman. The vast majority, it seems, were selfish, but their selfishness could express itself either as a love of cosy cushions or as an obsession with the cult of martyrdom. The mission's new, more disciplined religion is also dismissed: in so far as it existed, its roots were in late-medieval Christianity and the changed circumstances of life under a Protestant monarch, rather than in the agenda of the Counter-Reformation. In any case, the religion of many English Catholics, particularly in parts of the north, remained thoroughly traditional, based around the worship of communion bread, Latin prayers, the sign of the cross, and so forth.[49]

The most readable history may be written at the extremes of the interpretative spectrum, but the most reliable history is not. There seems little doubt that a more plausible explanation of the development of Elizabethan Catholicism is to be found in a blend of the two arguments, as Patrick McGrath and others have suggested. Bossy's case certainly neglects the importance of the Marian clergy and the conforming Catholic laity during the first decades of Elizabeth's reign. Even Edmund Campion, a leading missionary, found them impressive, writing in 1580 that 'The country priests are virtuous and learned; they have raised such an opinion of our society that all Catholics do us exceeding reverence.' Many Catholics were also well aware of a sense of obligation to their late-medieval ancestors, and therefore of a need to hold onto the 'old' faith. When Cecily Stonor stood before her judges in 1581, accused of recusancy, she declared proudly 'I hold me still to that wherein I was born and bred; and find nothing taught in it but great virtue and sanctity; and so by the grace of God I will live and die in it.'[50] In the light of such examples, the notion of a radical and abrupt break with the past, inspired by the missionaries, looks rather extreme.

Haigh's counter-case is, however, equally exaggerated. It seems rather harsh, for example, to accuse the missionaries of hiding out in comfortable gentry retreats when so many of them were executed for their activities (125 out of 463). The argument that those who died sought martyrdom for equally selfish reasons can hardly paper over the holes in this thesis. It is equally unfair to castigate the missionaries for focusing their attentions on the south of England. It seems very likely that they did so not to avoid the hardships of the north, but because political power was at its most concentrated in and around London. They may well have felt that if inroads could be made at the heart of things, then the real prize – national reconversion – might one day follow. The fact that, ultimately, this strategy did not work should not blind us to its coherence and potential. Furthermore, it can quite legitimately be argued that priests who spent their time close to London during the 1580s and 1590s, when the laws against them were increasing in severity, were exhibiting courage rather than cowardice.

In conclusion, it seems that the relationship between the old and the new needs to be understood – as with the Lollard/Protestant case – primarily in terms of mutual and fruitful interaction. Of course, there were tensions too, but, on both sides of the Reformation divide, comparative novelty built upon solid tradition without completely crushing or supplanting it. Among the Catholics, the Marian clergy prevented the disintegration of the faith, encouraging traditionalism and some recusancy during the 1560s and 1570s. But no priest lives forever, and by the later 1570s Catholicism may well have needed a fresh infusion of ideas and personnel. Government control over the clergy and over church attendance was becoming more effective, and the partial conformity of Catholicism up until this date must have been growing more difficult to sustain (though it remained one viable option for decades). The missionaries did bring new emphases and new energy, substantially extending the infrastructure of protected communication that had already begun to evolve. But they too were descended from English Catholics of the previous generation. They were not, therefore, entirely or even predominantly alien, and all Catholics shared fundamental attitudes towards the Mass, the seven sacraments and the priesthood. They differed, and they sometimes did so fiercely, but an underlying and powerful unity also needs to be borne in mind.

Perhaps the quietist Catholic consensus that was growing in the early seventeenth century can be interpreted as a resurgence of this basic unity. By this time, it was clear that Catholicism had failed in its objective of reclaiming England, but interpretations which seek the reasons for this failure primarily within Catholicism itself are somewhat unbalanced. The passage 'from inertia to inertia' cannot be explained purely in terms of lack-lustre gentry, hedonistic missionaries, priestless peasants and strategic error. The relative strength and popularity of the reformed Church of England by 1600, assessed in the earlier chapters of this book, must also be taken into account.

Attitudes to Dissent

Many historians believe sixteenth-century England to have been a straightforwardly intolerant place, in which those who dissented from orthodoxy were shunned, reported and often executed. Keith Thomas, writing in 1971, was absolutely clear on the matter: 'Indeed if the records of Tudor and Stuart life leave any single impression, it is that of the tyranny of local opinion and the lack of tolerance displayed towards nonconformity or social deviation.'[51] Witches, foreigners and religious dissenters, it seems, could all expect to be cold-shouldered, and the experience of standing apart was profoundly uncomfortable.

The legal status of dissent further strengthens this impression. The subject presents us with a confusing maze of jurisdictions and forms of illegality, but it is safe to say that those who chose not to conform – physically, spiritually or both – could be prosecuted somehow or other. They fell foul of ecclesiastical law, simply for maintaining affiliations which seemed to undermine or contradict their required allegiance to the established church. Visitation articles often requested information on parishioners suspected of belonging to groups beyond the official church. Punishments available to ecclesiastical judges included public penance, the enforced wearing of a heretic's badge (used against some of the Lollards), and excommunication, which in its strictest form banned culprits from participation in Christian society. The church courts could not order execution, but they could pass serious cases over to secular justice if the death sentence seemed to be deserved.

Parliamentary statutes, for this reason and others, also played a significant role. Many people, for example, were investigated because of their alleged refusal to accept the conservative theological doctrines set down in the Act of Six Articles (1539). Under Henry and Mary, individuals holding unorthodox beliefs could be executed, or punished in other ways, under the terms of heresy laws passed in the fifteenth century. These laws were repealed successively by Edward and Elizabeth, but new statutes imposed fines and incarceration for a variety of offences seen as detrimental to the established church. The Act of Uniformity (1559) banned criticism of the Prayer Book and any obstruction of church services, including simple failure to attend. The severity of fines for absenteeism increased with time, being set at £20 a month by an Act of 1581. From this date, as the number of missionaries increased and England faced an intensifying threat from Spain, a succession of Acts imposed ever harsher penalties on practising Catholics, particularly members of the priesthood and their more active helpers. An Act of 1585 allowed the death penalty to be passed on those who did 'receive, relieve, comfort or maintain' any Jesuit, seminary priest or 'such other like disobedient persons'.[52]

In 1593, a statute against 'seditious sectaries & disloyal persons' aimed simultaneously at Catholics and Protestant separatists. With the revocation of the medieval heresy laws, it had become impossible to execute dissenters purely for their beliefs, but alternative pretexts could be found when necessary (sedition, treason, and so forth). Throughout the century, the system was reinforced, and gaps within it plugged, by royal proclamations, injunctions, occasional Acts of Attainder, direct Privy Council intervention, and ecclesiastical commissions set up for specific purposes (out of which grew the more permanent, and infamous, Court of High Commission). If the authorities wished to punish an individual dissenter, they could always find a way to do so. And if the statute book can serve as an index of sixteenth-century attitudes, then dissenters received little sympathy from their contemporaries.

One does not have to search the historical literature for long before encountering further evidence of hostility. If the work of Reformation historians conjures up any single image, to paraphrase Thomas, it is that of the religious nonconformist facing gruesome death in the flames or on the gallows. There are hundreds of examples. The Lollard teacher Thomas Denys was burned alive during the middle years of Henry's reign. His pupils were forced first to watch and then to throw their books onto the fire. Foxe helped to turn the burnings of Marian Protestants into the stuff of English nationalist legend, but all sixteenth-century regimes executed religious dissidents. During Elizabeth's reign, for example, a Catholic woman named Margaret Clitherow was crushed to death for refusing to plead when she was tried for harbouring a priest. In July 1575, two Dutch Anabaptists – foreign as well as fanatical – went into the flames at Smithfield, and 'died in great horror with roaring and crieng'.[53]

Numerous examples suggest the bitter resentment with which condemned heretics could be regarded by on-lookers. In the early 1530s, one man hurled a block of wood at Thomas Harding as he burned for his Lollard/Protestant beliefs. Another Protestant in trouble was reportedly spat upon and taunted by those who said 'it was a pity I was not burned already'. Thomas Bennet, facing execution in 1532, was apparently threatened with a burning bush on a pole. Someone in the crowd was reported to have yelled, 'Ah! whoreson heretic! Pray to Our Lady and say *Sancta Maria, ora pro nobis*, or by God's wounds I will make thee do it!' Equally lurid reportage surrounded the executions of Catholics under Elizabeth and James, though nobody collated and coloured it with quite the panache of the Protestant martyrologist John Foxe.

The theatre of investigation and execution was deliberately compelling, and provided a setting within which the rival voices of authority and heresy could compete for the sympathy of the people. In 1530, four Protestant Londoners were made to sit backwards on their horses and ride through the city, their clothes decorated with placards and copies of forbidden texts. They then had to throw the books onto a fire, before being set in the pillory. Under Mary, twenty-two Colchester Protestants were roped together and marched up to London to face examination for their suspected denial of transubstantiation. Their ordeal inspired one of the most famous pictures in Foxe's *Book of Martyrs*. Throughout this period, banned books were periodically burned in large public bonfires, such as the one that took place at St. Paul's Cross on 26 September 1546.[54]

Such events could not have happened without the existence of people who were prepared to pass incriminating information on to the authorities. The governmental system, with no professional police force, was reliant upon such channels of communication. It is impossible, therefore, to argue that the persecution of dissenters had little or no grassroots impetus. Hundreds of suspects could be rounded up at a time. We can

rarely trace the source of the information with any precision, but conspicuous incidents and expressions, dotted through the sources, suggest some of
the interpersonal contexts within which a 'sinister report' might be generated. Lollards and early Protestants sometimes admitted that they would
not have attended official church services at all, 'if it were not for the speech
of the people'. One feared that, after his execution, his wife would face the
pointing fingers and wagging tongues of her neighbours: 'yonder goeth the
heretic's wife'. In 1538, a neighbour of John Harrydance, an evangelical
bricklayer, threatened to throw a bowling ball at his head unless he stopped
expounding the Gospel from a tree in his garden. There were mothers who
disowned their heretical offspring, and children whose parents encouraged
them to throw sticks into the flames. One Marian Protestant was reported
on more than one occasion by his own wife.[55]

Under Elizabeth and James, Catholic suspects could be treated with
equal contempt by Protestants. When ninety or more Catholics died in a
tragic accident at a church service in 1623, gloating crowds were said to
have thrown mud and stones at the wounded. By this date, in the words of
Martin Ingram, anti-Catholicism 'appears to have been fully absorbed into
the national consciousness', blending with xenophobia, providentialism
and a latent millenarianism to form a potent cocktail.[56]

Much of this evidence suggests an extreme and pervasive intolerance of
deviance. One of the most striking official expressions of this attitude was
in the ecclesiastical regulations governing the treatment of excommunicates, whose 'nonconformity' could range from sexual misbehaviour to a
principled refusal to attend church. They were deemed to have placed
themselves beyond the church, and were consequently to be severed from
all Christian participation and contact. A peculiar entry in the parish
register of Ledbury (Herefordshire) in 1593 indicates that one community
at least took the matter seriously: 'Thomas Barker being an excommunicate person, was putt into a grave out of Christian burial and was not
buried the VII day of April.' This, it seems, was a kind of anti-burial.[57]

There is, however, another tale to tell. From most modern perspectives,
it is a more attractive tale, and historians warn one another repeatedly
about the dangers of importing modern liberalism, or flexible Anglicanism, into sixteenth-century sources. This is, of course, a valid point, but it
should not be used as an excuse for glossing over the counter-evidence as if
it hardly existed. It also seems to present a somewhat suspect vision of the
present, in which English people look benevolently upon those who do not
share their beliefs. Admittedly, intolerance with roots that are principally
religious has faded with organised religion itself, but it is perfectly possible

to argue that we have simply found other foci for the same instincts. Historians of all periods might do better to construct models which can accommodate the simultaneous power of tolerance and intolerance, amity and enmity, rather than relying so heavily upon 'either/or' interpretations. It may be valuable to assess dissent's second story with this observation in mind.

When convicted dissenters prepared to depart this world at the violent hands of the state, the attendant crowds were certainly not unanimous in their happiness to see them go. Brigden, writing about the Protestant martyrdoms, argues that 'for the most part, the evidence from both persecutors and persecuted is of sympathy for the victims' (Haigh disagrees, however). In 1531, the execution in Norwich of Protestant preacher and local-boy-made-bad, Thomas Bilney, was certainly not greeted with cheers by on-lookers. When a group of Anabaptists died 'boldely, or chearefullye' in 1535, some neutrals were so impressed that they wondered whether it proved the validity of the heretics' cause. In 1555, people wept as they witnessed the burning of John Rogers at Smithfield. Those present at the execution of seven London Protestants in the same decade reportedly crowded close to the stake in consolement.[58] For some, this sympathy grew out of a shared doctrinal affiliation. For others, it was stimulated by the impressive bravery of the condemned. For others again, there were conscientious reasons for regretting the execution of neighbours who seemed honest and deserving of respect.

This emerges more clearly if we trace the judicial process back a step or two, to the point at which people decided whether or not to report the dissenters in their neighbourhood to the authorities. That word – 'neighbourhood' – will prove an important one. Several historians have argued that the bulk of England's conformist population was in fact reluctant to persecute the dissenters who lived amongst them. Robert Whiting has remarked that 'most of the known Protestants in the Henrician South-West seem not to have been delivered to the courts by their neighbours', despite the strong traditionalism of the region. Gina Alexander, writing of the Marian Protestants, asserts that 'the sympathetic silence of the majority of their neighbours' prevented their destruction. Duffy has little to say about the martyrs, but he does remark that 'Neighbourhood was neighbourhood' and that it was powerful enough to generate distaste for the Marian persecution. Susan Brigden has found 'almost no evidence' to suggest that Londoners turned their Protestant neighbours over to the authorities, particularly after the revival of the heresy laws placed the death penalty on the judicial menu.

Familists in the following reign were seldom presented to the church courts by their neighbours, though their affiliations must often have been well known. Elizabethan Catholics have also been portrayed, by Robin Clifton and others, as a group whose members were not, in the main, treated by their neighbours with anything like the severity which the law allowed. Anti-Catholicism was an ideological construct, passionate in the abstract or at isolated flashpoints, rather than something that was applied on a daily basis to the people next door. It seems, therefore, that much of the information presented against sixteenth-century dissenters was provided by a small number of informers or 'promotours', some of whom were professional. One such individual may have been Leonard Romsye, who supplied the Elizabethan authorities with (often dubious) information against radical puritans and members of the Family of Love.[59]

Some of the anecdotal evidence is indeed suggestive. In 1556, the mayor of Exeter, though a convinced Catholic, behaved kindly towards his Protestant neighbours, 'and did, both friendly and lovingly, bear with them and wink at them'. His name, somewhat inappropriately, was Walter Staplehead. Whiting presents him as more representative of the local population at this date than those who were bent on persecution. We might also mention the parish constable who advised a suspected Protestant to tell her judges exactly what they wished to hear, even that 'the crow is white', in order to save her skin. Around the same time, two London women stood surety for one of the suspects, not because they shared her faith but because, if she died, her children 'were like to perish'. It appears that the Henrician Protestant Richard Hilles had some justification for arguing that even his fiercest critics were reluctant to inform on him because they had no desire 'to be regarded in the sight of all as guilty of treachery against their neighbours'. The doctrine of neighbourhood could indeed cut across confessional divisions.[60]

It is also becoming increasingly apparent that sixteenth-century conformists did not necessarily shun their dissenting neighbours, nor even treat them with circumspection. Indeed, it is hardly likely that the dissenters' habit of 'infiltrating' local office, already discussed, would have been possible amongst people whose stance was suspicious or hostile. The benevolent treatment of dissenters was noted anxiously by Sir Thomas More in the 1520s. He observed that, 'among good Catholic folk', the heretics were increasingly 'suffered boldly to talk unchecked'. At the other end of the century, the social relations between recusant Catholics and conformists were often relatively harmonious. Catholic testators in Linton (Cambridgeshire) felt able to ask their non-Catholic neighbours to witness their wills, which were usually written in intimate domestic surroundings during a period of sickness. The compliment went the other way too. The fines for non-attendance seem to have been exacted only rarely. Nor were Catholics in Linton barred from access to the church's rites of passage. Instead, according to Andrzej Bida, they were 'full members' of the community. Some conformist parishioners even named their offspring after the most eminent of the local Catholics, Ferdinand Paris. Members of the Elizabethan Family of Love in numerous communities were also treated with considerable respect across half a century.[61]

A final indicator of the flexibility of attitude that existed in many local communities concerns the treatment of excommunicates. Although, as we have seen, they could be dealt with fiercely, there is also considerable evidence that local opinion avoided the most severe of dealings, except in extreme cases. Many excommunicates, Collinson has suggested, probably 'drifted back into good standing without making formal peace with the archdeacon'. Several cases from Herefordshire, discovered by Moir, suggest that the regulations concerning the burial of excommunicates were frequently waived by local people. Such cases were recorded only when higher authority reacted to breaches of the rules. In Sarnesfield, during the early seventeenth century, the body of an excommunicated recusant was buried in the churchyard. The judges ordered its urgent removal, and its burial in 'some other place, viz. in the heighwaie, diche or common field nexte adjoyninge, to the terror – and example – of others who doe or shall hereafter persist in the Sentence of excommunication'. People evidently needed to be told that the tolerant treatment of dissenters was officially unacceptable.[62]

It would also be misleading, however, to present the evidence as reflective of a clash of opinions between intolerant governors and accommodating subjects. The voice of authority also had its more gentle register, and the horrific burnings need to be weighed against numerous episodes in which suspects were handled with flexibility and even leniency. Philippa Tudor has remarked that the consumers of Protestant books during Mary's reign were often 'remarkably lightly treated'. Muriel McClendon finds that the mayor and aldermen of Norwich were 'generally reluctant to punish religious offenders harshly' during the sixteenth century. Several scholars have argued that even the regimes most commonly associated with cruelty, such as Mary's, aimed at persuasion and reconciliation, not at physical destruction. The vast majority of suspects were not executed, but were given plentiful opportunities to see, or to say they saw, the light. Those who died were usually resistant and defiant.[63]

Horst has described the English authorities as 'more tolerant of radical religion than any other country in Europe', and his wider perspective is informative. Elizabethan Catholics frequently did not pay the full fines to which they were liable, and MacCulloch has argued that, from the 1590s onward, 'persecuted gentry and government persecuting machinery seem usually to have settled down to a rather surprising degree of symbiosis'. Members of the Family of Love, too, were regularly dealt with quietly and gently by ecclesiastical court judges. The extraordinary flexibility of the system is well illustrated by the example of the leading Familist Robert Seale, who was granted the right to collect recusancy fines from wealthy Catholics![64]

In conclusion, there is probably little point in attempting to choose between the two sets of evidence. The exercise of deciding which was more representative of contemporary opinion is likely to prove a sterile one, however tempting the challenge might seem. Instead, it may be advisable to think in terms of an almost schizophrenic religious culture, in which contradictory instincts jostled for supremacy. There were good reasons, some principled and some pragmatic, for a degree of tolerance or accommodation. But there were also sound grounds for persecution. Many official pronouncements encouraged people to inform the authorities of the dissenters in their midst, but others urged that wrangling over religious matters was un-Christian and to be avoided. Ordinary people gave expression to the same contradiction, sometimes turning against their nonconformist neighbours and sometimes regarding them with a kind of passive tolerance. This tolerance was usually articulated in mundane actions rather than words, and it tends therefore to be underplayed by historians who regard verbal expression as supremely important. Tolerance was not tolerance unless it was spoken and recorded. The evidence certainly demonstrates, however, that a doctrine of Christian neighbourhood was one of the most robust features of sixteenth-century popular religion. It seems to have encouraged a widespread capacity to compromise or suspend judgement in matters relating to the treatment of dissenters. This in turn contributed to a surprising measure of fluidity and flexibility within religious culture at the grassroots.

Inevitably, in such a turbulent period, this fluidity sometimes caused great anxiety to those most fervently committed to the promotion of one religious system over another. Thomas More was not alone in wishing to see the lines between truth and falsehood more clearly drawn. There may have been a fear that people in general were in danger of becoming neither one thing nor the other if they persisted in coexisting with Lollards,

Familists and recusants. The evidence of 'mixed' beliefs found in the heads of conformists and dissenters alike suggests that this fear was not wholly without basis. Under Mary, to add one further example, two Suffolk Protestants were reported to have exhibited the burnt bones of a martyr, William Pygott, as relics.[65] Behind even so poignant a symbol of intolerance as a nonconformist's ashes, there lay hints of interchange and flexibility. Arguably, there was a certain vagueness or ambivalence close to the heart of popular religion.

Bitterness and benevolence towards dissenters must often have coexisted not merely within communities but within the minds of individual parishioners. The nature of the surviving sources means that this cannot often be demonstrated. Thomas Teversham of Balsham (Cambridgeshire), however, provides a good Jacobean illustration. He was a conformist, perhaps with puritan leanings, but he lived in a village that was well-stocked with members of the Family of Love. His conduct toward them was contradictory, to say the least. In 1602, Teversham can be glimpsed cooperating cordially with Edmund Rule, one of the Familists. Rule asked Teversham to witness an important legal transaction for him, and the latter complied. In 1609, however, Teversham expressed a very different instinct when he forcibly removed the gravestone from the resting place of a different, recently deceased member of the Family. He subsequently became entangled in a row with Edmund Rule's son, during which he reported Rule and his co-religionist John Taylor to the church courts, 'named uppon a common fame to be of the familye of Love'. This was the first time the Balsham Familists had been reported in this way, and the judge dealt leniently with them. It was extraordinary, given this background, that when the Familist Taylor made his will in 1616, he called Teversham to his deathbed to act as a witness. Teversham duly performed this intimate and neighbourly service, along with Edmund Rule's son! In this Jacobean village, tolerance and intolerance, love and hate, conflict and reconciliation seem to have followed one another around, like the seasons.[66]

Dissent and Popular Religion

Sixteenth-century dissent was driven by a variety of motives. For the majority of those involved, the roots of it all were to be found, first and foremost, in theological conviction. They felt that God could not be reached through the beliefs and practices required by the established church. But nonconformity met other aspirations too. In turbulent times, when the world feels unsettled, people are often particularly in need of an intense sense of belonging. Perhaps this is an advanced version of the instinct found amongst certain animals, who huddle together for security when a predator looms. For early-modern dissenters, the desire to experience a feeling of fellowship, warm and distinctive, was a powerful motivating factor. In the early eighteenth century, Isaac Watts spoke eloquently of dissent as 'A Garden wall'd around / Chosen and made peculiar Ground.' It is a paradoxical fact that many dissenters probably considered themselves to be fleeing from the emergent confessional confrontations of their age, rather than contributing actively to them. In their own minds, they were building a garden rather than a battleship. One Marian congregation in Islington was reported to distance itself simultaneously from Protestantism and Catholicism.[67] A few decades later, apologists for the Family of Love were explicit in claiming that confessional antagonism was one of the factors that had moved them to mystical dissent. Their religion can indeed be interpreted as a retreat inwards, both socially and psychologically. Nevertheless, dissent *was* also a battleship, and all participants must from time to time have experienced an urge to bear witness to truth by confronting falsehood more directly. Moments in which this instinct moved from the back to the front of the nonconformist psyche have already been described.

One further factor deserves mention. All forms of dissent were expressions of lay energy, and some embodied a desire for an unusually high degree of independent lay involvement in religious matters. This point can be exaggerated, for ordained clergymen played a vital role in many groups, and – as we have already seen – there were plenty of opportunities for active lay initiative within and alongside the church. But the spiritual energy of the laity bubbled with particular vigour amongst the dissenters. This was perhaps especially true of the early Protestants, whose ministers actively encouraged lay engagement with the Scriptures, and of the radicals, whose leaders were often layfolk themselves. Amongst such people, one of the main objectives of their spiritual lives was to break free from traditional clerical control. In 1526, John Parkyns of St Andrews Eastcheap allegedly spoke out against the Bishop of London's campaign to confiscate all copies of Tyndale's New Testament: 'he doth it because we should have no knowledge but keeps it all secret to himself '. His view was doubtless shared by the group of laypeople in Deal whose parson spoke to them about the dangers of studying the Scripture: 'you ought not to read it, it doth pass your capacity'. One Marian cleric chose his metaphor quite deliberately when he said scornfully of the ironically-named Protestant Agnes Priest that 'she was out of her wit, and talked of the scripture as a dog rangeth far off from his master when he walketh in the fields'.[68]

In milder forms, the energy of the laity also found expression amongst the Elizabethan Catholics. They remained spiritually dependent upon contact with the priesthood, but the domestic focus of their faith in post-Reformation circumstances meant that the dependence went the other way too. Seigneurial Catholicism was, by definition, household-centred, and priests who minister in the homes of laypeople are in a subtly different position from those who do so in their own churches. The power relationship must have shifted somewhat in favour of the laity. The changing culture of Catholicism also meant that women often came to occupy positions of considerable influence, and sometimes even recorded an awareness of the distinctive and important role of their sex. One of the three female Catholics to suffer execution during Elizabeth's reign had defended her action in organising the escape of a priest. Boldly, she declared that 'she believed the Queen herself, if she had the bowels of a woman, would have done as much, if she had known the ill-treatment he underwent'.[69] It is arguable, therefore, that Catholic dissent, like Protestant dissent, presented members of the laity with opportunities to exert greater control over their religious lives than was typically possible within an established church.

We are, however, in danger of forgetting that these opportunities were grasped by only a small minority of the population. The compelling nature of nonconformist evidence can easily carry historians away with it. It may be instructive to return, finally, to the issues raised at the outset. What can the history of dissent in the sixteenth century tell us about the nature of popular religion in general? The first point to make is that the over-whelming majority of people were reasonably content to participate in the religion established by law, even though it changed so frequently. A proportion of them at any one time must have been either too scared to dissent, or not alienated quite profoundly enough to take radical steps. Overall, however, there is little reason to modify the basically positive account of religion within and alongside the church that was given earlier in this book. Once again, we are left to ponder the apparent adaptability of majority religion.

The complexities and contradictions of the relationship between dissenters and conformists are perhaps its most striking feature. The evidence suggests that nonconformists were viewed by their neighbours with a curious mixture of hostility and sympathy. Expressions of bitterness were tempered by more positive feelings, sometimes even by a surprising degree of respect. It is difficult to see how else one can account for the cases in which conformists invited dissenters to attend them at their deathbeds. The later seventeenth century, as Bill Stevenson has shown, was to provide many comparable examples.[70] The mixed nature of the relationship requires some explanation. It can be argued that dissent, in a sense, evolved out of majority religion, and that it thus came to be regarded simultaneously with the anger that flows towards those who betray their roots, and with the familiarity that attaches itself to those with whom the past is shared. Although there may sometimes have been such things as local nonconformist dynasties, most dissenters had their origins amongst the conformists. This in itself may suggest the general warmth of religious commitment that existed amongst the majority. In the local context, moreover, these shared roots often covered not only religion but land, lifestyles and family inter-relationships. This, surely, was one of the reasons why dissenters tended to stay put. By doing so, they may have been able to tip the scales in favour of generally positive relations.

A more tangible explanation can be found in the powerful ethic of neighbourhood. As we have already seen, this was a prominent feature of popular religion throughout the sixteenth century, transcending the divisions of the Reformation to a considerable extent. Evidence of strong neighbourhood values can be found in the cheap print of the period, in the ways in which people made use of the church courts, and in attitudes towards participation in the Mass or Holy Communion. It is also present in many of the church's official homilies. The 'Sermon against contention and brawling', for example, is a comprehensive call for sympathy, modesty and patience in all human dealings, even those in which religious enemies come face to face. 'There is but one Faith, and how can we then say, he is of the old Faith, and he is of the new Faith?' 'And above all things,' listeners are told, 'keepe peace and unity.' Neighbourliness was a construct with a robust Christian foundation in the minds of ordinary people. Very few can have built upon it an articulate modern-style belief in the rights of religious dissenters to pursue their deviant interests in peace. Nevertheless, many evidently felt that dissenting neighbours deserved respect and a kind of tolerance, as long as their behaviour was not in itself considered 'unneighbourly'. The pregnant Lollard woman who spat upon one of her helpers during labour for asking the Blessed Virgin Mary to ease her pain had obviously forfeited her neighbourly dues, and she found herself in trouble. In contrast, the Familist William Taylor, who in 1598 'did...fetch a loade of corne wch lay in danger of spoilinge by cattell oute of his neighbors yearde into his owne yarde', enjoyed a long life in his village without ever being punished for his beliefs.[71]

This set of attitudes, negotiated informally amongst neighbours, operated as a substantial counterweight to more hostile instincts. These, too, were understandable. Dissenters deliberately set themselves apart by holding beliefs and gatherings that did not embrace the wider community. This could be seen as un-neighbourly, and it sometimes justified action against the offenders. Dissenters, simply by defining themselves consciously, also caused others to become somewhat more aware of the spiritual borderlines. This, in turn, could generate hostility. Such hostility was periodically encouraged by the church's leaders, and a fragile communal balance could easily be tipped. There was, to put it another way, a small bottle of poison bobbing in the village well. Everybody knew it was there, and that it would break if struck too forcefully by a visiting bucket. In this sense, neither tolerance nor intolerance can properly be presented as the 'norm', since both were continually present. Keith Thomas was right to argue that neighbours were continually on the look-out for one another's idiosyncrasies; but, in a different sense of the expression, they were also 'looking out' for one another. The 'tyranny of local opinion' had its benevolent side.

5

CONCLUSIONS: THE COMPLIANCE CONUNDRUM

Sir Thomas More, that most heroic of Henrician Catholics, believed that English devotion to the saints was 'so planted by goddes owne hande in the hertes of the hole church, that is to wit, not the clargie only, but the hole congregacion of all Christen people, that if the spiritualtie werc of the myndc to leve it, yet wolde not the temporaltie suffre it'. In othcr words, he held the view that any official attempt to undermine the cult of the saints would be met by stubborn rcsistance from the laity. But, in the decades after More's execution, the saints came under fierce reformist fire, and the vast majority of England's pcople put up with it. By 1600, a nation of once contented traditionalists had come to acccpt an essentially Protestant church, and the number of people who had lost their lives in the process was small by continental standards. Many communitics had, of couroc, cnduicd serious internal conflict along the way, and relatively few had come to be numerically dominated by Protestants of the more zealous variety. The English Reformation, therefore, had been neither fully peaceful nor fully successful. In a majority of settlements, however, it had happened, or was happening, and religious quarrels had generally not gone much beyond the inevitable 'grudge murmor and debates' reported in Henrician Suffolk. It was, then, with some justification that Elizabeth I offered thanks to God for 'the good things I have enjoyed until now to thy honor and the relief of thy church, while my nearest neighbours have felt the evils of bloody warfare'. The people of England may not exactly have taken the Reformation in their stride, but most of them had somehow managed to stay on their feet.[1]

Historians, with good reason, are increasingly aware that the problem of explaining majority acquiescence in an unwanted religious transformation is an acute one. It becomes still more so as an appreciation of the late-medieval church's basic popularity gathers weight. Even Christopher Haigh, who is concerned to emphasise grassroots resistance to Protestant reform, concedes that it is 'slightly surprising' that there was not more of it. For Patrick Collinson, the quiet compliance of thousands of communities is 'more than a little mysterious, for these onslaughts on time-out-of-mind religion were not trivial'. Thus far, historiographical attempts to solve the compliance conundrum seem to have lacked credibility, if not conviction. It is as if nobody has been willing to set all of the puzzle's pieces in place at once. Duffy's explanation, for example, incorporates several of the most important elements: the inevitable fading of traditionalist memories across the generations; the continuities that existed within the Elizabethan settlement; the power of the Tudor state; and the natural tendency of people to follow the path of least resistance. From the perspective of a social historian, however, these points are not always developed with sufficient intensity, and other necessary factors are severely neglected. The potential appeal of Protestantism to ordinary people earns no more than a passing and somewhat reluctant reference. Within the context of Duffy's book as a whole, the possibility of popular Protestantism appears out of the blue on page 586. To change the metaphor, it is a flower without roots. Overall, the question remains: if England's people were, in Scarisbrick's phrase, 'profoundly addicted to the old ways', why were their withdrawal symptoms not more agonising?[2] The following pages will attempt to provide a rounded answer to this question.

The Relative Popularity of Old and New

Our field of research is currently dominated by scholars who emphasise the hold of late-medieval Christianity over the people of England, while playing down the appeal of Protestantism. This insight characterises the work of Scarisbrick, Haigh, Duffy, Whiting and others. There is certainly no reason to deny its basic validity. There may, however, be some cause to study the picture a little more critically, and perhaps to tone down some of its more vibrant colours. In a sense, any such adjustment would of course be regrettable, for colour catches and holds the eye. It may, nevertheless, help us to understand the nature of the English Reformation.

We cannot, for instance, be quite sure that extravagant phrases such as 'profoundly addicted' are entirely warranted in describing the attitude of ordinary laypeople to the pre-Reformation church. Certainly, they were attached to the institution, as their readiness to invest in its material well-being suggests. Contemporary commentators often remarked on the high esteem in which traditional religion stood during the first half of the century. In 1539, for example, the French ambassador noted the 'great joy' with which the conservative Act of Six Articles had been greeted by the people, who were 'much more inclined to the old religion than to the new opinions'.[3]

Yet we have also encountered indications that the depth of popular devotion can be overstated. Under reformist pressure, levels of investment and involvement seem to have fallen away just a little too readily for the comfort of those reading the glowing accounts by Duffy and Haigh. Is it possible that a negative fear of purgatorial suffering had played a larger part in motivating people to charity than we have recently been led to believe? When people watched as their church interiors were radically simplified, could it be that they experienced, alongside an undeniable and predominant sense of loss, a paradoxical feeling of release from the claustrophobic clutter of traditional Christianity? The question seems almost unthinkable in the light of recent research, but it may need to be asked if we are to understand why people tolerated changes they did not consciously seek. Perhaps historians are too ready to assume that individuals respond clearly and decisively to stressful stimuli, when in reality they often experience contradictory reactions. In those contradictions may lie part of the explanation for majority compliance in the process of reform. A sense of sadness was surely the primary emotion, but the likelihood of its generating a widespread and militant spirit of resistance may have been reduced by subsidiary feelings of liberation, excitement or simple curiosity.

Just as some Tudor commentators remarked upon the resilience of traditionalist faith, so others noted what seemed to be its lack of depth or genuine popularity. The author Richard Whitford, for example, was aware in the early 1530s that those whose piety was profound and serious would be mocked by their contemporaries. And under Mary, several foreign observers considered that the people of England were unhappy with the restoration of Catholicism, and that they conformed 'from fear rather than from will'. Overall, the majority of people may have 'thought well of' the church, as implied by the quotation at the front of this book, without necessarily being 'profoundly addicted' to it.[4]

It may also be wise to modify the view that Protestantism had very little appeal to ordinary people in mid-sixteenth-century England. Haigh has

built a characteristically forceful case, insisting that the key Protestant
doctrines were too demanding and dangerously divisive, that an emphasis
on the printed Bible was hopelessly misplaced in a largely illiterate society,
and that godly attempts to reform popular recreations inspired only contempt. All of these arguments, when carried to extremes ('the English
people *could not* be made Protestants'), become questionable. They underestimate the capacities of our predecessors; they misunderstand the fluid
nature of early-modern culture; and they measure the impact of Protestantism according to standards set by the most zealous of puritans. Such
people, almost by definition, believed themselves to be failing, and their
perspective cannot be read as straightforward, factual evidence. If Haigh's
arguments are valid, then it also becomes extremely difficult to explain the
impact of Protestantism in a country such as Hungary, where the people
apparently took to it 'without a nudge' from their rulers.[5]

There is no point denying that theologically knowledgeable and zeal-
ously committed Protestants were a small minority throughout the sixteenth century, even in the south-east of the country. The reformist
programme may, however, have been a little less objectionable to commonplace Christians than Haigh would have us believe. Their very compliance is one obvious indication of this, and Byford is surely right to argue
that we should judge popular Protestantism by the unexceptional actions
of ordinary people, rather than merely by the intellectual knowledge they
did, or (more often) did not, acquire. It is possible to like something, and to
respond accordingly, without necessarily comprehending it in full. For this
reason, insists Byford, Protestantism 'could be had at a price low enough
for most individuals to afford'.[6] The shepherd who, with such regret,
recorded Henry VIII's decision to ban people of his lowly status from
reading the Bible would surely have agreed. Protestantism could offer
vernacular services, congregational singing, fuller participation in the
communion, a road to salvation that did not involve centuries of purgatorial suffering, a more direct relationship with God, and a reduction in
reliance upon the priesthood. These features may not have been instantly
attractive to the majority, but neither were they wholly repulsive. There
must also have been something appealing in the reformist emphasis upon
the rights of ordinary people to hold the vernacular Bible in their hands, to
confess directly to God, and so forth. This implied a high opinion of their
worth and their capabilities, even if it was not completely realistic. The
propagandist notion of the traditional church as an institution intent upon
holding the people in ignorance soon became a prominent feature of
English anti-Catholicism. Once again, personal reactions to all this must

have been mixed, and in such circumstances people are usually more likely to comply with change than to resist it.

Suggestions that Protestantism enjoyed a little more popularity than is often assumed are frequently encountered. The sermons of early reformers were reportedly attended by enthusiastic crowds, and in 1535 a traditionalist London curate complained that the people had ceased to accept the teachings of the priesthood, 'but when a new-fangled fellow doth come and show them a new story him they do believe'. One Protestant in Edwardian London reported that 'the truth is especially flourishing', and the humble status of many of the Marian martyrs needs no reiteration. In 1559, the Spanish ambassador at Elizabeth's court estimated that England's Catholic party was 'two-thirds larger than the other'. For what it is worth, this implies that 37.5% of the population was receptive to reform. And while most people probably disliked the later godly campaign against traditional recreations, they did not necessarily feel a hostility to Protestantism as a whole. In 1575, 'certain good-hearted men' from Coventry complained to the queen about the suppression of their 'Hock Tuesday Play'. They did not understand why it had been discontinued, 'unless it were by the zeal of certain [of] their preachers: men very commendable for their behaviour and learning, and sweet in their sermons, but somewhat too sour in preaching away their pastimes'. These petitioners, it seems, had traditionalist instincts, but also a measure of respect for their godly Protestant ministers. This balanced attitude, combining attachment to the old with a certain and partial receptivity to the new, may well have been extremely common, as other sections in this book have indicated. If so, it can improve our perspective on the way in which the English Reformation – unwanted but not wholly unwelcome – made its way.[7]

The Roots of Obedience

Recent research has left us in little doubt that, broadly speaking, the people of sixteenth-century England responded to official religious commands by doing what they were told. Churchwardens up and down the land snuffed out candles, removed statues and whitewashed walls with remarkable obedience. Then they reversed the whole process in a similar spirit. Then they repeated it once again. Robert Whiting mentions royal commissioners and justices who, at various dates, found the people 'very quiet and conformable' (1553), 'sufficiently well disposed towards religion'

(1559), or 'in very good and dutiful obedience, peace and quiet' (1569).[8] Moreover, these comments all related to Devon and Cornwall, counties whose people were strongly traditionalist in their religious tastes. Such people, along with hundreds of testators from all over the country, generally expressed those tastes only 'if the law will suffer it'.

Some of England's people were, of course, perfectly capable of defiance in the face of official orders. The compliant west country, for example, was shaken by a thoroughly conservative rising in 1549. And many wore compliance as a mask, behind which they grumbled against authority and subverted its commands. When the injunctions of 1538 prohibited the burning of candles in front of images, some parishes simply used garlands of flowers in their place. We have already encountered the Elizabethan clergymen who 'counterfeited' the Mass while using the Book of Common Prayer, and the local officers who hid images in and around the church, rather than destroying them. Others simply dragged their feet, or demanded to see official documentation before dismantling their rood lofts, or undertook the work of stop-start reform in a mood of bewilderment. In early Elizabethan London, outlawed images 'were burned with great wonder'.[9] But all over the country, with variations in speed and enthusiasm, the work was done.

The roots of this obedience do not tend to receive quite the attention they deserve, partly because some of them are perceived as somewhat shallow or essentially negative. People complied in order to protect their livelihoods, or because it simply required less effort, or because they feared the humiliation (or worse) that might follow upon public disobedience. Such attitudes were perfectly understandable in view of the punishments sometimes meted out against those who defied the state: in 1548, one 'traitor of Cornwall' was hanged and quartered, and one of the quarters was then put on public display. Contemporary politicians and divines sometimes scorned popular obedience in religious matters as superficial and unprincipled. In 1549, Sir William Paget asserted that 'what countenance so ever men make outwardly was to please them in whom they see the power resteth'. A few decades later, the godly Elizabethan author George Gifford condemned those who seemed to be 'of no religion, but looke whatsoever any Prince doth set foorth, that will they professe'.[10] The ordinary folk of England were repeatedly criticised by godly ministers for their tendency in religious matters to 'do as others do', thus avoiding danger and the necessity of committed personal engagement with the issues at stake.

As Patrick Collinson has pointed out, however, there was more to 'doing as others do' than a blind herd instinct. As a policy, it was not only safer and less challenging, 'but more charitable, more public-spirited'. In a sense, therefore, 'doing as others do' was a religious principle in itself, and can be related to the emphasis people placed upon communal harmony and the maintenance of charity. A comparable emphasis has also found a prominent place in recent continental scholarship. We have encountered this vital feature of popular religion at numerous points during this survey, and we shall do so again. For now, it may be valuable to remember that 'doing as others do' was also one of the ethical foundations of the Mass, and of 'common prayer'.[11]

Obedience to authority was a duty that, for sixteenth-century people, had sturdy spiritual foundations, as Robert Whiting has emphasised. In 1559, Bishop Scott of Chester felt reluctant to voice his traditionalist misgivings about the emerging religious settlement because of his respect for Queen Elizabeth, 'unto whom I do acknowledge that I owe obedience, not only for wrath and displeasure's sake, but for conscience sake, and that by the Scriptures of God'. Ordinary people were told the same thing repeatedly, by Protestants and Catholics alike, and there is little reason to suppose that it made no impression. Gifford clearly believed that a stubborn sense of loyalty to the prince, regardless of his or her religious policy, was one of the characteristics of Elizabethan popular religion. In his fictional dialogue, it is Atheos (the no-hoper) who warns Zelotes (the godly man) that he should be more obedient to authority: 'it were good that you Puritans should consider your selves, and become better subjects to the Prince'. Zelotes's attempt to parry the charge is rather unconvincing.[12]

The clergy were authority-figures too, and most of them could anticipate that the lead they offered in religious matters would be followed by a majority of their parishioners. In fact, it is one of the ironies of Reformation history that the success of the late-medieval church in encouraging people to look respectfully and obediently to the clergy for leadership came, in time, to benefit the Protestants. 'In the early Reformation', writes Brigden, 'very few parishioners, even those moving toward reform, were yet used to trusting their individual conscience or to finding faith only in Scripture; rather they were accustomed to authority and looked, as always before, to their parish clergy for guidance.'[13] If the clergy accepted the religious changes, then the people were more likely than not to follow suit.

Thus, it can be seen that the factors encouraging obedience to authority were varied and powerful. They were not overwhelming or irresistible, and sixteenth-century people could, and sometimes did, defy their supposed leaders. The fourth chapter of this book is full of examples, and it was not only religious radicals who were prepared to stand up for their rights in sixteenth-century England. Ordinary people regularly protested over a variety of economic and agrarian grievances, while in 1577 thirty women of Brentwood (Essex), armed with a formidable selection of domestic and agricultural implements, barricaded themselves into a chapel to prevent the local esquire from pulling it down. They allegedly beat up the schoolmaster in the process.[14] In the light of such colourful evidence, it is undoubtedly significant that the Reformation did not provoke communal protest on a much wider scale. It seems that governors who played their cards right could expect that most of their orders, even those that lacked active popular support, would be implemented. Their authority might find itself in serious danger when one or more of three situations arose. The alarm bells would ring if there were rival, and reasonably well-matched, claimants to the throne; or if official orders alienated either the clergy or the magistracy as a body; or if the required local changes were too extreme, or enforced with too heavy and violent a hand. Popular obedience was not, therefore, unconditional, but if the leading governors in church and state could successfully negotiate these three parallel tight-ropes (not an easy exercise), then change, even substantial change, could be brought about without extreme civil strife.

Reformist Tactics

The approaches adopted by Protestant reformers to the task of converting a nation from one system of faith to another may therefore provide us with another important piece of the puzzle. Sixteenth-century English Protestantism was marked by complex disagreements over policy, rather more damagingly than by theological disputes. For the sake of clarity, we can perhaps discern two principal attitudes, one characterised by an uncompromising zeal and the other by a more gentle mood of caution. In general, historians who treat the English Reformation as a deeply unpopular failure (the 'catastrophist school', as Collinson has dubbed it) are concentrating in their assessment upon the fiercer of the two strategies, which was led by clerics who by the close of the century were known to their contemporaries as 'puritans'.

One of the earlier proponents of this more militant approach was John Hooper, the 'fiery spirit' who became Bishop of Gloucester in 1551. He clearly felt that the Reformation could only be worked in the hearts of the traditionalist majority through the adoption of a radical, uncompromising strategy. By his standards, only 79 of the 311 clergy whose qualities he assessed were considered adequate to the task.[15] Hooper was executed in 1555. His heirs are to be found amongst the puritan ministers of Elizabethan England, men like George Gifford who cajoled and criticised the majority of his contemporaries, complaining vehemently about what were perceived as the Pelagian and papistical features of popular religion. These preachers, 'learned, zealous and godly', yearned to witness a thunderbolt conversion of the English nation, and they grew more and more frustrated as they realised that it was not happening.

Christopher Haigh's extremely negative account of the impact of reform upon the people of Elizabethan England draws heavily upon such writing, and upon the sometimes angry responses of those whom the puritans confronted. For Haigh, the reformed Church of England was oppressive, far too demanding, and disastrously intolerant of human nature. The average minister 'may have come to seem an outsider rather than a member of the community, who intruded only to complain about alehouses and present fornicators at visitation'. Such clergymen provoked lay hostility 'and turned laymen to sullen indifference towards established religion or to separatism'.[16] Indeed, it is difficult not to see this strand of the reformist strategy as hopelessly ambitious, excessively fiery and ultimately limited in its general impact. The circumstances were certainly not auspicious. The Edwardian and Elizabethan Reformations had to rely upon clergymen and magistrates who clearly were not zealous to a man, as Hooper knew only too well. The problems involved in training and dispersing a new battalion of unequivocally Protestant preachers were extremely serious, and real progress may not have been made until the last decades of the century, or even later in large areas of the north. Conditions in England's border zones certainly offered little encouragement to religious educators of either brand.

It is also arguable that the English state lacked the machinery for the enforcement of a zealous Reformation. Indeed, recent writing on the progress of reform during the mid-century often seems to reveal a somewhat inflated impression of the executive power of contemporary governments. In Scarisbrick's view, Tudor government could be 'astonishingly effective and formidable'.[17] Few religious historians, it seems, would disagree with the argument that the sheer force of official will, backed by muscle and teeth, can go a long way towards solving the compliance conundrum. While it is an established fact that the English nation was more self-conscious and centralised than most of its neighbours in this period, it is surely going too far to present governmental commandments as practically irresistible.

Members of Tudor Privy Councils can in fact be heard lamenting their *lack* of effective power. In 1550, it seemed that provincial magistrates were failing to enforce orders, while many people in some shires 'have never heard of divers of his majesty's proclamations'. The fact that official instructions were not generally resisted (when they got through) cannot be attributed primarily to the brutal power of the state, though fear of the consequences of defiance was of course a significant motivating factor. In practice, the system of government depended heavily upon implementation of orders by the locals themselves, as Ingram's work on the church courts under Elizabeth and James has made abundantly plain. The specially appointed commissioners of the mid-sixteenth century clearly did often perform their duties with great energy, but that energy cannot have carried the Reformation almost on its own. There was official surveillance, but it was 'rarely close at hand'.[18] For this reason too, Hooper's strategy was unlikely to achieve its comprehensive objectives, though he would presumably have argued that only an aggressive, unyielding approach could overcome the obstacles littering the path of Protestants. In reality, it seems more likely that the products of this approach were the vibrant puritan minority amongst the laity, whose members we have already encountered.

There was, however, another Reformation, characterised by a 'softly softly' approach to the task of converting the nation to Protestantism. Its most famous early champion was Thomas Cranmer, Archbishop of Canterbury under Henry VIII and Edward VI. He clashed forcefully with Hooper in 1550–1, insisting on the need for the retention of certain ceremonies in the Prayer Book, 'lest the people, not having yet learned Christ, should be deterred by too extensive innovations from embracing his religion'. Such ceremonies were also designed as a middle path between those 'addicted to their old customs' and those 'so new-fangled that they would innovate all thing'. Cranmer hoped that they would all walk the path together.[19]

This more sensitive appreciation of popular tastes was shared by substantial numbers of Elizabethan governors and clerics on all levels. The Privy Council sometimes intervened in local disputes over maypoles and morris dancing, siding with the majority against the puritans in defence of 'those pastimes of recreation'. In 1580, the Council advised one bishop to deal gently with people whose attachment to traditional components of holy communion remained strong. He was told 'charitabley to tollerate them (that esteem wafer bread) as children, with milke'. A comparable sense of tact seems to have characterised the reforming efforts of many catechists and ecclesiastical judges, examined by Ian Green and Martin Ingram respectively. The queen herself also deserves mention. She combined a deeply conservative form of Protestantism with a basic temperamental caution in matters of policy. Elizabeth I was not one to force the Protestant pace, and her personal faith touched that of her people at many points. This, too, was a vital factor in encouraging general conformity, and in shaping the nature of post-Reformation Christianity in England. In the words of Alexandra Walsham, 'The Church of England was to be a nursery in which the masses were gently weaned, not roughly snatched, from popery.'[20]

The gradualist strategy also had an important accidental aspect. The repeated reversals of official religious policy, caused by political expediency, royal ambivalence and dynastic turnover, meant that the English Reformation, in practice, was a piecemeal affair. It 'picked off targets one by one', across several decades.[21] There was, for example, a fifteen-year delay between Henry VIII's assumption of the royal supremacy and his son's repudiation of the Mass. This may have meant that people and communities had a certain amount of time in which to grow accustomed to the idea that change, in directions that had once seemed unimaginable, was becoming a real possibility. We should not exaggerate this point, of course, for the stuttering and contradictory nature of religious developments must also have bred deep confusion and disorientation. As Haigh has argued, the middle decades of the century revealed little coherent sense of direction to those who lived through them.

Through this combination of policy and circumstance, it was probably the second of these two models that dominated the contact most people had with Protestant reform. The 'softly softly' approach, godly without being 'puritan', had a good deal to recommend it in the conditions of sixteenth-century England. It fitted reasonably well with other, older trends, but did not attempt to force their pace with excessive aggression. Protestantism interacted with slowly rising levels of lay literacy, with developments in the sophistication of the state, and with an intensifying consciousness of nationhood in a way that often worked to its advantage. It can be argued that once Protestantism and Englishness became welded in the popular mind, the battle for the hearts and minds of the people was halfway to being won. John Aylmer knew the importance of forging this link when, in 1559, he explained in *An Harborowe for Faithfull and Trewe Subiectes* that 'God is English.'[22] The Protestant message, which urged the diversion of charitable funds from the church to the poor, was also well-suited to a society in which levels of poverty were rising quickly. Theologically, Protestantism can also be said to have built upon the late-medieval trend towards a more Christo-centric faith, exemplified in the colourful celebration of the feast of Corpus Christi. Of course, none of these relationships was clear-cut or straightforward, and there is little cause to suppose that, had the political situation been different, Catholicism could not have responded equally well. But in the strange atmosphere of Tudor England, it was eventually Protestantism that benefited from wider trends.

The gentler strategy also meant that religious change could be conducted (just about) within the parameters of the acceptable in many of England's varied communities. It attempted to enforce basic physical and liturgical changes, and did so with a firm hand. Beyond this, however, it allowed parishes to set their own pace to a considerable degree. This revealed a sensitive understanding, not shared by more radical strategists, of the ways in which local government operated, and of what it could be expected to achieve. Collinson has referred to 'the implementation, negotiation and internalisation of religious changes initially made above the heads and consciences of ordinary testators'. Lastly, Cranmer's approach made use of basic generational transfer – the inevitable round of deaths and births – in encouraging the English population, predominantly conservative by instinct, to absorb the changes across several decades. This was evidently what happened in Heydon (Essex), and only the more cautious of our two persuasive strategies can account for the way in which a traditionalist priest like William Sheppard steadily converted his flock to a form of Protestantism, not by a thunderbolt conversion 'but by a series of conforming experiences'.[23]

Nevertheless, the 'softly softly' strategy had weaknesses, as Hooper and his heirs were acutely aware. It compromised the Protestant message by leaving bits and pieces of the past in place, and by deliberately not driving that message home with force. The results of this were seen in the church papists' habit of treating the Elizabethan Prayer Book almost as if it was just another version of the old Catholic liturgy. We have also noticed the mixed nature of early seventeenth-century popular religion as it found expression in the cheaper forms of print. And the quieter approach to reform frustrated a potentially dangerous minority of more militant Protestant tacticians. As a result, the stability for which Elizabeth I offered her gratitude to God was somewhat precarious, and was to become much more so in the middle decades of the seventeenth century, when frustration turned to alienation and gathered new momentum.

Continuities

One important feature of the gradualist strategy, as we have already seen, was a sensitivity to the popular need for continuities. No attempt to account for the basic compliance of the English people in the process of Reformation can omit this, and numerous examples have been cited throughout this book. Continuities, whether they were present by accident or by design, performed a vital function in tempering the impact of radical change. The retention of sufficient familiar things rendered an unrequested transformation significantly more tolerable, probably persuading thousands of traditionalists, in Andrew Brown's phrase, to 'follow the ship of state without rocking the boat'.[24]

Some of the most powerful continuities were so basic to Christianity that the coming of Protestantism did not shake their foundations, though it did of course seek to alter the theological context within which they operated. The fundamental importance within sixteenth-century popular religion of charity amongst Christians, the maintenance of neighbourly values, and the preservation of the moral 'community' has emerged at many points in this study. In 1500, to give another example, the Leathersellers of London acknowledged that 'amongst all things most pleasant to Our Lord God in this transitory world, after due love had unto him, is the love, amity, and good accord to be had amongst Christian people'. Henry VIII agreed, lamenting the strain that was being placed upon 'the special foundation of our religion, being charity between man and man'.[25] The coming of Protestantism, in its more moderate forms at least, clearly did not mount any purposeful assault upon this ideal, as the official homilies and liturgy of the reformed church make plain. The records of village life in the Elizabethan period remain full of comments reflecting the continuing primacy of 'charity'. As change followed change in the sixteenth century, the spiritual duty of promoting local peace and harmony was a vital element in guiding parochial reactions, and more often than not it encouraged compliance.

Other continuities existed either for strategic reasons, or because to deny them would have involved a measure of upheaval that was scarcely practicable. The system of church government – based on bishops, deacons and priests, parishes and dioceses, canon law, convocation and church courts – survived intact. Medieval church buildings could not realistically be abandoned, however desirable this might seem to extreme Protestant purists. As a result, the reformed services of the Edwardian and Elizabethan churches were conducted in surroundings which, though

substantially redecorated, had also been the sacred centre for the traditionalist piety of previous generations. At a personal level, there must have
been something potent in the knowledge that one's grandparents had
offered thanks to God in the same holy space. In a great many parishes,
the clergymen who led the new services had also ministered to the
Catholics of Henrician or Marian England. A comparable continuity of
personnel can be detected amongst the lay officers of the church, chosen
from within the congregation. The liturgical performances which they
helped to organise had been transformed in many important ways, becoming essentially Protestant, but here too there were numerous pieces of the
past. Puritans supplied a comprehensive list of these in their 'View of
popish abuses yet remaining in the English Church' (1572): private communion, special holy day services, kneeling at communion, wafer cakes,
surplice and cope, the 'churching' of women, the baptismal sign of the
cross, the wedding ring, kneeling at the name of Jesus, and many more
besides.[26]

It is difficult to exaggerate the significance of these continuities in
promoting mass acquiescence in the process of reform. Historians on
both sides of the theological fence sometimes underplay the number and
significance of liturgical survivals, arguing that the changes were so mas-
sive that any minor continuities pale into insignificance alongside them.
Duffy and MacCulloch have both aimed this point at the 'Anglo-Catholic'
tradition, whose adherents have attempted to argue that the Elizabethan
church was simply the late-medieval church cleansed of its worst excesses.
This old-fashioned thesis is indeed highly questionable, but aggressive
repudiations of it run the alternative risk of failing to identify or sufficiently
acknowledge one of the most important factors in explaining such widespread compliance. It can even be argued that, the more traumatic the
changes, the more important are the continuities. A child being sent far
away from home needs a familiar teddy (or computer game) more intensely than one who is merely popping next door. It is thus important that
historians analyse the significance of the numerous and various continuities with clear heads and open minds.

Other pieces of the past survived against the wishes of the leading
reformers, or only with their reluctant allowance. Parishioners and clergymen in conservative areas of the country attempted to retain elements of
the old liturgy that were not officially permitted in the new. Many people,
including the queen, persisted in using highly traditional expletives such as
'By our Lady', 'By St Mary' and 'By my faith' – much to the disquiet of
their most Protestant contemporaries. In most parishes, some at least of

the traditional church imagery survived in bench-ends, misericords, carved pillars, gargoyles and stained-glass windows. Even in Cockfield, the Suffolk parish dominated for several decades by the puritan minister John Knewstub, there survives to this day a glass picture of St Anne teaching the Blessed Virgin Mary to read.[27] Traditional pictures also migrated to find a new place on the pages of the cheapest forms of literature. In a parallel development, festive rituals that had been banned from the church itself moved out into the homes and fields of traditionalist parishioners where, it seems, they were often tolerated. Eventually, two centuries later, they were still being used by locals who thought of themselves as Protestants.

Historians have also noted continuities that were less straightforward but equally fascinating. Scholars have occasionally detected curious connections between enthusiastic medieval traditionalism and committed Elizabethan godliness in the same localities (Norwich and Coventry, for example). As we have already seen, medieval pilgrimage sites sometimes became the settings for well-attended Protestant sermons, while medieval guilds and early-modern conventicles had more in common than we might think. In various ways, therefore, old energies and impulses found expression through new objects, implying that there was rather more to contemporary religious identities than a dogged adherence to one theological code or the other. In a multitude of aspects, people interpreted the coming of largely unsought reform in a way that prevented their sense of spiritual fulfilment from being comprehensively eroded. The official Reformation, furthermore, often seemed to encourage this approach. This was simultaneously its genius and its most dangerous flaw

The Flexibility of Faith

In the mid-sixteenth century, England's people were called upon, rather abruptly, to make religious choices that were more stark and stressful than any they had been required to make before. Successive regimes, furthermore, displayed a greater will to monitor and enforce these choices than any of their governmental predecessors. The resultant tensions, conflicts and martyrdoms are the stuff of Reformation mythology. These fractures even occurred at school, and the pupils at Bodmin in 1548 reportedly confronted one another in Protestant and Catholic gangs.[28]

Such playground polarities cannot, however, be taken unaccompanied to represent the nature of popular responses to intensified pressure. A broader analysis must recognise that, as Walsham has argued, it was often the *refusal* of people to make the brutal choices with which they were presented that infuriated the most committed commentators on either side. Thomas More, perhaps revising the view quoted earlier, observed that the common folk were 'blown about like a weathercock' with the 'wind of every new doctrine'. Later in the century, godly writers spoke frustratedly of the people who agreed to wear any religious coat given to them, or who 'quietly enjoy the world; they care not what religion comes'. Such neutrals, said Henry Peacham in 1638, were discarded by Protestants and Catholics alike. For John Jewel, writing at the opening of Elizabeth's reign, the problem was not so much that people would believe anything as that they would believe nothing taught by either side, having 'so hardened their hearts'.[29]

These comments portray popular religion, variously, as superficial, blindly obedient, unprincipled and resistant. In other equally hostile remarks, however, there are hints that we should consider a more positive interpretation. The seminary priest John Radford criticised the practice of church papists, and referred to 'such as say they may be saved in any sect, or religion'. Such, in Walsham's words, were 'the excuses of those who rendered redundant denominational polemic'. Ralph Buckland, another priest, was just as scornful of those who would not come off the fence, those who said instead, 'What? we be al Christians, beleeve in one Saviour, expect one heaven, and enjoy our redemption. Have not al men soules to save: little differences make no great square, in the foundation we agree.'[30] There were, it seems, certain ethical supports, rarely articulated and probably rather vague, beneath the commonly condemned refusal of people to choose. The weathercock had principles. Bearing these suggestions in mind, we can perhaps deconstruct More's metaphor in search of contrary meanings. After all, the weathercock's flexibility owes everything to the strong, stable, stationary pivot about which it rotates. Popular religion, too, had its constant core.

Indeed, there is plentiful evidence to suggest that, in many respects, the popular response to the pressures of the period was marked by a certain flexibility, a syncretic instinct and a reluctance to abandon what was becoming the middle ground in a tense confrontation between Catholicism and Protestantism, old and new, the past and the future. People on all social levels might refuse to make a decisive choice between traditionalism and reform. One Elizabethan writer condemned a popular instinct to 'conceive a mixt Religion, compounded of that which is best in both'. The result, complained another, was a religious 'hodge podge of altogither'. They might also, as we have seen, display a reluctance to report on the dissenters who lived amongst them, on condition that those dissenters conducted themselves with neighbourly moderation. When the Elizabethan bishop Richard Curteys required two justices of the peace to swear that they would not keep company with religious conservatives, they objected that 'we cannot take knowledge of every mans religion and conscience that cometh into our company'. The Privy Council, significantly, intervened by rebuking the bishop for his rigorous attitude. The highest governors in the land understood, as Curteys did not, that an important priority for hundreds of lesser magistrates, thousands of churchwardens and millions of ordinary folk was that of 'holding their peace' in circumstances that placed it in severe danger.[31]

The same attitudes lay behind the syncretism already detected in the cheap print of the period, and in a substantial minority of wills. Such sources suggest that bits and pieces of old and new could come together without necessarily engendering any uncomfortable qualms over theological consistency. Any account of sixteenth-century popular religion that overlooks such evidence will risk gross distortion. As one wise observer of the later Reformation warned, 'whosoever shall behold the papistes with puritane spectacles, or the puritan with papistical, shal see no other certeynte, than the multiplication of false images'.[32]

It is also inadequate, in view of the evidence presented above, to treat common compliance as merely a shallow, 'follow-my-leader' attitude. Sometimes, undeniably, it was just that. But in many circumstances it was rather more, even if its extra depth was rarely articulated in the explicit, verbal terms that we have come to demand. It was founded upon a capacity for some degree of flexibility and accommodation, which itself owed a great deal to a powerful instinct for the preservation of social harmony within the locality. These characteristics seem to have enabled popular piety to adjust and re-position itself in a changing world. Of course, there were always those who stood apart from the fragile consensus, either refusing to shift ground or insisting on doing so at high speed. Blood was shed. Amongst the majority, however, a mode of piety adjusted gradually and partially. This religion, in the words of zealots on both sides, was 'neither hot nor cold', but it was possessed of a warmth that slowly came to settle around new services and new symbols. This was also a fairly positive form of compliance. Near the opening of Elizabeth's reign, David Augustine Baker observed that the people in Abergavenny, his native town, were not deeply troubled by the changes, 'And so easily digested the new religion and accommodated themselves hereto.' The system and the religious culture also allowed a measure of creativity in compliance, and it has been shrewdly observed by John Craig that, 'even in conformity, royal and ecclesiastical policies were tempered and sometimes transformed by a sense of what husbandmen and yeomen deemed important or unnecessary'.[33] The result, by c.1600, was a nation whose members, in the main, attended the reformed Church of England and thought of themselves as Protestants – even if they were generally a little hazy about what this meant in precise theological terms.

Popular Religion Through the Reformation

The current generation of religious historians is dominated by those who present the changes of the sixteenth century in a gloomy light. For Haigh they brought satisfaction only to a tiny few, destroyed the 'amicable coexistence' of late-medieval Christians, and left a legacy of 'breaches and bitterness'. Duffy's people adjust to the Reformation, but they do so only with a profound and sorry reluctance. Whiting's Reformation is a journey from religious enthusiasm and involvement towards 'conformism, inactivity and even disinterest'. For Scarisbrick, the changes created a religion that was heavy, serious and empty of support: 'People were more exposed than ever before.' He does, however, detect an early seventeenth-century resurgence of older, pre-Reformation instincts, which – with Laud's capable assistance – brought colour and spiritual comfort back into the church. Collinson, too, though his perspective is in many ways different, sees the results of the Reformation programme as 'the consequences of failure, not of success'.[34]

Evidence for these negative assessments is frequently taken from contemporary remarks concerning the state of popular religion as it seemed to be in the decades after 1550. One puritan commentator alleged that less than one in forty people were 'good and devout gospellers'. Another exclaimed, in 1588, 'what a pitiful thing it is to come into a congregation of one or two thousand souls and not to find above four or five that are able to give an account of their faith in any tolerable manner'. Many of the zealous godly felt that those who were 'either indifferent or plain neuter' were depressingly numerous.[35]

This widespread historiographical habit of assessing the Reformation through the eyes of its most fiery proponents is not, of course, without its problems. In Haigh's account, the terms 'Protestant' and 'puritan' are synonymous, even though this was demonstrably not the case for many contemporaries. Scarisbrick assumes that the stark doctrine of double predestination was central to the contact people had with Protestant reformers, but Ian Green has shown that this was not the case. An emphasis is frequently placed upon assessing what people comprehended in theological terms, rather than upon analysing their actions, allegiances and 'inarticulate' convictions. There is, therefore, a danger of developing a warped perspective regarding the impact of Protestant reform in the lives of the majority. It is perfectly possible to present Gifford's 'men [and women] indifferent' as people who were in the process of making a necessarily gradual shift from one religious system to another, and who were doing so, as far as possible, without endangering their relations with their Christian neighbours. Even Atheos, the parishioner of George Gifford's nightmares, felt a great love for the Prayer Book and Homilies of the Elizabethan church. If we compensate for the undeniable exaggerations of puritan writing on popular religion, then we may find ourselves left with essentially positive and conformist Christians, who had some grasp of the basics at the heart of Christian theology, and who had at least the potential to become the 'Prayer Book Protestants' of Judith Maltby's account.

This book has drawn much of its inspiration from a gathering body of work that concentrates more sensitively upon the experiences of the rarely articulate majority, and in consequence presents a rather more positive view of their responses to the changes of the period. This marks no return to the old Protestant triumphalism, for most writers now accept that the English Reformation was not held 'by popular demand', and that its progress was slow and partial. It may well be that the denominational dimension, which has often led historians to write on behalf of one camp or the other, is also beginning to fade, though we cannot expect that it will ever do so completely. The work of Watt, Byford, Ingram, Green, Alldridge, Boulton and Maltby also applies different standards in the analysis of the Reformation's impact. We are beginning to assess the changes in terms of what was possible in the circumstances, rather than in terms of what was considered ideally desirable by Gifford and his allies.

The result of these shifting perspectives is a Reformation which, though initially unwanted, gradually and steadily worked its way into popular culture, even as the puritans lamented its failure. Back in 1553, Lord Paget had remarked that Protestantism was 'not yet printed in the stomachs of eleven of twelve parts of the realm'. By the early seventeenth century, however, there is strong evidence that Protestantism had found a place 'in the... gut-reactions of the masses', as Collinson has recently put it. Providentialism, justification by faith, anti-Catholicism and the vernacular Bible all became important features of that culture. The transformation was never wholesale, for people did not allow the images and ideas of the past to fade away in their entirety. Popular religion as it emerged was hardly zealous, but it was warm and committed: we need not shrink from calling it 'piety'. A glance back to the troubled middle decades of the sixteenth century suggests that we should be cautious about treating the Reformation as a failure. Given the basic unpopularity of Protestant change at its outset, and the many disruptions it brought, it is perhaps remarkable that there was not more conflict, bitterness and alienation from organised religion. The vast majority maintained a basic conformity to the requirements of the changing church. At both ends of the century, they attended its services with regularity, if not always with rapt devotion. They married their chosen partners, baptised their babies, and buried their dead according to its rites, and they apparently did so without reluctance. Respect for the church, shaken by the upheaval of mid-century, was recovering again by 1600. People continued to administer the affairs of their local churches with acceptable diligence, and to uphold largely consensual moral standards through their cooperation with the ecclesiastical courts.

These observations reflect well on the capacity of people to adjust positively to changes they had not sought, and indeed on the moderate official policies that had enabled and encouraged this adjustment. England's people may not have wanted the Reformation, but they had accepted it, negotiated it, shaped it, compromised it, and they had managed to make from it something that still satisfied their essential spiritual needs. Above all, they had striven – with a considerable measure of success – to promote communal harmony in circumstances that often encouraged discord. The majority would have agreed with the moderate preacher who, in the middle of the seventeenth century, taught that true religion was 'not to hear, and talk, and fill the world with noise and confusion, not to exercise ourselves in things too high for us; but to fight against our lusts and trouble none but ourselves'. Such ministers aimed to pass their wisdom on to the people, but perhaps they had learnt something from the people too. Popular piety was certainly, in Ingram's words, 'unspectacular' and 'inconspicuous'. It was also, as Watt has argued, more 'post-Reformation' than strictly 'Protestant'.[36] But it was no less important for this. It is clearly true that the fractured nature of the English Reformation bred tensions that contributed to the outbreak of civil war in the middle of the next century. Perhaps we should add, however, that the fundamental, 'unspectacular' solidity of majority religion helped to carry the country through that crisis.

In the latter part of the fifteenth century, an East Anglian artisan named Robert Reynes compiled a manuscript 'commonplace book', designed as a record of the things that were important to him in his everyday life. There are good reasons for agreeing with Eamon Duffy that the text provides a reasonably reliable summary of the religious outlook and priorities of the majority of English people at this time.[37] As Duffy has explained, Reynes's book includes a substantial body of information on secular matters (prices, taxes and local events), but is dominated by its religious contents. These reveal a keen interest in the liturgy and calendar of the late-medieval church. Reynes clearly valued the sacraments highly. His orthodox devotion was also sustained through an attention to colourful stories about the saints, religious plays, the rosary, the life of the Blessed Virgin, the Ten Commandments, the seven deadly sins, and so forth. Reynes was preoccupied with divine judgement, and particularly with purgatory. He believed that the performance of good works and the avoidance of swearing were the best methods for softening God's wrath. Indeed, 'a sober and conformist morality' had a place 'somewhere near the heart' of his religion. There is little to suggest, however, that Reynes was either interested in, or knowledgeable about, the intricacies of theology. Nor was his piety deeply introspective. Lastly, the waters of his orthodoxy were muddied somewhat by his interest in charms, divination and zodiacal prognostication. Reynes was a warm and committed conformist, but this religion was quite definitely his own.

Over a century later, a rather better known man named John Taylor, 'the water poet', supplemented his income as a London boatman by publishing a wonderful series of writings. He was of humble origins, though he rose to fame, and Bernard Capp argues convincingly that Taylor's religious outlook can be taken to represent that of many of his contemporaries.[38] It is important to note that he had been born in 1578, and so belonged to the first generation of English people who had never known officially-sanctioned Catholicism. His works, published in the early and mid-seventeenth century, provide us with 'a rare glimpse into the mind of an unsophisticated layman', or a veritable bucketful of gold dust.

Capp's sensitive reconstruction of Taylor's beliefs also enables us to draw a comparison with the earlier world of Robert Reynes.

In many ways, Taylor's attitudes reveal the profound impact of Protestantism upon popular religion. He identified himself as 'a plain Protestant', and had no doubt that the official services of the Church of England were not only 'reformed' but fundamentally true. His devotion to the established church was unequivocal, and he regarded it as 'authentic old'. Taylor produced some fierce anti-Catholic polemic, and placed emphasis upon the Bible, salvation by faith in Jesus Christ, the sanctity of the Sabbath, preaching and providence. Within the head of this lively, creative, but otherwise unexceptional man, the Reformation had obviously happened.

Taylor's faith was, however, far more eclectic and temperate than this brief summary suggests. For Capp, it reveals clearly 'the syncretic character of lay religion'. Although Taylor exhibited signs of a puritanical disposition, he also found spiritual comfort in some of the same things that had succoured Robert Reynes. He was a devoted friend of the great Christian festivals, especially Christmas, and a stout defender of the merry-making that traditionally accompanied them. He viewed honest recreation of all sorts, including drinking (but not, of course, drunkenness), as aspects of the religious life because they fostered community and charity. We can be sure that Reynes shared this view: the difference was that he felt under no pressure to spell it out. The church services attended by Taylor were less colourful and ritualised than those familiar to Reynes, but the ceremonial features that remained – including the surplice, the baptismal sign of the cross, the wedding ring, the kneeling and the music – aroused his passion and nurtured his devotion. Taylor, like Reynes, was an 'instinctive loyalist', and the roots of his love for the established church lay partially in the very fact that it was the *established* church. He also followed Reynes in mixing the sacred and the secular without a sense of contradiction, and in drawing upon astrological thought in his search for sense in the world. He even held the Virgin Mary in high reverence, and criticised Protestants for neglecting her.

Taylor's vision of the world was bolstered by a strong morality and a powerful urge to condemn sin. This insistence on virtuous conduct was itself informed by a familiarity with the Ten Commandments and the more traditionalist seven deadly sins. Furthermore, he blended his reformist emphasis upon faith in Jesus Christ with an apparent belief that prayer and good works could be efficacious in the human quest for salvation. His religion lacked theological sophistication, and his understanding of predestination was shaky at best. One senses that Taylor and Reynes, despite their differences, could have shared an 'honest' drink or two and held a convivial conversation. Indeed, Taylor's fiery anti-Catholicism was tempered by a somewhat gentler, if patronising, attitude to ordinary Catholics at home. As he plied his trade on the Thames, this 'plain Protestant' did not discriminate, preferring to ferry (and charge) passengers, 'be they of what religion they will'.

GLOSSARY

Advowson the right of appointment to an ecclesiastical living.

Ale, church a communal festivity, held in order to raise funds for the local church.

Anabaptists radical Protestants who denied the validity of infant baptism (the term was often applied very loosely, however).

Antinomian holding the radical belief that the moral law does not apply to those who are predestined to salvation.

Apparitor an official messenger on behalf of the ecclesiastical courts, responsible for summoning parties to appear and for executing orders.

Arian holding the radical belief that Christ was not truly divine.

Barrowist a follower of Henry Barrow (died 1593), whose teachings justified and encouraged congregational independence and separatism.

Bedesman the holder of the pre-Reformation local ecclesiastical office that conveyed responsibility for remembering the souls of parish benefactors.

Both kinds, in refers to the reception of holy communion in the form of both bread and wine.

Brownist a follower of the Elizabethan separatist leader Robert Browne (died 1633), but sometimes applied more loosely.

Censer a container used for the burning of incense during Mass.

Chantry an endowment for the maintenance of priests to say or sing Masses on behalf of one's soul.

Church papist a post-Reformation Catholic who decided to attend the Protestant services of the established church, while dissenting in conscience.

Churching the ceremony, both pre- and post-Reformation, by which a woman was welcomed back to the services of the church following childbirth.

Classes conferences held by radical puritan ministers, especially during the 1580s.

Conduct one, usually a clergyman, who was engaged to read prayers in church or, more commonly, in a college chapel.

Consistory court the bishop's court for the administration of ecclesiastical justice within his diocese.

Creeping to the cross pre-Reformation ritual, performed on Good Friday, in which bare-footed parishioners and priests approached the altar on their knees and kissed the crucifix.

Decalogue an alternative name for the Ten Commandments.

Elect belonging to those whom God has chosen. The term is often associated particularly strongly with Calvinists, though it was also used by others.

Elevation of the Host the lifting of the sacred elements in the Mass, following their consecration (pre-Reformation).

Eschatology the branch of theology that deals with the ultimate destiny of souls.

Excommunication a punishment under ecclesiastical law which excluded miscreants from participation in the life of the church.

Familist a follower of the sixteenth-century Dutch mystic Hendrick Niclaes (or, more loosely, one suspected of a variety of perfectionist beliefs).

Family of Love the mystical religious fellowship whose members adhered to the teachings of the Dutch visionary Hendrick Niclaes ('HN').

Freewiller   one who professed belief in the freedom of humans to choose good or evil, in opposition to the predestinarian teachings of other mid-sixteenth-century Protestants.

Guild (or confraternity)   before the Reformation, a local fellowship of Christians (mainly members of the laity) supportive of the parish church and usually dedicated to a specific saint.

Holy bread   before the Reformation, a blessed loaf that was distributed amongst the congregation at the end of Mass (not to be confused with the Host itself).

Hornbook   an early teaching aid, which presented letters, words or phrases (often religious) on a small hand-held board.

Host   the consecrated bread in the Mass or Holy Communion.

Instance causes   ecclesiastical court cases in which one party sued another (similar to modern civil litigation).

Lamp   pre-Reformation, a candle lit before an altar, crucifix, or image of a saint.

Lectureship   post-Reformation, an unofficial preaching post established by committed Protestant laypeople (usually in an urban setting) in order to improve the number and quality of sermons.

Libertine   one suspected of a variety of heretical beliefs, often including antinomianism and pantheism.

Litany   a set form of prayers comprising petitions spoken by a clergyman and congregational responses.

Lollard   a follower of John Wycliffe (*c.*1330–84), who criticised many of the teachings and ceremonies of the late-medieval church. The term came to be applied somewhat less precisely to those suspected of heresy in the century before the Reformation.

Mortuary fee   pre-Reformation, a payment due to the local priest following the death of a parishioner.

Office causes   ecclesiastical court cases in which the church prosecuted those suspected of breaching its laws (comparable to modern criminal litigation).

Paxbred   in the Mass, a small disc bearing a religious illustration that was passed from the priest to the congregation, and kissed by each parishioner in turn.

Pluralism   the much-criticised clerical practice of holding more than one benefice simultaneously.

Predestination   the divine decree by which certain individuals are chosen for salvation (while others, in the strictest interpretations, are selected for damnation). After the Reformation, a rigorous emphasis upon this decree was associated particularly with Calvinist thinkers.

Presbyterianism   a form of church government which rests ultimately upon the principle that a congregation should choose its own minister, and which generates a hierarchy of courts from the bottom up.

Primer   a devotional book containing various prayers, psalms and liturgical extracts.

Prophesyings   preaching conferences organised in Elizabethan England by puritan clergy, especially in Essex and East Anglia.

Providence   the protective and punitive care of God, which leads Him to intervene directly in human affairs.

Psalter   a version of the Book of Psalms.

Pyx   pre-Reformation, the vessel in which the consecrated wafer was placed.

Recusant   one who refused to attend the post-1559 services of the Church of England (most commonly applied to Catholics).

Rogationtide   before and after the Reformation, the period of the Rogation days in early summer. These were associated particularly with official prayers for the harvest, and with a ceremony in which the borders of the parish were walked ('beating of the bounds').

Rood screen   the screen dividing the nave from the chancel in parish churches. Before the Reformation, it was usually decorated with colourful and imposing religious imagery.

Sacrament   defined in the official Elizabethan catechism as 'an outward and visible sign of an inward and spiritual grace given unto us'. Roman Catholics of the period recognised seven (Baptism, Confirmation, the Eucharist, Penance, Extreme Unction, Ordination and Matrimony).

The post-Reformation church accepted only Baptism and the Eucharist as full sacraments.

Sacring bell pre-Reformation, a bell rung during Mass (especially at the Elevation of the Host) in order to focus the congregation's attention.

Sexton an assistant to the parish clerk, with responsibility for cleaning the church, ringing the bell and preparing graves.

Sidesman (also questman) an assistant to the parochial churchwardens.

Simony the buying and selling of ecclesiastical offices for profit.

Solifidianism the doctrine of justification by faith alone, vigorously promoted by Protestant theologians.

Surplice a loose, white, sleeved vestment worn by clergymen.

Tithe the payment by the laity to the clergy of one tenth of all produce of the land.

Transubstantiation during the Mass, the conversion of bread and wine into the body and blood of Christ (a process denied by Protestant reformers).

Visitation the inspection of a diocese or ecclesiastical province by a bishop or archbishop.

Visitation articles the points of enquiry that were circulated in the localities prior to a visitation.

NOTES AND REFERENCES

1 Introduction

1. The examples are from W. M. Palmer, 'Fifteenth-Century Visitation Records of the Deanery of Wisbech', *Proceedings of the Cambridge Antiquarian Society*, XXXIX (1940) pp. 69–75.

2. Examples from Cambridge University Library, Ely Diocesan Records [hereafter cited as CUL, EDR], B/2/26.

3. CUL, EDR, B/2/10, fols 1, 5, 8, 77, 112–15; Cambridgeshire County Record Office, Ely Consistory Court original will (William Akers, 1590).

4. Eamon Duffy, *The Stripping of the Altars* (New Haven, CT, and London, 1992) pp. 1–8.

5. John Earle, cited by Patrick Collinson, *The Religion of Protestants* (Oxford, 1982) p. 192; A. L. Rowse, cited by D. M. Palliser, 'Popular Reactions to the Reformation During the Years of Uncertainty, 1530–70', in Christopher Haigh (ed.), *The English Reformation Revised* (Cambridge, 1987) p. 108.

6. Ralph Houlbrooke, 'The Puritan Death-Bed, *c*.1560–*c*.1660', in Christopher Durston and Jacqueline Eales (eds), *The Culture of English Puritanism, 1560–1700* (Basingstoke, 1996) p. 143.

7. Margaret Spufford, *Contrasting Communities* (Cambridge, 1974) p. 319.

8. Peter Clark, *English Provincial Society from the Reformation to the Revolution: Religion, Politics and Society in Kent, 1500–1640* (Brighton, 1977) p. 154; Susan Brigden, *London and the Reformation* (Oxford, 1989) pp. 252–3.

9. J. S. Craig, 'Cooperation and Initiatives: Elizabethan Churchwardens and the Parish Accounts of Mildenhall', *Social History*, vol. 18, no. 3 (October 1993) pp. 378–80; M. S. Byford, 'The Price of Protestantism: Assessing the Impact of Religious Change on Elizabethan Essex' (Oxford D.Phil, 1988) pp. 72–4, 84, 428.

10. John Gough, cited by G. L. Barnes, 'Laity Formation: the Role of Early English Printed Primers', *Journal of Religious History*, vol. 18, no. 2 (December 1994) p. 154.

11. Robert Whiting, *The Blind Devotion of the People* (Cambridge, 1989); Keith Thomas, *Religion and the Decline of Magic* (1971; Harmondsworth, 1978).
12. Margaret Aston, *England's Iconoclasts* (Oxford, 1989) p. 16.
13. A. G. Dickens, *The English Reformation* (1964; 2nd edn, London, 1989) pp. 241, 385.
14. Ibid., p. 377.
15. A. G. Dickens, *Lollards and Protestants in the Diocese of York* (1959; London, 1982) p. 235.
16. For readers with no interest in football, Jack Charlton is the Englishman who managed the Irish national team during a period of unprecedented success in the late 1980s and early 1990s.
17. J. J. Scarisbrick, *The Reformation and the English People* (Oxford, 1984) pp. 7–9.
18. Christopher Haigh, *English Reformations* (Oxford, 1993) pp. 14, 45, 279.
19. Duffy, *Stripping*, and Eamon Duffy, 'The Godly and the Multitude in Stuart England', *The Seventeenth Century*, 1 (1986) pp. 31–55; Margaret Spufford (ed.), *The World of Rural Dissenters, 1520–1725* (Cambridge, 1995).
20. Whiting, *Blind Devotion*, p. 171; Brigden, *London*; for a selection of Collinson's works, see the Bibliography.
21. Tessa Watt, *Cheap Print and Popular Piety, 1550–1640* (Cambridge, 1991); J. P. Boulton, 'The Limits of Formal Religion: the Administration of Holy Communion in Late Elizabethan and Early Stuart London', *London Journal*, 10 (1984) pp. 135–54; N. Alldridge, 'Loyalty and Identity in Chester Parishes, 1540–1640', in S. J. Wright (ed.), *Parish, Church and People: Local Studies in Lay Religion, 1350–1750* (London, 1988) pp. 85–125; Martin Ingram, *Church Courts, Sex and Marriage in England, 1570–1640* (Cambridge, 1987); Craig, 'Cooperation and Initiatives'; Eric Carlson, 'The Origins, Function, and Status of the Office of Churchwarden, with Particular Reference to the Diocese of Ely', in Spufford (ed.), *World of Rural Dissenters*, pp. 164–207; Judith Maltby, 'By This Book: Parishioners, the Prayer Book and the Established Church', in Kenneth Fincham (ed.), *The Early Stuart Church, 1603–1642* (Basingstoke, 1993) pp. 115–39 (a monograph from Maltby is also imminent); Byford, 'Price of Protestantism'.
22. Alexandra Walsham, *Church Papists* (Woodbridge, 1993); Ian Green, *The Christian's ABC: Catechisms and Catechising in England c.1530–1740* (Oxford, 1996). Green is currently working on other aspects of early-modern religious education.
23. Haigh, *English Reformations*, part I.
24. Ibid., p. 179.
25. Diarmaid MacCulloch, *The Later Reformation in England, 1547–1603* (Basingstoke, 1990) p. 152.
26. Cited by Keith Wrightson, *English Society, 1580–1680* (London, 1982) p. 51; David Levine and Keith Wrightson, *The Making of an Industrial Society: Whickham 1560–1765* (Oxford, 1991) pp. 280–1.
27. James Shirley, *The Brothers, A Comedie* (London, 1652) p. 44.
28. Peter Blickle, *Communal Reformation. The Quest for Salvation in Sixteenth-Century Germany* (1985; translated by Thomas Dunlap, London, 1992). My quotations are from pp. 193 and 183 respectively. I am grateful to Scott Dixon for suggesting that I consider this comparison.

2   Layfolk within the Church

1. Claire Cross, *Church and People 1450–1660* (Glasgow, 1976); J. J. Scarisbrick, *The Reformation and the English People* (Oxford, 1984); N. Alldridge, 'Loyalty and Identity in Chester Parishes, 1540–1640', in S. J. Wright (ed.), *Parish, Church and People. Local Studies in Lay Religion, 1350–1750* (London, 1988).

2. C. P. Graves, 'Social Space in the English Medieval Parish Church', *Economy and Society*, xviii (1989) pp. 297–322; Martin Ingram, 'From Reformation to Toleration: Popular Religious Cultures in England, 1540–1690', in Tim Harris (ed.), *Popular Culture in England, c.1500–1850* (Basingstoke, 1995) p. 100; Margaret Aston, *England's Iconoclasts* (Oxford, 1989), p. 16.

3. Cheshire Record Office, EDC5, 1606.33; J. S. Craig, 'Cooperation and Initiatives: Elizabethan Churchwardens and the Parish Accounts of Mildenhall', *Social History*, vol. 18, no. 3 (October 1993) p. 378, notes 120 and 121.

4. Eamon Duffy, *The Stripping of the Altars* (New Haven, CT, and London, 1992), p. 475.

5. Cited by Christopher Haigh, *English Reformations* (Oxford, 1993) p. 141.

6. Cited by Duffy, *Stripping*, p. 590; Judith Maltby, 'By this Book: Parishioners, the Prayer Book and the Established Church', in Kenneth Fincham (ed.), *The Early Stuart Church*, 1603–1642 (Basingstoke, 1993).

7. David Cressy, 'Purification, Thanksgiving and the Churching of Women in Post-Reformation England', *Past and Present*, 141 (November, 1993) pp. 106–46; Anthony Fletcher, *Gender, Sex and Subordination in England, 1500–1800* (New Haven, CT, 1995) p. 348.

8. Craig, 'Cooperation and Initiatives', p. 376, note 108; CUL, EDR, D/2/10a, fol. 79.

9. Duffy, *Stripping*, pp. 2, 52.

10. Based on ibid., ch. 3.

11. Scarisbrick, *Reformation*, p. 41.

12. Duffy, *Stripping*, p. 117.

13. Ibid., p. 126.

14. Cited by Nicholas Temperley, *The Music of the English Parish Church* (Cambridge, 1979) p. 44.

15. *The Prayer-Book of Queen Elizabeth 1559* (The Ancient and Modern Library of Theological Literature, London, 1890) pp. 92–106.

16. Temperley, *Music of the English Parish Church*, p. 45.

17. See, for example, Christopher Haigh, 'Anticlericalism and the English Reformation', in Christopher Haigh (ed.), *The English Reformation Revised* (Cambridge, 1987) pp. 73–4; Duffy, *Stripping*, p. 112.

18. Temperley, *Music of the English Parish Church*, p. 76.

19. J. P. Boulton, 'The Limits of Formal Religion: the Administration of Holy Communion in Late Elizabethan and Early Stuart London', *London Journal*, 10 (1984) p. 138.

20. Gerald Bray (ed.), *Documents of the English Reformation* (Cambridge, 1994) pp. 347–8.

21. Duffy, *Stripping*, ch. 1.

22. Haigh, *English Reformations*, p. 164; Ronald Hutton, *The Rise and Fall of Merry England* (Oxford, 1994) p. 80.
23. Hutton, *Rise and Fall of Merry England*, p. 123, and Ronald Hutton, 'The English Reformation and the Evidence of Folklore', *Past and Present*, 148 (1995) pp. 115–16.
24. Duffy, *Stripping*, p. 395; Robert Whiting, *The Blind Devotion of the People* (Cambridge, 1989) pp. 38, 71.
25. Keith Thomas, *Religion and the Decline of Magic* (1971; Harmondsworth, 1978) pp. 190, 204; Peter Clark, *English Provincial Society from the Reformation to the Revolution: Religion, Politics and Society in Kent, 1500–1640* (Brighton, 1977) p. 156; Duffy, *Stripping*, p. 465; Scarisbrick, *Reformation*, p. 163.
26. Patrick Collinson, 'Sir Nicholas Bacon and the Elizabethan *via media*', *Historical Journal*, 23, 2 (1980) p. 268; Whiting, *Blind Devotion*, p. 166.
27. Ingram, 'From Reformation to Toleration', pp. 111–12; Eric Carlson, 'The Origins, Function, and Status of the Office of Churchwarden, with Particular Reference to the Diocese of Ely', in Margaret Spufford (ed.), *The World of Rural Dissenters 1520–1725* (Cambridge, 1995) pp. 167, 172–3; Patrick Collinson, *The Religion of Protestants* (Oxford, 1982) pp. 199–231; Alldridge, 'Loyalty and Identity'; John Morrill, 'The Church in England, 1642–9', in John Morrill (ed.), *Reactions to the English Civil War* (London, 1982) pp. 89–114; Donald Spaeth, 'Common Prayer? Popular Observance of the Anglican liturgy in Restoration Wiltshire', in S. J. Wright (ed.), *Parish, Church and People: Local Studies in Lay Religion, 1350–1750* (London, 1988) pp. 125–46.
28. Margaret Bowker, *The Henrician Reformation: The Diocese of Lincoln under John Longland, 1521–1547* (Cambridge, 1981) p. 50; R. N. Swanson, *Church and Society in Late-Medieval England* (Oxford, 1989) p. 252; N. Tanner, *The Church in Late-Medieval Norwich* (Toronto, 1984) p.9; Colin Richmond, 'Religion and the Fifteenth-Century English Gentleman', in Barrie Dobson (ed.), *The Church, Politics and Patronage in the Fifteenth Century* (Gloucester, 1984) p. 194.
29. Robert Whiting, 'Local Responses to the Henrician Reformation', in Diarmaid MacCulloch (ed.), *The Reign of Henry VIII* (Basingstoke, 1995) p. 213.
30. Whiting, *Blind Devotion*.
31. Collinson, *Religion of Protestants*, p. 209; CUL, EDR, B/2/10a, fol. 107; Keith Wrightson and David Levine, *Poverty and Piety in an English Village* (1979; Oxford, 1995) p. 157; Martin Ingram, *Church Courts, Sex and Marriage in England, 1570–1640* (Cambridge, 1987) p. 106.
32. Ingram, 'From Reformation to Toleration', pp. 111–12; Alexandra Walsham, *Church Papists* (Woodbridge, 1993) p. 100; Alldridge, 'Loyalty and Identity', p. 98; Dewey D. Wallace Jr, 'George Gifford, Puritan Propaganda and Popular Religion', *Sixteenth Century Journal*, IX, 1 (1978) p. 37.
33. Andrzej Bida, 'Papists in an Elizabethan Parish: Linton, Cambridgeshire, *c.*1560–*c.*1600' (Diploma in Historical Studies, Cambridge University, June 1992) p. 38.
34. Thomas, *Religion and the Decline of Magic*, p. 191; Duffy, *Stripping*, p. 118; CUL, EDR, B/2/35, fol. 137; Ingram, 'From Reformation to Toleration', p. 114.
35. Whiting, *Blind Devotion*, p. 93; CUL, EDR, D/2/18, fol. 142.
36. Duffy, *Stripping*, pp. 126–7.

37. CUL, EDR, D/2/18, fols. 137, 149; B/2/18, fol. 126v; Ingram, *Church Courts*, p. 112.
38. Ingram, *Church Courts*, p. 116; Wallace, 'George Gifford', p. 30.
39. Duffy, *Stripping*, pp. 98, 126.
40. M. S. Byford, 'The Price of Protestantism: Assessing the Impact of Religious Change on Elizabethan Essex' (Oxford D. Phil, 1988) p. 428; Maltby, 'By this Book', pp. 118–28.
41. CUL, EDR, D/2/32, fol. 57; Ingram, 'From Reformation to Toleration', p. 116; Duffy, *Stripping*, pp. 23 and 93–4; Margaret Spufford (ed.), *World of Rural Dissenters*, p. 89; Arnold Hunt, 'The Lord's Supper in Early Modern England'. I am grateful to Dr Hunt for allowing me to read this so-far unpublished piece.
42. David Cressy and Lori Anne Ferrell (eds), *Religion and Society in Early Modern England: A Sourcebook* (London, 1996) p. 108; Hunt, 'Lord's Supper'; John Aubrey, cited by Hunt.
43. Boulton, 'Limits of Formal Religion'; Hunt, 'Lord's Supper'; John Panke, cited by Hunt.
44. D. M. Palliser, *Tudor York* (Oxford, 1979) p. 258; Cambridgeshire County Record Office, Ely St Mary, churchwardens' accounts (loose papers, various); Hunt, 'Lord's Supper'; Jeremiah Dyke, cited by Hunt.
45. Patrick Collinson, *The Birthpangs of Protestant England* (Basingstoke, 1988) p. 51; Whiting, *Blind Devotion*, p. 71; Duffy, *Stripping*, p. 29; Hutton, *Rise and Fall of Merry England*, pp. 142–3; Spaeth, 'Common Prayer?', p. 140; CUL, EDR, B/2/33, fol. 36v; Collinson, *Religion of Protestants*, p. 209.
46. Scarisbrick, *Reformation*, p. 7; Duffy, *Stripping*, p. 114; F. G. Emmison (ed.), *Essex Wills...1569–78* (Chelmsford, 1994) no. 831.
47. Whiting, 'Local Responses', p. 214.
48. Collinson, *Birthpangs*, p. 40, Clive Burgess, 'A Fond Thing Vainly Invented: an Essay on Purgatory and Pious Motive in Later Medieval England', in Wright (ed.), *Parish, Church and People*, pp. 73–4.
49. Peter Marshall, *The Catholic Priesthood and the English Reformation* (Oxford, 1994) p. 41.
50. Scarisbrick, *Reformation*, p. 164.
51. Beat Kümin, *The Shaping of a Community* (Aldershot, 1996).
52. Scarisbrick, *Reformation*, p. 164.
53. William Nicholson (ed.), *The Remains of Edmund Grindal* (Parker Society, Cambridge, 1843) p. 133.
54. Collinson, *Birthpangs*, p. 55.
55. Duffy, *Stripping*, p. 550; G. Mayhew, 'Religion, Faction and Politics in Reformation Rye', *Sussex Archaeological Collections*, 120 (1982) p. 152; Susan Brigden, *London and the Reformation* (Oxford, 1989) pp. 555, 585.
56. Scarisbrick, *Reformation*, p. 89. See also, Hutton, *Rise and Fall of Merry England*, and Whiting, *Blind Devotion*.
57. Whiting, *Blind Devotion*, pp. 81, 184.
58. Ibid., p. 172.
59. William Harrison, *The Description of England* (1587; Washington, DC, 1994) pp. 35–6; Peter White, 'The Via Media in the Early Stuart Church', in Kenneth Fincham (ed.), *The Early Stuart Church, 1603–1642* (Basingstoke,

1993) p. 223; Patricia Crawford, *Women and Religion in England 1500–1720*
(London, 1993) p. 54; Aston, *England's Iconoclasts*, p. 337; Morrill, 'Church in
England', p. 94.

60. *The Journal of William Dowsing...*, *1643–44* (Ipswich, 1885).

61. Tessa Watt, *Cheap Print and Popular Piety, 1550–1640* (Cambridge, 1991) p. 137.

62. Scarisbrick, *Reformation*, p. 14; Whiting, 'Local Responses', p. 209.

63. White, 'Via Media', p. 228; George Yule, 'James VI and I: Furnishing the
    Churches in his Two Kingdoms', in Anthony Fletcher and Peter Roberts (eds),
    Religion, Culture and Society in Early-Modern Britain (Cambridge, 1994) pp. 182–
    209; Patrick Collinson, 'Ecclesiastical Vitriol: Religious Satire in the 1590s and
    the Invention of Puritanism', in John Guy (ed.), *The Reign of Elizabeth I* (Cam-
    bridge, 1995) p. 151; Diarmaid MacCulloch, 'The Myth of the English
    Reformation', *Journal of British Studies*, 30 (January, 1991) pp. 13–14; Kümin,
    Shaping of a Community, pp. 221–2.

64. Yule, 'James VI and I', pp. 189–90.

65. CUL, EDR, D/2/23, fol. 107v.

66. These subjects will all be discussed in more detail below.

67. Tanner, *Church in Late-Medieval Norwich*, pp. 29, 170; M. Moir, 'Church
    and Society in Sixteenth-Century Herefordshire' (M.Phil thesis, Leicester,
    1984) pp. 55–6; Haigh, *English Reformations*, p. 29; Whiting, 'Local Responses',
    p. 210; Andrew Brown, *Popular Piety in Late Medieval England* (Oxford, 1995)
    pp. 226–7; Diarmaid MacCulloch, 'England', in Andrew Pettegree (ed.), *The
    Early Reformation in Europe* (Cambridge, 1992) p. 177.

68. Brown, *Popular Piety*, p. 254; Duffy, *Stripping*, pp. 96, 135, 347.

69. Burgess, 'A Fond Thing', pp. 76–7; Duffy, *Stripping*, pp. 160–1.

70. Glanmor Williams, *Renewal and Reformation: Wales c.1415–1642* (Oxford, 1993)
    p. 125; Scarisbrick, *Reformation*, p. 41; Duffy, *Stripping*, p. 346; Moir, 'Church
    and Society', pp. 55–6.

71. Moir, 'Church and Society', p. 62.

72. F. G. Emmison (ed.), *Essex Wills...1591–97* (Chelmsford, 1991) no. 770;
    Ingram, *Church Courts*, p. 116.

73. Ingram, 'From Reformation to Toleration', p. 115.

74. H. Munro Cautley, *Suffolk Churches* (1937; Woodbridge, 1982) p. 29.

75. Kümin, *Shaping of a Community*, pp. 41–2; CUL, EDR, D/2/19, fol. 83.

76. W. E. Tate, *The Parish Chest* (1946; Cambridge, 1951) p. 106; Scarisbrick,
    Reformation, p. 165; Kümin, *Shaping of a Community*, p. 41; Alldridge, 'Loyalty
    and Identity'; Carlson, 'Origins, Function, and Status of the Office of Church-
    warden', p. 171.

77. Kümin, *Shaping of a Community*, p. 41.

78. Eric Carlson, 'Origins, Function, and Status of the Office of Churchwarden',
    and Eric Carlson, *Marriage and the English Reformation* (Oxford, 1994) p. 151;
    Cheshire Record Office, EDC5, 1582.48.

79. Kümin, *Shaping of a Community*, pp. 29–31, 236; Alldridge, 'Loyalty and Iden-
    tity', pp. 104–5; Brown, *Popular Piety*, p. 245.

80. Whiting, *Blind Devotion*, p. 91; Carlson, 'Origins, Function, and Status of the
    Office of Churchwarden', p. 183.

81. CUL, EDR, D/2/10a, fol. 124; B/2/29; B/2/24, fol. 41.

82. Craig, 'Cooperation and Initiatives', p. 365; CUL, EDR, fol. 95.

83. Carlson, 'Origins, Function, and Status of the Office of Churchwarden', pp. 204–5; CUL, EDR, D/2/18, fol.273; B/2/14, fol. 15.
84. CUL, EDR, D/2/19, fol. 215.
85. Carlson, 'Origins, Function, and Status of the Office of Churchwarden', pp. 173–4; Devon Record Office, Chanter 860, fol. 320.
86. Ingram, *Church Courts*, p. 328.
87. Alldridge, 'Loyalty and Identity', pp. 111–12; Martha Carlin, *Medieval Southwark* (London, 1996) p. 98; Craig, 'Cooperation and Initiatives', pp. 372–5.
88. Kümin, *Shaping of a Community*, p. 248.
89. Ibid., p. 214; Carlson, 'Origins, Function, and Status of the Office of Churchwarden', p. 187.
90. Duffy, *Stripping*, p. 60. This section draws extensively upon Duffy's discussion of confession.
91. Thomas, *Religion and the Decline of Magic*, p. 185.
92. Whiting, *Blind Devotion*, p. 24.
93. Marshall, *Catholic Priesthood*, pp. 26, 53.
94. Patrick Collinson, 'Shepherds, sheepdogs and hirelings', *Studies in Church History*, 26 (1989) pp. 216–20; Burgess, 'A Fond Thing'.
95. Thomas, *Religion and the Decline of Magic*, p. 188.
96. The following brief discussion is based on Ian Green, *The Christian's ABC: Catechisms and Catechising in England c.1530–1740* (Oxford, 1996).
97. Moir, 'Church and Society', p. 46; Ingram, *Church Courts*, p. 121; Green, *Christian's ABC*, p. 236, note 27.
98. Brigden, *London*, p. 47; Haigh, *English Reformations*, p. 294; Tanner, *Church in Late-Medieval Norwich*, pp. 25–6; Ian Green, 'Career Prospects and Clerical Conformity in the Early Stuart Church', *Past and Present*, 90 (February 1981), p. 87.
99. M. Keeling, 'The Reformation in the Anglo-Scottish Borders', *Northern History*, 15 (1979) p. 29; Byford, 'Price of Protestantism', ch. 1; W. J. Sheils, *The Puritans in the Diocese of Peterborough 1558–1610* (Northampton, 1979) p. 20; D. M. Palliser, 'Popular Reactions to the Reformation During the Years of Uncertainty, 1530–70', in Christopher Haigh (ed.), *The English Reformation Revised* (Cambridge, 1987) p. 112.
100. Byford, 'Price of Protestantism', p. 21.
101. Cited in ibid.; Green, 'Career prospects', p. 90.
102. A. G. Dickens, *The English Reformation* (1964; 2nd edn, London, 1989) p. 321; Cord Oestmann, *Lordship and Community: The Lestrange Family and the Village of Hunstanton in the First Half of the Sixteenth Century* (Centre of East Anglian Studies, 1994) p. 241.
103. Ingram, *Church Courts*, pp. 89, 91, 114; Sheils, *Puritans*, pp. 10–11; Walsham, *Church Papists*, p. 55; Byford, 'Price of Protestantism', ch. 1.
104. Green, *Christian's ABC*, pp. 252, 258, 568.
105. Dickens, *English Reformation*, p. 55; Christopher Haigh, 'Anticlericalism and the English Reformation', in Haigh (ed.), *English Reformation Revised*, and Haigh, *English Reformations*, part I.
106. Haigh, *English Reformations*, pp. 45, 279.
107. Marshall, *Catholic Priesthood*, p. 235.
108. Brigden, *London*, pp. 50–1, 534; Whiting, *Blind Devotion*, pp. 131, 144; Haigh, *English Reformations*, p. 250.

109. CUL, EDR, B/2/11, fol. 146v; B/2/24, fol. 16v; Ingram, *Church Courts*, p. 110.

110. R. N. Swanson, 'Problems of the Priesthood in Pre-Reformation England', *English Historical Review*, 105 (October 1990) p. 868.

111. Whiting, 'Local Responses', pp. 207–9.

112. Rosemary O'Day, *The English Clergy: The Emergence and Consolidation of a Profession, 1558–1642* (Leicester, 1979), pp. 21–3, 132, 136, 244; Green, 'Career Prospects', pp. 86–7.

113. O'Day, *The English Clergy*, pp. 206–7; Whiting, *Blind Devotion*, p. 132.

114. W. K. Jordan, *Philanthropy in England, 1480–1660* (London, 1959) pp. 309–14; Scarisbrick, *Reformation*, p. 188.

115. Dickens, *English Reformation*, p. 241; Scarisbrick, *Reformation*, p. 70; Whiting, 'Local Responses', p. 207.

3   Layfolk alongside the Church

1. Ronald Hutton, *The Rise and Fall of Merry England* (Oxford, 1994) ch. 1. This section draws extensively on Hutton's account.

2. Eamon Duffy, *The Stripping of the Altars* (New Haven, CT, and London, 1992) p. 15.

3. Ibid., p. 149.

4. Robert Whiting, *The Blind Devotion of the People* (Cambridge, 1989) p. 59.

5. Miri Rubin, *Corpus Christi* (Cambridge, 1991), and 'Corpus Christi: Inventing a Feast', *History Today*, 40 (July 1990) p. 19.

6. Patrick Collinson, 'William Shakespeare's Religious Inheritance and Environment', in Patrick Collinson, *Elizabethan Essays* (London, 1994) p. 226; David Englander *et al.* (eds), *Culture and Belief in Europe, 1450–1600* (Oxford, 1990) pp. 8–16.

7. Whiting, *Blind Devotion*, p. 92.

8. M. Moir, 'Church and Society in Sixteenth-Century Herefordshire' (M. Phil thesis, Leicester, 1984) p. 57; Whiting, *Blind Devotion*, p. 199; Imogen Luxton, 'The Reformation and Popular Culture', in Felicity Heal and Rosemary O'Day (eds), *Church and Society in England: Henry VIII to James I* (London, 1977) p. 60.

9. Duffy, *Stripping*, p. 68.

10. Ibid., p. 138.

11. Patrick Collinson, *The Birthpangs of Protestant England* (Basingstoke, 1988) p. 105.

12. The impact of reform upon festivity is discussed in Hutton, *Rise and Fall of Merry England*, chs 2–4.

13. Martin Ingram, 'From Reformation to Toleration: Popular Religious Cultures in England, 1540–1690', in Tim Harris (ed.), *Popular Culture in England, c.1500–1800* (Basingstoke, 1995) p. 115.

14. Ronald Hutton, 'The English Reformation and the Evidence of Folklore', *Past and Present*, 148 (1995) p. 115.

15. David Cressy, *Bonfires and Bells: National Memory and the Protestant Calendar in Elizabethan and Stuart England* (Berkeley, 1989); M. S. Byford, 'The Price of Protestantism: Assessing the Impact of Religious Change on Elizabethan Essex' (Oxford D. Phil, 1988) p. 408.
16. Martin Ingram, *Church Courts, Sex and Marriage in England, 1570–1640* (Cambridge, 1987) p. 105; Patrick Collinson, *The Religion of Protestants* (Oxford, 1982) p. 225; Eric Carlson, *Marriage and the English Reformation* (Oxford, 1994) p. 173.
17. Christopher Fetherston, *A Dialogue agaynst Light, Lewde, and Lascivious Dauncing* (London, 1582); Hutton, *Rise and Fall of Merry England*, pp. 128–34; Keith Wrightson and David Levine, *Poverty and Piety in an English Village: Terling, 1525–1700* (1979; Oxford, 1995) pp. 179–80.
18. Ingram, *Church Courts*, pp. 101, 104; David Cressy and Lori Anne Ferrell (eds), *Religion and Society in Early Modern England: A Sourcebook* (London, 1996) p. 149.
19. Hutton, *Rise and Fall of Merry England*, p. 237; Andrew Brown, *Popular Piety in Late Medieval England: The Diocese of Salisbury, 1250–1550* (Oxford, 1995) p. 241.
20. Ingram, *Church Courts*, p. 3. The following section makes extensive use of Ingram's work. See also Ralph Houlbrooke, *Church Courts and the People During the English Reformation* (Oxford, 1979).
21. Patrick Collinson, 'England', in Bob Scribner *et al.* (eds), *The Reformation in National Context* (Cambridge, 1994) pp. 90–1.
22. C. Harper-Bill, 'A Late-Medieval Visitation – the Diocese of Norwich in 1499', *Proceedings of the Suffolk Institute of Archaeology*, xxxiv (1977) pp. 35–47; Ingram, *Church Courts*, p 68
23. A. G. Dickens, *The English Reformation* (1964; 2nd edn, London, 1989) p. 279.
24. Whiting, *Blind Devotion*, p. 127; Collinson, 'William Shakespeare', p. 248; CUL, EDR, B/2/39, fol. 167.
25. J. Sharpe, 'Defamation and Sexual Slander in Early Modern England: the Church Courts of York', *Borthwick Papers*, 58 (1980).
26. Carlson, *Marriage*, p. 150; Ingram, *Church Courts*, p. 336.
27. Brown, *Popular Piety*, p. 243.
28. J. J. Scarisbrick, *The Reformation and the English People* (Oxford, 1984) pp 23, 25; W. M. Palmer, 'Village Guilds of Cambridgeshire', *Transactions of the Cambridgeshire and Huntingdonshire Archaeological Society*, i (1902) pp. 337–8.
29. Barbara Hanawalt and Ben McRee, 'The Guilds of Homo Prudens in Late Medieval England', *Continuity and Change*, 7 (August 1992) pp. 170–1; Ben McCree, 'Religious Guilds and the Regulation of Behaviour', in J. Rosenthal and C. Richmond (eds), *People, Politics and Community in the Late Middle Ages* (Gloucester, 1987) pp. 116–17; B. Hanawalt, 'Keepers of the Light: Late Medieval English Parish Guilds', *Journal of Medieval and Renaissance Studies*, xiv (1984) p. 29.
30. Palmer, 'Village Guilds', pp. 346–8.
31. My examples are drawn from the articles mentioned in note 29, above, and from Judith M. Bennet, 'Conviviality and Charity in Medieval and Early-Modern England', *Past and Present*, 36 (February 1992) p. 38.
32. Scarisbrick, *Reformation*, p. 165.
33. Duffy, *Stripping*, p. 150; Hanawalt and McRee, 'Guilds', pp. 166–7; Scarisbrick, *Reformation*, pp. 25, 29, 165–6.

34. Christopher Haigh, *English Reformations* (Oxford, 1993) p. 36; Duffy, *Stripping*, p. 152; Gervase Rosser, 'Communities of Parish and Guild in the Late Middle Ages', in S. J. Wright (ed.), *Parish, Church and People: Local Studies in Lay Religion, 1350–1750* (London, 1988) p. 36.

35. W. M. Palmer, 'Fifteenth-Century Visitation Records of the Deanery of Wisbech', *Proceedings of the Cambridge Antiquarian Society*, XXXIX (1940) p. 241; Robert Whiting, 'Local Responses to the Henrician Reformation', in Diarmaid MacCulloch (ed.), *The Reign of Henry VIII: Politics, Policy and Piety* (Basingstoke, 1995) pp. 211–12.

36. Rosser, 'Communities'; Duffy, *Stripping*, pp. 146, 149.

37. Susan Brigden, *London and the Reformation* (Oxford, 1989) p. 582; Whiting, 'Local Responses', p. 212, and *Blind Devotion*, p. 109.

38. Scarisbrick, *Reformation*, p. 99.

39. Duffy, *Stripping*, pp. 167, 191, 197, 204.

40. Whiting, *Blind Devotion*, p. 72.

41. Collinson, *Birthpangs*, p. 21; Collinson *Religion of Protestants*, p. 260; Patrick Collinson, *The Elizabethan Puritan Movement* (Oxford, 1967) p. 150.

42. Clive Holmes, *Seventeenth-Century Lincolnshire* (Lincoln, 1980) p. 42.

43. Wrightson and Levine, *Poverty and Piety*, p. 206; William Hunt, *The Puritan Moment: The Coming of Revolution in an English County* (Cambridge, MA, 1983) p. 146.

44. Ingram, *Church Courts*, p. 95; W. J. Sheils, *The Puritans in the Diocese of Peterborough, 1558–1610* (Northampton, 1979) pp. 85, 145; Arthur Dent, *The Plaine Man's Pathway to Heaven* (London, 1601) p. 287.

45. Margaret Spufford, 'Puritanism and Social Control?', in A. Fletcher and J. Stevenson (eds), *Order and Disorder in Early Modern England* (Cambridge, 1985) pp. 41–57; Ingram, *Church Courts*, p. 116; Collinson, *Religion of Protestants*, pp. 193–4.

46. Nicholas Tyacke, 'Popular Puritan Mentality in Late Elizabethan England', in P. Clark *et al.* (eds), *The English Commonwealth 1547–1640* (Leicester, 1979) pp. 78, 81–3, 90–1; Dent, *Plaine Man's Pathway*, p. 269; Collinson, *Birthpangs*, p. 97.

47. F. G. Emmison, *Essex Wills... 1591–97* (Chelmsford, 1991) pp. 139–40; Collinson, *Birthpangs*, pp. 43–4.

48. Collinson, 'William Shakespeare', p. 237; Ingram, 'From Reformation to Toleration', p. 102; R. C. Richardson, *Puritanism in North-West England* (Manchester, 1972) pp. 82–3.

49. Collinson, *Religion of Protestants*, p. 256.

50. Ibid., pp. 261, 266; Patrick Collinson, 'Elizabethan and Jacobean Puritanism as Forms of Popular Religious Culture', in Christopher Durston and Jacqueline Eales (eds), *The Culture of English Puritanism, 1560–1700* (Basingstoke, 1996) p. 50; Arnold Hunt, 'The Lord's Supper in Early Modern England' (see Chapter 2, note 41).

51. Collinson, *Religion of Protestants*, p. 269.

52. Essex Record Office, Quarter sessions roll, Q/SR, 222/12; Dent, *Plaine Man's Pathway*, p. 245.

53. David Lloyd, *Cabala: or, The Mystery of Conventicles Unvail'd* (London, 1664) p. 35.

54. See, for example, Collinson, *Religion of Protestants*, pp. 248–52.

55. Rosser, 'Communities', p. 46.

56. N. Tanner, *The Church in Late-Medieval Norwich* (Toronto, 1984) pp. 170–1.

57. N. Alldridge, 'Loyalty and Identity in Chester Parishes, 1540–1640', in S. J. Wright (ed.), *Parish, Church and People: Local Studies in Lay Religon, 1350–1750* (London, 1988) p. 117.

58. W. A. Pantin, 'Instructions for a Devout and Literate Layman', in J. J. G. Alexander and M. T. Gibson (eds), *Medieval Learning and Literature* (Oxford, 1976) pp. 398–422.

59. Anthony Fletcher, 'The Protestant Idea of Marriage in Early Modern England', in Anthony Fletcher and Peter Roberts (eds), *Religion, Culture and Society in Early Modern England: Essays in Honour of Patrick Collinson* (Cambridge, 1994) pp. 163, 181; Ian Green, *The Christian's ABC: Catechisms and Catechising in England c.1530–1740* (Oxford, 1996) p. 209; Patricia Crawford, *Women and Religion in England, 1500–1720* (London, 1993) p. 37.

60. Wisbech and Fenland Museum, Wisbech corporation records, 1566–99.

61. W. K. Jordan, *Philanthropy in England, 1480–1660* (London, 1959) p. 16.

62. For some recent discussions, see Haigh, *English Reformations*, p. 200; Hutton, *Rise and Fall of Merry England*, pp. 94, 102; Caroline Litzenberger, 'Local Responses to Changes in Religious Policy based on Evidence from Gloucestershire Wills', *Continuity and Change*, 8 (December 1993) pp. 417–39.

63. Whiting, 'Local Responses', p. 216; Peter Clark, *English Provincial Society from the Reformation to the Revolution: Religion, Politics and Society in Kent, 1500–1640* (Brighton, 1977) pp. 58–9; Brigden, *London*, p. 629; Hutton, *Rise and Fall of Merry England*, p. 102.

64. Duffy, *Stripping*, ch. 15.

65. Peter Heath, 'Urban Piety in the Later Middle Ages: the Evidence of Hull Wills', in Barrie Dobson (ed.), *The Church, Politics and Patronage in the Fifteenth Century* (Gloucester, 1984) p. 214.

66. Haigh, *English Reformations*, p. 160; Gina Alexander, 'Bonner and the Marian Persecution', in Christopher Haigh, *The English Reformation Revised* (Cambridge, 1987) p. 168; Brigden, *London*, p. 483; see above, p. 90.

67. Litzenberger, 'Local Responses', p. 421.

68. Duffy, *Stripping*, p. 514; A. G. Dickens, *Lollards and Protestants in the Diocese of York* (1959; London, 1982) p. 217; John Craig and Caroline Litzenberger, 'Wills as Religious Propaganda: the Testament of William Tracy', *Journal of Ecclesiastical History*, 44, 3 (July 1993) p. 429.

69. M. Moir, 'Church and Society in Sixteenth-Century Herefordshire' (M. Phil thesis, Leicester, 1984) p. 89.

70. Ingram, *Church Courts*, p. 115.

71. Margaret Spufford, *Contrasting Communities* (Cambridge, 1974) p. 343; J. G. Davies, *The Secular Use of Church Buildings* (London, 1968) p. 159; Christopher Marsh, 'In the Name of God? Will-making and Faith in Early Modern England', in G. H. Martin and P. Spufford (eds), *The Records of the Nation* (Woodbridge, 1990) pp. 224–5.

72. Cambridgeshire Record Office, Ely Consistory Court original will (George Wilson, 1628); Brigden, *London*, p. 631.

73. Brigden, *London*, p. 482; Green, *Christian's ABC*, p. 472.

74. Jordan, *Philanthropy*, pp. 254, 298, 368.

75. See, for example, William G. Bittle and R. Todd Lane, 'Inflation and Philan-
    thropy in England: a Re-assessment of W. K. Jordan's Data', *Economic History
    Review*, 2nd series, xxix, no. 2 (1976) pp. 203–10, and the articles by Hadwin,
    Coleman, Gould, and Bittle/Lane in *Economic History Review*, 2nd series, xxxi
    (1978).
76. Scarisbrick, *Reformation*, p. 53.
77. Marsh, 'In the Name of God?', p. 225.
78. David Cressy, *Literacy and the Social Order* (Cambridge, 1980) pp. 118–29, 176–7.
79. Margaret Spufford, 'First Steps in Literacy', *Social History*, 4 (1979) pp. 407–35;
    CUL, EDR, B/2/24, fol. 82.
80. Green, *Christian's ABC*, p. 242; Duffy, *Stripping*, p. 205; Haigh, *English Reforma-
    tions*, p. 157.
81. Tessa Watt, *Cheap Print and Popular Piety, 1550–1640* (Cambridge, 1991) p. 69.
82. Dickens, *English Reformation*, p. 93; Whiting, *Blind Devotion*, p. 194; Dent, *Plaine
    Man's Pathway*, p. 409.
83. Haigh, *English Reformations*, pp. 151, 161; Whiting, *Blind Devotion*, pp. 189–90.
84. Duffy, *Stripping*, p. 214.
85. Margaret Spufford (ed.), *The World of Rural Dissenters* (Cambridge, 1995)
    pp. 72–5.
86. Watt, *Cheap Print*, p. 326; Duffy, *Stripping*, pp. 68–87, 211.
87. Haigh, *English Reformations*, p. 161.
88. Luxton, 'Reformation and Popular Culture', p. 75; Spufford (ed.), *World of
    Rural Dissenters*, p. 53; Ingram, 'From Reformation to Toleration', p. 98;
    Collinson, 'William Shakespeare', p. 251; Watt, *Cheap Print*, p. 326.
89. See, for example, Bob Scribner, 'Is a History of Popular Culture Possible?',
    History of European Ideas, 10, 2 (1989) pp. 175–91.
90. Peter Lake, 'Deeds Against Nature: Cheap Print Protestantism and Murder in
    Early Seventeenth-Century England', in K. Sharpe and P. Lake (eds), *Culture
    and Politics in early Stuart England* (Basingstoke, 1994) p. 273.
91. G. L. Barnes, 'Laity Formation: the Role of Early English Printed Primers',
    Journal of Religious History, vol. 18, no. 2 (December 1994) pp. 140–57; Duffy,
    Stripping, pp. 538, 542–3; Elizabeth K. Hudson, 'The Plain Man's Pastor:
    Arthur Dent and the Cultivation of Popular Piety in Early Seventeenth-
    Century England', *Albion*, 25 (Spring 1993) p. 23; Byford, 'Price of Protestant-
    ism', p. 21.
92. Watt, *Cheap Print*. Not all historians find Watt's interpretation quite so persuas-
    ive: Ian Green will shortly be arguing that she substantially exaggerates the
    presence of Protestant theology within cheap literature.
93. See, for example, George Gifford, *A briefe discourse of certaine points of the religion,
    which is among the common sort of Christians which may be termed the Countrey Divinitie*
    (London, 1612).
94. Keith Thomas, *Religion and the Decline of Magic* (1971; Harmondsworth, 1978)
    pp. 219, 761–3.
95. Ibid., pp. 48–9, 216–18, 275, 648–9; Duffy, *Stripping*, p. 286; Crawford, *Women
    and Religion*, p. 101.
96. Scarisbrick, *The Reformation*, p. 179; Public Record Office, Prerogative Court of
    Canterbury, 46 Leicester; Luxton, 'Reformation and Popular Culture', p. 65;
    Thomas, *Religion and the Decline of Magic*, pp. 209, 353; Ingram, *Church Courts*, p. 97.

97. Duffy, *Stripping*, pp. 189, 277.
98. Ibid., pp. 277, 283; Thomas, *Religion and the Decline of Magic*, p. 254.
99. Thomas, *Religion and the Decline of Magic*, p. 307.
100. Alan Macfarlane, *Witchcraft in Tudor and Stuart England* (London, 1970) p. 62.
101. Marianne Hester, 'Patriarchal Reconstruction and Witch Hunting', in Jonathan Barry *et al.* (eds), *Witchcraft in Early Modern Europe: Studies in Culture and Belief* (Cambridge, 1996) pp. 288–309; J. Sharpe, 'Witchcraft and Women in Seventeenth-Century England: some Northern Evidence', *Continuity and Change*, 6 (1991) p. 183; Malcolm Gaskill, 'Witchcraft in Early Modern Kent: Stereotypes and the Background to Accusations', in Barry *et al.* (eds), *Witchcraft*, pp. 257–87.
102. Ingram, 'From Reformation to Toleration', p. 107; F. G. Emmison, *Essex Wills... 1596–1603* (Chelmsford, 1990) no. 772.
103. Alexandra Walsham, 'The Fatal Vesper: Providentialism and Anti-popery in Late Jacobean London', *Past and Present*, 144 (August 1994) pp. 36–87; Luxton, 'Reformation and Popular Culture', pp. 72–3; Malcolm Gaskill, 'Fiction in the English Archives'. I am grateful to the author for allowing me to read this so-far unpublished piece.
104. Thomas, *Religion and the Decline of Magic*, pp. 81, 316.
105. Luxton, 'Reformation and Popular Culture', p. 71; Ingram, *Church Courts*, pp. 96–7; Thomas, *Religion and the Decline of Magic*, p. 645; W. L. Sachse, *The Diary of Roger Lowe* (London, 1938) pp. 76–7.
106. Thomas, *Religion and the Decline of Magic*, pp. 422, 757. On astrology, see also Bernard Capp, *Astrology and the Popular Press: English Almanacs, 1500–1800* (London, 1979).
107. Ibid., pp. 189–98, 318, 761–2.
108. Duffy, *Stripping*, pp. 72–3; Clark, *English Provincial Society*, p. 155; Margaret Spufford, 'Importance of Religion', in Margaret Spufford (ed.), *The World of Rural Dissenters, 1520–1725* (Cambridge, 1995) p. 53; Dewey D. Wallace Jr, 'George Gifford, Puritan Propaganda and Popular Religion', *Sixteenth Century Journal*, IX: 1 (1978) p. 34; James Sharpe, *Instruments of Darkness: Witchcraft in England, 1550–1750* (London, 1996), p. 66; Ingram, 'From Reformation to Toleration', p. 107.

4 Layfolk beyond the Church

1. Patrick Collinson, 'Towards a Broader Understanding of the Early Dissenting Tradition', in C. Robert Cole and Michael E. Moody (eds), *The Dissenting Tradition* (Ohio, 1975) pp. 3–5; Christopher Hill, 'From Lollards to Levellers', in M. Cornforth (ed.), *Rebels and their Causes* (London, 1978) p. 49.
2. W. J. Sheils, *The Puritans in the Diocese of Peterborough, 1558–1610* (Northampton, 1979) p. 137; M. Moir, 'Church and Society in Sixteenth-Century Herefordshire' (M.Phil thesis, Leicester, 1984) p. 97; Martin Ingram, 'From Reformation to Toleration: Popular Religious Cultures in England, 1540–1690' in Tim Harris (ed.), *Popular Culture in England, c.1500–1850* (Basingstoke,

1995) p. 105; Martin Ingram, *Church Courts, Sex and Marriage in England, 1570–1640* (Cambridge, 1987) p. 95.

3. Christopher Haigh, *English Reformations* (Oxford, 1993) p. 248.

4. A. G. Dickens, *The English Reformation* (1964; 2nd edn, London, 1989) p. 314; J. J. Scarisbrick, *The Reformation and the English People* (Oxford, 1984) p. 137.

5. Dickens, *English Reformation*, p. 216; Susan Brigden, *London and the Reformation* (Oxford, 1989) p. 82; I. B. Horst, *The Radical Brethren: Anabaptism and the English Reformation to 1558* (Nieuwkoop, 1972) pp. 138–9.

6. John Bossy, *The English Catholic Community, 1570–1850* (London, 1975) p. 192.

7. Haigh, *English Reformations*, p. 54.

8. Patrick Collinson, *The Birthpangs of Protestant England* (Basingstoke, 1988) p. 30.

9. Ibid., p. 53; Margaret Spufford (ed.), *The World of Rural Dissenters* (Cambridge, 1995) pp. 40–64; Robert Whiting, 'Local Responses to the Henrician Reformation', in Diarmaid MacCulloch (ed.), *The Reign of Henry VIII: Politics, Policy and Piety* (Basingstoke, 1995) p. 223; J. F. Davis, *Heresy and Reformation in Southeast England, 1520–59* (London, 1983) p. 2; Anne Hudson, *The Premature Reformation. Wycliffite Texts and Lollard History* (Oxford, 1988) p. 456; J. W. Martin, *Religious Radicals in Tudor England* (London, 1989) ch. 3; Dickens, *English Reformation*, p. 295; Michael Watts, *The Dissenters. From the Reformation to the French Revolution* (Oxford, 1978) ch. 1; Christopher W. Marsh, *The Family of Love in English Society, 1550–1630* (Cambridge, 1994) p. 7; John Bossy, 'The Map of Christianity in Early-Modern England', in Edward Royle (ed.), *Regional Studies in the History of Religion in the Later Middle Ages* (Conference of Regional and Local Historians, 1984) pp. 8–22.

10. D. M. Palliser, 'Popular Reactions to the Reformation during the Years of Uncertainty, 1530–70', in Christopher Haigh (ed.), *The English Reformation Revised* (Cambridge, 1987) p. 103; Christopher Haigh, 'The Continuity of Catholicism in the English Reformation', in Christopher Haigh (ed.), *The English Reformation Revised* (Cambridge, 1987) pp. 176–209; Bossy, 'Map', pp. 9, 11; Diarmaid MacCulloch, *The Later Reformation in England, 1547–1603* (Basingstoke, 1990) p. 149.

11. Horst, *Radical Brethren*, p. 134; J. Strype, *Annals of the Reformation* (new edn, Oxford, 1824) vol. III, part i, pp. 21–2; Spufford, *World of Rural Dissenters*, chs 1, 2, 5, 8; Brigden, *London*, pp. 90–1.

12. Horst, *Radical Brethren*, p. 178; Marsh, *Family of Love*, pp. 150–7, 252–8; Scarisbrick, *Reformation*, pp. 156–9; Alexandra Walsham, *Church Papists* (Woodbridge, 1993) p. 92.

13. Andrzej Bida, 'Papists in an Elizabethan Parish: Linton, Cambridgeshire, 1560–1600' (Diploma in historical studies, Cambridge University, June 1992) pp. 30–1; Diarmaid MacCulloch, *Suffolk and the Tudors* (Cambridge, 1987) p. 129; Haigh, *English Reformations*, pp. 265–6.

14. Haigh, *English Reformations*, pp. 196–7; Patricia Crawford, *Women and Religion in England, 1500–1720* (London, 1993) pp. 26, 62; Dickens, *English Reformation*, p. 305.

15. Dickens, *English Reformation*, pp. 334–7; Susan Brigden, *London*, p. 618, and 'Youth and the English Reformation', *Past and Present*, xcv (1982) pp. 37–67; John Fines, 'Studies in Lollard Heresy' (Sheffield Ph.D, 1964) p. 144.

16. Dickens, *English Reformation*, p. 54.

17. Scarisbrick, *Reformation*, p. 6; Hudson, *Premature Reformation*, p. 469.
18. Hudson, *Premature Reformation*, pp. 194, 469–70.
19. Ibid., pp. 151, 165, 468, 469; Dickens, *English Reformation*, p. 54; Moir, 'Church and society', pp. 67–8; Fines, 'Studies in Lollard Heresy', p. 210; Brigden, *London*, p. 94.
20. Eamon Duffy, *The Stripping of the Altars* (Newhaven, CT, and London, 1992) p. 197; Brigden, *London*, pp. 86, 94; Hudson, *Premature Reformation*, p. 172.
21. G. Walker, 'Heretical sects in pre-Reformation England', *History Today*, 43 (1993) pp. 42–8; Brigden, *London*, p. 405.
22. Paul Seaver, 'Community Control and Puritan Politics in Elizabethan Suffolk', *Albion*, 9 (1977) p. 313; Sheils, *Puritans*, pp. 136–40; Keith Thomas, *Religion and the Decline of Magic* (1971; Harmonsworth, 1978) p. 157.
23. This paragraph draws principally upon Horst, *Radical Brethren*.
24. Martin, *Religious Radicals*, chs 3, 4, 10, 11, 12; Marsh, *Family of Love*, ch. 2.
25. Haigh, 'Continuity', p. 204; John Bossy, 'The Character of Elizabethan Catholicism', in T. Aston (ed.), *Crisis in Europe, 1560–1660* (London, 1965) pp. 223–46; Palliser, 'Popular Reactions', pp. 103–4; Haigh, *English Reformations*, p. 253.
26. Hudson, *Premature Reformation*, pp. 153, 179; Robert Whiting, *The Blind Devotion of the People* (Cambridge, 1989) p. 161; Philippa Tudor, 'Protestant Books in London in Mary Tudor's Reign', *London Journal*, 15, 1 (1990) p. 20; Spufford (ed.), *World of Rural Dissenters*, p. 79; Marsh, *Family of Love*, pp. 89–93.
27. Haigh, *English Reformations*, p. 264; Scarisbrick, *Reformation*, pp. 138, 156, 178; Haigh, 'Continuity', p. 206; Walsham, *Church Papists*.
28. Brigden, *London*, p. 604; I owe the quotation to John Craig.
29. Spufford (ed.), *World of Rural Dissenters*, p. 55; Dickens, *English Reformation*, pp. 55–6; Richard G. Davies, 'Lollardy and Locality', *Transactions of the Royal Historical Society*, 6th series, 1 (1991) pp. 191–212.
30. Davis, *Heresy and Reformation*, p. 138; Scarisbrick, *Reformation*, pp. 142, 157; Marsh, *Family of Love*, p. 74.
31. Dickens, *English Reformation*, p. 303; D. M Loades, 'The Essex Inquisitions of 1556', *Bulletin of the Institute of Historical Research*, xxxv (1962) pp. 93–4; Duffy, *Stripping*, p. 490.
32. Hudson, *Premature Reformation*, pp. 479–80; Derek Plumb, 'The Social and Economic Status of the Later Lollards', in Spufford (ed.), *World of Rural Dissenters*, pp. 106, 124–5; Andrew Brown, *Popular Piety in Late Medieval England: The Diocese of Salisbury, 1250–1550* (Oxford, 1995) p. 225; Marsh, *Family of Love*, pp. 170–3; Walsham, *Church Papists*, pp. 83–4; Bida, 'Papists', pp. 31–3; Patrick Collinson, 'The English Conventicle', in W. J. Sheils and Diana Wood (eds), *Voluntary Religion: Studies in Church History*, 23 (1986) p. 253.
33. Silvana Seidel Menchi, 'Italy', in Bob Scribner *et al.* (eds), *The Reformation in National Context* (Cambridge, 1994) pp. 192–4; Tudor, 'Protestant Books', p. 21; Hudson, *Premature Reformation*, p. 143; Marsh, *Family of Love*, p. 145; Fines, 'Studies in Lollard Heresy', p. 178; Haigh, *English Reformations*, p. 253.
34. Brigden, *London*, p. 628.

35. Peter Holmes, *Resistance and Compromise: The Political Thought of the English Catholics* (Cambridge, 1982); Brigden, *London*, pp. 545–6; Marsh, *Family of Love*, p. 166.
36. Marsh, *Family of Love*, pp. 147–8; Brigden, *London*, pp. 420–1.
37. Davies, 'Lollardy', p. 198; Marsh, *Family of Love*, pp. 159–61; Martin, *Religious Radicals*, p. 50; Walsham, *Church Papists*, pp. 30–2; Collinson, *Birthpangs*, p. 145.
38. Haigh, *English Reformations*, p. 67; Margaret Aston, *Faith and Fire: Popular and Unpopular Religion 1350–1600* (London, 1993) pp. 231–60; Gina Alexander, 'Bonner and the Marian Persecution', in Haigh, *English Reformation Revised* p. 170; Brigden, *London*, pp. 96, 120, 548, 550; Patrick Collinson, 'England', in Scribner *et al.* (eds) *The Reformation in National Context*, p. 85.
39. Moir, 'Church and Society', p. 95; Crawford, *Women and Religion*, p. 63; Marsh, *Family of Love*, pp. 37–8.
40. Walsham, *Church Papists*, pp. 71–2, 83–4.
41. Spufford (ed.), *World of Rural Dissenters*, pp. 23–37 and ch. 7.
42. Ibid., p. 391.
43. Ibid., p. 394.
44. Dickens, *English Reformation*, pp. 52, 56–8.
45. A. G. Dickens, *Lollards and Protestants in the Diocese of York* (1959; London, 1982) p. 243; Hudson, *Premature Reformation*, p. 507.
46. G. Mayhew, 'Religion, faction and politics in Reformation Rye', *Sussex Archaeological Collections*, 120 (1982) p. 143.
47. Hudson, *Premature Reformation*, p. 479; Horst, *Radical Brethren*, pp. 79, 109–11; Martin, *Religious Radicals*, chs 3 and 4; Marsh, *Family of Love*, pp. 58–63.
48. Bossy, 'Character of Elizabethan Catholicism', and John Bossy, *The English Catholic Community 1570–1850* (London, 1975); J. C. H. Aveling, *The Handle and the Axe* (London, 1976); Dickens, *English Reformation*, pp. 365–7.
49. Haigh, 'Continuity'.
50. Patrick McGrath, 'Elizabethan Catholicism: a Reconsideration', *Journal of Ecclesiastical History*, xxxv (1984) pp. 414–28; Alan Dures, *English Catholicism, 1558–1642* (Harlow, 1983) pp. 90–1, 94.
51. Thomas, *Religion and the Decline of Magic*, p. 629.
52. Dures, *English Catholicism*, p. 30.
53. Hudson, *Premature Reformation*, p. 472; Patrick Collinson, 'William Shakespeare's Religious Inheritance and Environment', in Patrick Collinson, *Elizabetah Essays* (London, 1994) p. 233; John Stow, *The Annals of England* (1580; 2nd edn, London, 1592) p. 1162.
54. Haigh, *English Reformations*, pp. 51, 68, 166; Brigden, *London*, pp. 183–4, 625.
55. Brigden, *London*, pp. 163, 190, 273; Haigh, *English Reformations*, p. 232.
56. Alexandra Walsham, 'The Fatal Vesper: Providentialism and Anti-popery in Late Jacobean London', *Past and Present*, 144 (August 1994) pp. 55–6; Ingram, 'From Reformation to Toleration', p. 99.
57. Moir, 'Church and Society', p. 197.
58. Brigden, *London*, p. 625; Haigh, *English Reformations*, p. 67; Horst, *Radical Brethren*, pp. 65–6; Dickens, *English Reformation*, p. 297.
59. Whiting, *Blind Devotion*, p. 169; Alexander, 'Bonner', p. 167; Duffy, *Stripping*, p. 561; Brigden, *London*, pp. 625–6; Marsh, *Family of Love*, pp. 35, 82–3 and chs 6 and 7; Robin Clifton, 'Fear of Popery', in Conrad Russell (ed.), *The Origins of*

the English Civil War (London, 1973) pp. 144–67; Martin, *Religious Radicals*, pp. 135, 139.

60. Whiting, *Blind Devotion*, pp. 169–70; Brigden, *London*, pp. 321, 620, 626.
61. Brigden, *London*, p. 126; Bida, 'Papists'; Marsh, *Family of Love*.
62. Patrick Collinson, *The Religion of Protestants* (Oxford, 1982) p. 216; Moir, 'Church and Society', p. 195.
63. Tudor, 'Protestant Books', p. 21; Muriel McClendon, 'Religious Toleration and the Reformation: the Case of Norwich in the Sixteenth Century' (paper read at Neale Lecture and Colloquium, 1996); Brigden, *London*, p. 572.
64. Horst, *Radical Brethren*, p. 159; MacCulloch, *Later Reformation*, p. 152; Marsh, *Family of Love*, pp. 165, 230.
65. MacCulloch, *Suffolk*, p. 172.
66. Marsh, *Family of Love*, pp. 218–34.
67. Spufford (ed.), *World of Rural Dissenters*, p. 91; David Loades, *Revolution in Religion: The English Reformation 1530–1570* (Cardiff, 1992) p. 52.
68. Haigh, *English Reformations*, p. 60; Collinson, *Birthpangs*, p. 37; Whiting, *Blind Devotion*, p. 196.
69. Crawford, *Women and Religion*, p. 63.
70. Bill Stevenson, 'The Social Integration of Post-Restoration Dissenters, 1660–1725', in Spufford (ed.), *World of Rural Dissenters*, pp. 360–87.
71. *Certaine Sermons or Homilies* (1562; London, 1623) vol. I, pp. 90, 98; Brigden, *London*, p. 96; Marsh, *Family of Love*, p. 189.

5   Conclusions: The Compliance Conundrum

1. Eamon Duffy, *The Stripping of the Altars* (New Haven, CT, and London, 1992) p. 165; Diarmaid MacCulloch, *Suffolk and the Tudors* (Cambridge, 1987) pp. 169–70; G. W. Bernard, 'The Church of England, *c.* 1529–*c.*1642', *History*, 75 (June 1990) p. 107.
2. Christopher Haigh, *English Reformations* (Oxford, 1993) p. 172; Collinson, 'England', in Bob Scribner *et al.* (eds), *The Reformation in National Context* (Cambridge, 1994) p. 88; J. J. Scarisbrick, *The Reformation and the English People* (Oxford, 1984) p. 54.
3. Susan Brigden, *London and the Reformation* (Oxford, 1989) p. 306.
4. Haigh, *English Reformations*, p. 27; A. G. Dickens, *The English Reformation* (1964; 2nd edn, London, 1989) p. 292.
5. Katalin Peter, 'Hungary', in Bob Scribner *et al.* (eds), *Reformation in National Context* (Cambridge, 1994) pp. 156–67.
6. M. S. Byford, 'The Price of Protestantism: Assessing the Impact of Religious Change on Elizabethan Essex' (Oxford D.Phil, 1988) p. 434.
7. Brigden, *London*, pp. 257, 462; Dickens, *English Reformation*, p. 349; Patrick Collinson, *The Birthpangs of Protestant England* (Basingstoke, 1988) p. 100.
8. Robert Whiting, *The Blind Devotion of the People* (Cambridge, 1989) pp. 39, 44, 47.

9. Haigh, *English Reformations*, pp. 157, 242.
10. Whiting, *Blind Devotion*, p. 185; Brigden, *London*, p. 425; Dewey D. Wallace Jr, 'George Gifford, Puritan Propaganda and Popular Religion', *Sixteenth Century Journal*, IX: 1 (1978) p. 30.
11. Collinson, 'England', p. 83; see, for example, Peter Blickle, *Communal Reformation: The Quest for Salvation in Sixteenth-Century Germany* (1985; translated by Thomas Dunlap, London, 1992) p. 83.
12. Dickens, *English Reformation*, p. 353; Wallace, 'George Gifford', p. 42.
13. Brigden, *London*, p. 403.
14. Essex Record Office, Q/SR 64/46.
15. Diarmaid MacCulloch, 'England', in Andrew Pettegree (ed.), *The Early Reformation in Europe* (Cambridge, 1992) p. 168; Haigh, *English Reformations*, pp. 178–9. D. G. Newcombe has recently explained just how misleading Hooper's standards can be to historians. See his 'John Hooper's Visitation and Examination of the Clergy in the Diocese of Gloucester, 1551', in Beat A. Kümin (ed.), *Reformations Old and New: Essays on the Socio-economic Impact of Religious Change, c.1470–1630* (Aldershot, 1996) pp. 57–70.
16. Christopher Haigh, 'Anticlericalism and the English Reformation', in Christopher Haigh (ed.), *The English Reformation Revised* (Cambridge, 1987) p. 74.
17. Scarisbrick, *Reformation*, p. 81.
18. Duffy, *Stripping*, p. 468; Collinson, 'England', p. 88.
19. Haigh, *English Reformations*, p. 179; Patrick Collinson, 'Sir Nicholas Bacon and the Elizabethan *via media*', *Historical Journal*, 23, 2 (1980) p. 256.
20. Haigh, *English Reformations*, p. 280; Alexandra Walsham, *Church Papists* (Woodbridge, 1993) p. 17.
21. Scarisbrick, *Reformation*, p. 61.
22. Collinson, *Birthpangs*, p. 4.
23. Collinson, 'England', pp. 87–8; Byford, 'Price of Protestantism', p. 82.
24. Andrew Brown, *Popular Piety in Late Medieval England: The Diocese of Salisbury, 1250–1550* (Oxford, 1995) p. 243.
25. Brigden, *London*, pp. 26, 378.
26. David Cressy and Lori Anne Ferrell (eds), *Religion and Society in Early Modern England: A Sourcebook* (London, 1996) pp. 82–90.
27. H. Munro Cautley, *Suffolk Churches* (1937; Woodbridge, 1982) p. 254.
28. D. M. Palliser, 'Popular Reactions to the Reformation during the Years of Uncertainty, 1530–70', in Haigh (ed.), *English Reformation Revised*, p. 107.
29. Walsham, *Church Papists*, pp. 8, 99, 106–07; Brigden, *London*, pp. 181, 636; Whiting, *Blind Devotion*, p. 268.
30. Walsham, *Church Papists*, p. 41.
31. Ibid., pp. 40–1; Penry Williams, *The Later Tudors, 1547–1603* (Oxford, 1995) p. 470.
32. Walsham, *Church Papists*, pp. 118–19.
33. Glanmor Williams, *Renewal and Reformation: Wales, c.1415–1642* (Oxford, 1993) p. 306; John Craig, 'Cooperation and Initiatives: Elizabethan Churchwardens and the Parish Accounts of Mildenhall', *Social History*, vol. 18, no. 3 (October 1993) p. 378.

34. Haigh, *English Reformations*, p. 293; Duffy, *Stripping*, pp. 592–3; Whiting, *Blind Devotion*, p. 187; Scarisbrick, *Reformation*, pp. 172, 185–7; Collinson, *Birthpangs*, p. 154.

35. Patrick Collinson, *The Religion of Protestants* (Oxford, 1982) p. 200; Haigh, *English Reformations*, p. 269.

36. Anthony Farindon, cited in J. Sears McGee, *The Godly Man in Stuart England: Anglicans, Puritans and the Two Tables, 1620–1670* (New Haven, CT, 1976) p. 167; Martin Ingram, *Church Courts, Sex and Marriage in England, 1570–1640* (Cambridge, 1987) pp. 113, 123; Tessa Watt, *Cheap Print and Popular Piety, 1550–1640* (Cambridge, 1991) p. 327. Continental scholarship, too, is currently emphasising the compromises, negotiations and continuities that characterised the Reformation. See Bob Scribner and Trevor Johnson (eds), *Popular Religion in Germany and Central Europe, 1400–1800* (Basingstoke, 1996) pp. 1–15.

37. Based on Duffy, *Stripping*, pp. 71–4.

38. Based on Bernard Capp, *The World of John Taylor the Water-poet* (Oxford, 1994) ch. 6.

SELECT BIBLIOGRAPHY

Alexander, Gina, 'Bonner and the Marian persecution', in Christopher Haigh (ed.), *The English Reformation Revised* (Cambridge, 1987).

Alldridge, N., 'Loyalty and Identity in Chester Parishes, 1540–1640', in S. J. Wright (ed.), *Parish, Church and People: Local Studies in Lay Religion, 1350–1750* (London, 1988).

Aston, Margaret, *England's Iconoclasts* (Oxford, 1989).

——, *Faith and Fire: Popular and Unpopular Religion, 1350–1600* (London, 1993).

Aveling, J. C. H., *The Handle and the Axe* (London, 1976).

Bainbridge, Virginia, *Gilds in the Medieval Countryside* (Woodbridge, 1996).

Barnes, G. L., 'Laity Formation: the Role of Early English Printed Primers', *Journal of Religious History*, vol. 18, no. 2 (December 1994).

Barry, Jonathan *et al.* (eds), *Witchcraft in Early Modern Europe: Studies in Culture and Belief* (Cambridge, 1996).

Bennet, Judith M., 'Conviviality and Charity in Medieval and Early-Modern England', *Past and Present*, 36 (February 1992).

Bernard, G. W., 'The Church of England, *c.*1529–*c.*1642', *History*, 75 (June 1990).

Bida, Andrzej, 'Papists in an Elizabethan Parish: Linton, Cambridgeshire, 1560–1600' (Diploma in Historical Studies, Cambridge University, June 1992).

Bittle, William G., and R. Todd Lane, 'Inflation and Philanthropy in England: a Re-assessment of W. K. Jordan's Data', *Economic History Review*, 2nd series, xxix, no. 2 (1976).

Blickle, Peter, *Communal Reformation: The Quest for Salvation in Sixteenth-Century Germany* (1985; translated by Thomas Dunlap, London, 1992).

Bossy, John, 'The Character of Elizabethan Catholicism', in T. Aston (ed.), *Crisis in Europe, 1560–1660* (London, 1965).

——, *The English Catholic Community, 1570–1850* (London, 1975).

Boulton, J. P., 'The Limits of Formal Religion: the Administration of Holy Communion in Late Elizabethan and Early Stuart London', *London Journal*, 10 (1984).

Bowker, Margaret, *The Henrician Reformation: the Diocese of Lincoln under John Longland, 1521–1547* (Cambridge, 1981).

Bray, Gerald (ed.), *Documents of the English Reformation* (Cambridge, 1994).

Brigden, Susan, 'Youth and the English Reformation', *Past and Present*, 95 (1982).

——, *London and the Reformation* (Oxford, 1989).

Brown, Andrew D., *Popular Piety in Late Medieval England. The Diocese of Salisbury, 1250–1550* (Oxford, 1995).

Burgess, Clive, 'A Fond Thing Vainly Invented: an Essay on Purgatory and Pious Motive in Later Medieval England', in S. J. Wright (ed.), *Parish, Church and People: Local Studies in Lay Religion, 1350–1750* (London, 1988).

Burgess, Clive, and Beat Kümin, 'Penitential Bequests and Parish Regimes in Late-Medieval England', *Journal of Ecclesiastical History*, 44 (1993).

Byford, M. S., 'The Price of Protestantism: Assessing the Impact of Religious Change on Elizabethan Essex' (D.Phil, Oxford, 1988).

Capp, Bernard, *Astrology and the Popular Press: English Almanacs, 1500–1800* (London, 1979).

——, *The World of John Taylor the Water-poet* (Oxford, 1994).

Carlson, Eric, *Marriage and the English Reformation* (Oxford, 1994).

——, 'The Origin, Function and Status of the Office of Churchwarden, with Particular Reference to the Diocese of Ely', in Margaret Spufford (ed.), *The World of Rural Dissenters* (Cambridge, 1995).

Cautley, H. Munro, *Suffolk Churches* (1937; Woodbridge, 1982).

Certaine Sermons or Homilies (1562; London, 1623).

Christian, William A. Jr, *Local Religion in Sixteenth-Century Spain* (Princeton, NJ, 1981).

Clark, Peter, *English Provincial Society from the Reformation to the Revolution: Religion, Politics and Society in Kent, 1500–1640* (Brighton, 1977).

Clifton, Robin, 'Fear of Popery', in Conrad Russell (ed.), *The Origins of the English Civil War* (London, 1973).

Collinson, Patrick, *The Elizabethan Puritan Movement* (Oxford, 1967).

——, 'Sir Nicholas Bacon and the Elizabethan *via media*', *Historical Journal*, 23: 2 (1980).

——, *The Religion of Protestants* (Oxford, 1982).

——, 'The English Conventicle', in W. J. Sheils and Diana Wood (eds), *Voluntary Religion. Studies in Church History*, 23 (1986).

——, *The Birthpangs of Protestant England* (Basingstoke, 1988).

——, 'Shepherds, Sheepdogs and Hirelings', *Studies in Church History*, 26 (1989).

——, *Elizabethan Essays* (London, 1994).

——, 'England', in Bob Scribner *et al.* (eds), *The Reformation in National Context* (Cambridge, 1994).

——, 'Ecclesiastical Vitriol: Religious Satire in the 1590s and the Invention of Puritanism', in John Guy (ed.), *The Reign of Elizabeth I* (Cambridge, 1995).

——, 'Elizabethan and Jacobean Puritanism as Forms of Popular Religious Culture', in Christopher Durston and Jacqueline Eales (eds), *The Culture of English Puritanism, 1560–1700* (Basingstoke, 1996).

Craig, John Semple, 'Reformation Politics and Polemics in Sixteenth-Century East Anglian Market Towns' (Ph.D, Cambridge University, 1992).

Craig, John, 'Cooperation and Initiatives: Elizabethan Churchwardens and the Parish Accounts of Mildenhall', *Social History*, vol. 18, no. 3 (October 1993).

—— and Caroline Litzenberger, 'Wills as Religious Propaganda: the Testament of William Tracy', *Journal of Ecclesiastical History*, 44, 3 (July 1993).

Crawford, Patricia, *Women and Religion in England, 1500–1720* (London, 1993).

Cressy, David, *Literacy and the Social Order* (Cambridge, 1980).

——, *Bonfires and Bells: National Memory and the Protestant Calendar in Elizabethan and Stuart England* (Berkeley, CA, 1989).

——, 'Purification, Thanksgiving and the Churching of Women in Post-Reformation England', *Past and Present*, 141 (November 1993).

—— and Lori Anne Ferrell (eds), *Religion and Society in Early Modern England: A Sourcebook* (London, 1996).

Cross, Claire, *Church and People 1450–1660* (Glasgow, 1976).

Davies, J. G., *The Secular Use of Church Buildings* (London, 1968).

Davies, Richard G., 'Lollardy and Locality', *Transactions of the Royal Historical Society*, 6th series, I (1991).

Davis, J. F., *Heresy and Reformation in South-east England, 1520–59* (London, 1983).

Dent, Arthur, *The Plaine Man's Pathway to Heaven* (London, 1601).

Dickens, A. G., *Lollards and Protestants in the Diocese of York* (1959; London, 1982).

——, *The English Reformation* (1964; 2nd edn, London, 1989).

Dobson, Barrie (ed.), *The Church, Politics and Patronage in the Fifteenth Century* (Gloucester, 1984).

Dixon, C. Scott, *The Reformation and Rural Society: The Parishes of Brandenburg- Ansbach-Kulmbach, 1528–1603* (Cambridge, 1996).

Dowsing, William, *The Journal of William Dowsing, 1643–44* (Ipswich, 1885).

Duffy, Eamon, 'The Godly and the Multitude in Stuart England', *The Seventeenth Century*, 1 (1986).

——, *The Stripping of the Altars* (New Haven, CT, and London, 1992).

Dures, Alan, *English Catholicism, 1558–1642* (Harlow, 1983).

Durston, Christopher, and Jacqueline Eales (eds), *The Culture of English Puritanism, 1560–1700* (Basingstoke, 1996).

Emmison, F. G. (ed.), *Essex Wills... 1596–1603* (Chelmsford, 1990).

——, *Essex Wills... 1591–97* (Chelmsford, 1991).

——, *Essex Wills... 1569–78* (Chelmsford, 1994).

Englander, David *et al.* (eds), *Culture and Belief in Europe, 1450–1600* (Oxford, 1990).

Fincham, Kenneth (ed.), *The Early Stuart Church, 1603–42* (Basingstoke, 1993).

Fines, John, 'Studies in Lollard Heresy' (Ph.D, Sheffield, 1964).

Fletcher, Anthony, and Peter Roberts (eds), *Religion, Culture and Society in Early Modern England: Essays in Honour of Patrick Collinson* (Cambridge, 1994).

Fletcher, Anthony, 'The Protestant Idea of Marriage in Early Modern England', in Anthony Fletcher and Peter Roberts (eds), *Religion, Culture and Society* (see above).

——, *Gender, Sex and Subordination in England, 1500–1800* (New Haven, CT, 1995).

Foster, Andrew, *The Church of England, 1570–1640* (London, 1994).

Gaskill, Malcolm, 'Witchcraft in Early Modern Kent: Stereotypes and the Background to Accusations', in Jonathan Barry *et al.* (eds), *Witchcraft in Early Modern Europe: Studies in Culture and Belief* (Cambridge, 1996).

Gifford, George, *A briefe discourse of certaine points of the religion, which is among the common sort of Christians which may be termed the Countrey Divinitie* (London, 1612).

Graves, C. P., 'Social Space in the English Medieval Parish Church', *Economy and Society*, XVIII (1989).

Green, Ian, 'Career Prospects and Clerical Conformity in the Early Stuart Church', *Past and Present*, 90 (February 1981).

——, *The Christian's ABC: Catechisms and Catechising in England c.1530–1740* (Oxford, 1996).

Haigh, Christopher, *Reformation and Resistance in Tudor Lancashire* (Cambridge, 1975).

—— (ed.), *The English Reformation Revised* (Cambridge, 1987).

——, 'Anticlericalism and the English Reformation', in Haigh (ed.), *The English Reformation Revised* (Cambridge, 1987).

——, The Continuity of Catholicism in the English Reformation', in Haigh (ed.), *The English Reformation Revised* (Cambridge, 1987).

——, *English Reformations* (Oxford, 1993).

Hanawalt, B., 'Keepers of the Light: Late Medieval English Parish Guilds', *Journal of Medieval and Renaissance Studies*, XIV (1984).

—— and Ben McRee, 'The Guilds of Homo Prudens in Late-Medieval England', *Continuity and Change*, 7 (August 1992).

Harper-Bill, C., 'A Late-Medieval Visitation – the Diocese of Norwich in 1499', *Proceedings of the Suffolk Institute of Archaeology*, XXXIV (1977).

Harris, Tim (ed.), *Popular Culture in England, c.1500–1850* (Basingstoke, 1995).

Harrison, William, *The Description of England* (1587; Washington DC, 1994).

Heal, Felicity, 'The Parish Clergy and the Reformation in the Diocese of Ely', *Proceedings of the Cambridgeshire Antiquarian Society*, LXVI (1975–6).

Heath, Peter, *The English Parish Clergy on the Eve of the Reformation* (London, 1969).

——, 'Urban Piety in the Later Middle Ages: the Evidence of Hull Wills', in Barrie Dobson (ed.), *The Church, Politics and Patronage in the Fifteenth Century* (Gloucester, 1984).

Hester, Marianne, 'Patriarchal Reconstruction and Witch Hunting', in Jonathan Barry *et al.* (eds), *Witchcraft in Early Modern Europe: Studies in Culture and Belief* (Cambridge, 1996).

Hill, Christopher, 'From Lollards to Levellers', in M. Cornforth (ed.), *Rebels and Their Causes* (London, 1978).

Holmes, Clive, *Seventeenth-Century Lincolnshire* (Lincoln, 1980).

——, 'Women: Witnesses and Witches', *Past and Present*, 140 (1993).

Horst, I. B., *The Radical Brethren: Anabaptism and the English Reformation to 1558* (Nieuwkoop, 1972).

Houlbrooke, Ralph, *Church Courts and the People During the English Reformation* (Oxford, 1979).

——, 'The Puritan Death-bed, *c.*1560–*c.*1660', in Christopher Durston and Jacqueline Eales (eds), *The Culture of English Puritanism, 1560–1700* (Basingstoke, 1996).

Hudson, Anne, *The Premature Reformation: Wycliffite Texts and Lollard History* (Oxford, 1988).

Hudson, Elizabeth K., 'The Plain Man's Pastor: Arthur Dent and the Cultivation of Popular Piety in Early Seventeenth-Century England', *Albion*, 25 (Spring 1993).

Hunt, William, *The Puritan Moment: The Coming of Revolution in an English County* (Cambridge, MA, 1983).

Hutton, Ronald, *The Rise and Fall of Merry England* (Oxford, 1994).

——, 'The English Reformation and the Evidence of Folklore', *Past and Present*, 148 (1995).

Ingram, Martin, *Church Courts, Sex and Marriage in England, 1570–1640* (Cambridge, 1987).

——, 'From Reformation to Toleration: Popular Religious Cultures in England, 1540–1690', in Tim Harris (ed.), *Popular Culture in England, c.1500–1850* (Basingstoke, 1995).

Jacob, W. M., *Lay People and Religion in the Early Eighteenth Century* (Cambridge, 1996).

Jordan, W. K., *Philanthropy in England, 1480–1660* (London, 1959).

Keeling, M., 'The Reformation in the Anglo-Scottish Borders', *Northern History*, 15 (1979).

Kümin, Beat, *The Shaping of a Community: The Rise and Reformation of the English Parish, c.1400–1560* (Aldershot, 1996).

——(ed.), *Reformations Old and New. Essays on the Socio-economic Impact of Religious Change, c.1470–1630* (Aldershot, 1996).

Lake, Peter, 'Deeds Against Nature: Cheap Print Protestantism and Murder in Early Seventeenth-Century England', in K. Sharpe and P. Lake (eds), *Culture and Politics in Early Stuart England* (Basingstoke, 1994).

Lehmberg, Stanford E., *The Reformation of Cathedrals: Cathedrals in English Society, 1485–1603* (Princeton, NJ, 1988).

Levine, David, and Keith Wrightson, *The Making of an Industrial Society: Whickham 1560–1765* (Oxford, 1991).

Litzenberger, Caroline, 'Local Responses to Changes in Religious Policy based on Evidence from Gloucestershire Wills', *Continuity and Change*, 8 (December 1993).

Lloyd, David, *Cabala: or, The Mystery of Conventicles Unvail'd* (London, 1664).

Loach, Jennifer, 'Mary Tudor and the Re-Catholicisation of England', *History Today*, 44 (November 1994).

Loades, D. M., 'The Essex Inquisitions of 1556', *Bulletin of the Institute of Historical Research*, xxxv (1962).

——, *Revolution in Religion: The English Reformation, 1530–1570* (Cardiff, 1992).

Luxton, Imogen, 'The Reformation and Popular Culture', in Felicity Heal and Rosemary O'Day (eds), *Church and Society in England: Henry VIII to James I* (London, 1977).

McCree Ben, 'Religious Guilds and the Regulation of Behaviour', in J. Rosenthal and C. Richmond (eds), *People, Politics and Community in the Late Middle Ages* (Gloucester, 1987).

MacCulloch, Diarmaid, *Suffolk and the Tudors* (Cambridge, 1987).

——, *The Later Reformation in England, 1547–1603* (Basingstoke, 1990).

——, 'The Myth of the English Reformation', *Journal of British Studies*, 30 (January 1991).

——, 'England', in Andrew Pettegree (ed.), *The Early Reformation in Europe* (Cambridge, 1992).

——(ed.), *The Reign of Henry VIII: Politics, Policy and Piety* (Basingstoke, 1995).

Macfarlane, Alan, *Witchcraft in Tudor and Stuart England* (London, 1970).

McGee, J. Sears, *The Godly Man in Stuart England: Anglicans, Puritans and the Two Tables, 1620–1670* (London, 1976).

McGrath, Patrick, 'Elizabethan Catholicism: a Reconsideration', *Journal of Ecclesiastical History*, xxxv (1984).

Maltby, Judith, 'By This Book: Parishioners, the Prayer Book and the Established Church', in Kenneth Fincham (ed.), *The Early Stuart Church, 1603–42* (Basingstoke, 1993).

Marsh, Christopher, 'In the Name of God? Will-making and Faith in Early Modern England', in G. H. Martin and P. Spufford (eds), *The Records of the Nation* (Woodbridge, 1990).

——, *The Family of Love in English Society, 1550–1630* (Cambridge, 1994).

Marshall, Peter, *The Catholic Priesthood and the English Reformation* (Oxford, 1994).

Martin, J. W., *Religious Radicals in Tudor England* (London, 1989).

Mayhew, G., 'Religion, Faction and Politics in Reformation Rye', *Sussex Archaeological Collections*, 120 (1982).

Mertes, Kate, 'The Household as a Religious Community', in J. Rosenthal and C. Richmond (eds), *People, Politics and Community in the Later Middle Ages* (Gloucester, 1987).

Moir, M., 'Church and Society in Sixteenth-Century Herefordshire' (M.Phil thesis, Leicester, 1984).

Molen, R. L. de, '*Pueri Christi Imitatio*: the Festival of the Boy Bishop in Tudor England', *Moreana*, xl (1975).

Morrill, John, 'The Church in England, 1642–9', in John Morrill (ed.), *Reactions to the English Civil War* (London, 1982).

Nicholls, A. E., 'The Etiquette of Pre-Reformation Confession in East Anglia', *Sixteenth Century Journal*, XVII (1986).

Nicholson, William (ed.), *The Remains of Edmund Grindal* (Parker Society, Cambridge, 1843).

O'Day, Rosemary, *The English Clergy. The Emergence and Consolidation of a Profession, 1558–1642* (Leicester, 1979).

——, *The Debate on the English Reformation* (London, 1986).

Oestmann, Cord, *Lordship and Community: The Lestrange Family and the Village of Hunstanton in the First Half of the Sixteenth Century* (Centre of East Anglian Studies, 1994).

Palliser, D. M., *Tudor York* (Oxford, 1979).

——, 'Popular Reactions to the Reformation during the Years of Uncertainty, 1530–70', in Christopher Haigh (ed.), *The English Reformation Revised* (Cambridge, 1987).

Palmer, W. M., 'Village Guilds of Cambridgeshire', *Transactions of the Cambridgeshire and Huntingdonshire Archaeological Society*, I (1902).

——, 'Fifteenth-Century Visitation Records of the Deanery of Wisbech', *Proceedings of the Cambridge Antiquarian Society*, XXXIX (1940) pp. 69–75.

Pantin, W. A., 'Instructions for a Devout and Literate Layman', in J. J. G. Alexander and M. T. Gibson (eds), *Medieval Learning and Literature* (Oxford, 1976).

Parker, Kenneth, *The English Sabbath* (Cambridge, 1988).

Plumb, Derek, 'The Social and Economic Status of the Later Lollards', in Margaret Spufford (ed.), *The World of Rural Dissenters* (Cambridge, 1995).

Poos, L. R., 'Sex, Lies and the Church Courts of Pre-Reformation England', *Journal of Interdisciplinary History*, 25 (Spring 1995).

Richardson, R. C., *Puritanism in North-west England* (Manchester, 1972).

Richmond, Colin, 'Religion and the Fifteenth-Century English Gentleman', in Barrie Dobson (ed.), *The Church, Politics and Patronage in the Fifteenth Century* (Gloucester, 1984).

Rosser, Gervase, 'Communities of Parish and Guild in the Late Middle Ages', in S. J. Wright (ed.), *Parish, Church and People. Local Studies in Lay Religion, 1350–1750* (London, 1988).

Rubin, Miri, 'Corpus Christi: Inventing a Feast', *History Today*, 40 (July 1990).

——, *Corpus Christi* (Cambridge, 1991).

Scarisbrick, J. J., *The Reformation and the English People* (Oxford, 1984).

Scribner, Bob, 'Is a History of Popular Culture Possible?', *History of European Ideas*, 10: 2 (1989).

—— and Trevor Johnson (eds), *Popular Religion in Germany and Central Europe, 1400–1800* (Basingstoke, 1996).

—— *et al.* (eds), *The Reformation in National Context* (Cambridge, 1994).

Seaver, Paul, 'Community Control and Puritan Politics in Elizabethan Suffolk', *Albion*, 9 (1977).

——, *Wallington's World. A Puritan Artisan in Seventeenth-Century London* (Stanford, 1985).

Sharpe, J., 'Defamation and Sexual Slander in Early-Modern England: the Church Courts of York', *Borthwick Papers*, 58 (1980).

——, 'Witchcraft and Women in Seventeenth-Century England: Some Northern Evidence', *Continuity and Change*, 6 (1991).

——, *Instruments of Darkness. Witchcraft in England, 1550–1750* (London, 1996).

Sharpe K., and P. Lake (eds), *Culture and Politics in Early Stuart England* (Basingstoke, 1994).

Sheils, W. J., *The Puritans in the Diocese of Peterborough, 1558–1610* (Northampton, 1979).

Shirley, James, *The Brothers. A Comedie* (London, 1652).

Skeeters, Martha C., *Community and Clergy. Bristol and the Reformation, c.1530–c.1570* (Oxford, 1993).

Spaeth, Donald, 'Common Prayer? Popular Observance of the Anglican Liturgy in Restoration Wiltshire', in S. J. Wright (ed.), *Parish, Church and People: Local Studies in Lay Religion, 1350–1750* (London, 1988).

Spufford, Margaret, *Contrasting Communities* (Cambridge, 1974).

——, 'First Steps in Literacy', *Social History*, 4 (1979).

——, 'Puritanism and Social Control?', in A. Fletcher and J. Stevenson (eds), *Order and Disorder in Early Modern England* (Cambridge, 1985).

—— (ed.), *The World of Rural Dissenters* (Cambridge, 1995).

Stevenson, Bill, 'The Social Integration of Post-Restoration Dissenters, 1660–1725', in Margaret Spufford (ed.), *The World of Rural Dissenters* (Cambridge, 1995).

Stow, John, *The Annals of England* (1580, 2nd edn, London, 1592).

Strype, J., *Annals of the Reformation* (new edn, Oxford, 1824).

Swanson, R. N., *Church and Society in Late-Medieval England* (Oxford, 1989).

——, 'Problems of the Priesthood in Pre-Reformation England', *English Historical Review*, 105 (October 1990).

Tanner, N., *The Church in Late-Medieval Norwich* (Toronto, 1984).

Tate, W. E., *The Parish Chest* (1946; Cambridge, 1951).

Temperley, Nicholas, *The Music of the English Parish Church* (Cambridge, 1979).

Thomas, Keith, *Religion and the Decline of Magic* (1971; Harmondsworth, 1978).

Thomson, John A. F., *The Early Tudor Church and Society, 1485–1529* (London, 1993).

Tudor, Philippa, 'Protestant Books in London in Mary Tudor's Reign', *London Journal*, 15, 1 (1990).

Tyacke, Nicholas, 'Popular Puritan Mentality in Late Elizabethan England', in P. Clark *et al.* (eds), *The English Commonwealth, 1547–1640* (Leicester, 1979).

Wallace, Dewey D. Jr, 'George Gifford, Puritan Propaganda and Popular Religion', *Sixteenth Century Journal*, ix, 1 (1978).

Walker, G., 'Heretical Sects in Pre-Reformation England', *History Today*, 43 (1993).

Walsham, Alexandra, *Church Papists* (Woodbridge, 1993).

——, 'The Fatal Vesper: Providentialism and Anti-popery in Late Jacobean London', *Past and Present*, 144 (August 1994).

Watt, Tessa, *Cheap Print and Popular Piety, 1550–1640* (Cambridge, 1991).

Watts, Michael, *The Dissenters: From the Reformation to the French Revolution* (Oxford, 1978).

White, Peter, 'The Via Media in the Early Stuart Church', in Kenneth Fincham (ed.), *The Early Stuart Church, 1603–42* (Basingstoke, 1993).

Whiting, Robert, *The Blind Devotion of the People* (Cambridge, 1989).

Whiting, Robert, 'Local Responses to the Henrician Reformation', in Diarmaid MacCulloch (ed.), *The Reign of Henry VIII: Politics, Policy and Piety* (Basingstoke, 1995).

Williams, Glanmor, *Renewal and Reformation: Wales, c.1415–1642* (Oxford, 1993).

Williams, Penry, *The Later Tudors, 1547–1603* (Oxford, 1995).

Wright, S. J. (ed.), *Parish, Church and People: Local Studies in Lay Religion, 1350–1750* (London, 1988).

Wrightson, Keith, *English Society, 1580–1680* (London, 1982).

—— and David Levine, *Poverty and Piety in an English Village: Terling, 1525–1700* (1979; Oxford, 1995).

Yule, George, 'James VI and I: Furnishing the Churches in his Two Kingdoms', in Anthony Fletcher and Peter Roberts (eds), *Religion, Culture and Society in Early Modern England: Essays in Honour of Patrick Collinson* (Cambridge, 1994).

INDEX

90
128-38